ARCHITECTURAL LIGHTING for COMMERCIAL INTERIORS

ARCHITECTURAL LIGHTING for COMMERCIAL INTERIORS

PRAFULLA C. SORCAR

A Wiley-Interscience Publication
JOHN WILEY & SONS
New York • Chichester • Brisbane • Toronto • Singapore

Library of Congress Cataloging in Publication Data:

Sorcar, Prafulla C.
    Architectural lighting for commercial interiors.
    "A Wiley-Interscience publication"

    Bibliography: p.
    1. Lighting, Architectural and decorative.

I. Title.
TH7900.S67   1987   725'.2   87-2210
ISBN 0-471-01168-1

Printed and bound in the United States of America by Braun-Brumfield, Inc.

10 9 8 7 6 5

14995

2.2.9

To

my father, P. C. Sorcar (1913–1971),
the celebrated magician,
who kindled my interest in lighting;

my mother, Basanti Sorcar,
whose devotion enabled me to
complete my formal education;

my wife, Shikha,
for her patience and encouragement.

PREFACE

For many years the scientific side of lighting has been separated from the artistic, the utilitarian from the aesthetic, engineering from architecture. But lighting design combines these elements and more; the visual, psychological, and physiological, to name a few. Neither the mathematical formulas of the technicians nor the values of aestheticians can define it. The bottom line is that the mind must be satisfied.

Man is a dynamic creature; the eyes need constant variety for the stimulation required to stay alert and to admire the environment. No fixed level of lighting can satisfy this variety at all times. The many controversial issues such as the level of illuminance, brightness, uniform pattern, blanket of light, nonuniform pattern, and accent lighting are only contributing factors. Each application is different and has specific needs that must be evaluated on an individual basis, the ultimate goal of which is to create a balanced interior lighting.

In this book I have consolidated the many factors that are required to achieve that goal. For convenience it has been divided into four parts: *Foundation* deals with the fundamentals of the seeing process of light and color; *Engineering Tools* deals with the mathematics, science, and utility of the light sources; *Architectural Tools* consists of many important aspects such as the aesthetics, psychology, and physiology of light and color and the selection of fixtures; and *Application* provides some examples of implementation in office and merchandising environments.

I must confess that some of the issues I have dealt with are old concepts with a fresher look, but there are many others, particularly those under *Architectural Tools* and *Applications,* that will be new and stimulating to the creative designer. In addition, I have presented Chapters 11–13 in a minicatalog format to help the designer select light fixtures based on dimensions, finish, areas of application, advantages and disadvantages, and design tips. These fixtures are discussed from the standpoint that knowledge gained from this limited number will be applicable to others, for which, of course, manufacturer's catalogs must be consulted.

Although this book is written for lighting designers, consulting engineers, and architects, it should be equally useful to environmental designers, interior decorators, students of architectural engineering, luminaire manufacturers, and all other enthusiasts whose interest in lighting designs goes beyond the technical.

I am obliged and grateful to the following persons who took the time to review parts of the manuscript and to provide constructive criticism and helpful suggestions:

Dave L. DiLaura
Associate Professor, Adjunct
Civil, Environmental and Architectural Engineering
University of Colorado, Boulder.

Steve M. Stannard
Chairman
Calculation Procedures Committee
Illuminating Engineering Society of North America

Martin M. McCloskey
President
Lighting Technologies Inc., Boulder, Colorado

Stuart A. Ohlson, Architect
Ohlson Lavoie Corporation
Denver, Colorado

George W. Hazen, Architect
Lawrence and Hazen Architects
Seattle, Washington

I am grateful to the Illuminating Engineering Society of North America for giving permission to reproduce many of the tables and figures from the IES Handbooks. A heartfull of special thanks go to my business partner Howard W. Butterweck for reviewing the complete manuscript and to my wife Shikha for typing it.

PRAFULLA C. SORCAR

Denver, Colorado
April 1987

CONTENTS

ARCHITECTURAL LIGHTING
for COMMERCIAL INTERIORS

FOUNDATION

1

Light Story

God said "Let there be light," and there was light, but not enough to meet the need. Even though the sun gave light to all creatures in the universe, their normal activities under daylight came to a halt at sunset! Dependence on the moon, the stars, on lightning, or on the glow of fireballs—perhaps romantic—did not secure them from all manner of nightstalkers.

The invention of fire by the striking of flints represented a major breakthrough. For the first time light was produced by choice, for it was then that it was learned how to burn wood and other dry materials for heating, cooking, safety, and, of course, illumination!

History shows that for many centuries oil-wick lamps were common in eastern countries. A wick lying in a container of oil produced a tongue of flame as long as the oil lasted. In European countries light from woodburning fireplaces appeared to be the most popular and economical means, followed by home-made rush lights, tallow candles of mutton fat and beeswax.

Oil-wick and other "flame" lights were popular in western countries as well. Until the invention of the gas lamp they were used not only at home but on a larger scale in arenas, theaters, and other gathering places. This, of course, produced some adverse results. Lavoisier, the great eighteenth-century chemist, concluded in his experiments inside a theater that at least one-quarter of the oxygen available for breathing was consumed by the burning wicks.

In the late eighteenth and early nineteenth centuries gaslight served as the bridge between candlelight and electricity. Methane gas, naturally produced from animal waste, is today still an economical fuel for light and heat in the rural areas of many developing countries.

The mid-eighteenth and nineteenth centuries were glorious years of development in the utilization of electricity. In 1745 E. G. Von Kleist showed in his invention of the Leyden jar that he could collect small quantities of electricity generated by friction machines. Later several Leyden jars, connected in parallel by Benjamin Franklin, produced electrical discharges of various strengths that led to the establishment of series and parallel electrical circuits. In 1820 Hans Oersted discovered the deflection of a compass needle by forcing current to flow through a wire. André Marie Ampère later discovered that current passing through a coil produced a magnetic field. In 1825 George Simon Ohm stated that current

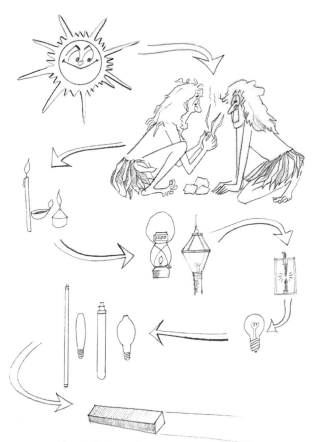

Figure 1-1. *Evolution of artificial light.*

Figure 1-2. *Disco: flasher, laser, and mirror ball.*

lamp lost up to 2 in. of carbon in one hour! About 1875 Charles F. Brush invented a slipping clutch controlled by the current flowing through the arc for adjusting the carbons of an arc lamp. This device provided stability and precise control of the arc position and an automatic changeover to new carbon rods but did not eliminate the problem of fast decay. Marks

flowing through a wire is directly proportional to its voltage but inversely proportional to its resistance. In the same year William Sturgeon built the first electromagnet. Six years later, in 1831, Michael Faraday found that when a copper disk was rotated between two poles of a permanent magnet it generated an electric current; this discovery served as the foundation for what would come to be known as the dynamo (dc-generator). To this invention were added the modifications that included sophisticated electric lighting.

Early attempts to produce electric light were confined primarily to the use of carbon rods connected across a battery to produce an arc. In 1808 Humphrey Davey demonstrated this miracle by passing current from a battery through two physically separated tips of horizontal carbon rods. Since that time, up until 1893, a number of scientists took an interest in the arc-lamp concept and made developments, but all had one common problem: the high cost of carbon rods so quickly used up; for example, a 10-A arc

Figure 1-3. *Indoor suntan.*

Figure 1-4. *Some lighting has no substitute.*

Figure 1-5. *Indoor sunbath for plants.*

then introduced an enclosed glass tube that housed the arc to restrict the flow of oxygen. This increased the power consumption somewhat but slashed the maintenance to one-fifth! About 1899 fluorides of magnesium, barium, strontium, and calcium were added to the carbon rods in the form of cores to produce a ''flame arc'' on various colors.

Around the same time another group of experimenters were working on alternative methods of electric lighting. As early as 1820 Warren de la Rue made the first attempt to make an incandescent lamp—a glass tube with a brass end cap, in which a platinum wire formed the filament, but a huge number of batteries was required to sustain the incandescence for even a few minutes. From 1831 to 1878 various types of incandescent lamp were developed and patented. In 1838 Jobert, a Belgian, heated a thin rod of carbon in a vacuum to maintain incandescence for a short time. Seven years later J. W. Starr, an American, tried a similar experiment, but all experiments had one thing in common: they needed a battery, or a constant-current dynamo for power to which all lamps could be connected in series. This produced a major disadvantage in that all lights would go out together when a lamp failed or was detached from the series circuit. In 1878 Thomas Alva Edison developed a ''constant voltage'' dynamo with which he could operate multiple lamps simultaneously, all with individual or collective switching control. In addition, he realized that a metal filament or carbon putty filament was not the answer and in 1879 turned his attention to natural fibers. It is said that in quest of the right filament he experimented with horsehair, bamboo fibers, fish line, grass fibers from home and abroad, fiber of trees, even hairs from the beards of some of his assistants and finally succeeded with carbonized sewing thread. The lamp continued to burn for 45 h— a record longevity for that time. In 1880 he patented his first high-resistance, carbon filament vacuum incandescent lamp, which is recognized as the ''foundation day'' for all practical incandescent lamps. Although Edison patented his work in 1880, it is interesting to note that 15 years earlier Joseph Wilson Swan, a New Castle chemist, had performed a similar experiment but did not patent his work until 1881. After a lawsuit the two men reconciled their differences by establishing the Edison and Swan United Electrical Light Company Ltd. To bring forward the history of incandescent lamps to recent times, in 1908 Coolidge produced tungsten in a ductile form and made lamps with efficiencies of 1.2 W/ cd, as opposed to 1.6, the previous best. In 1913 Irving Langmuir of General Electric suggested filling the bulb with an inert gas to prevent the lamp from blackening. In 1934 the coiled-coil filament was developed to improve the efficiency of a regular coiled filament by locking some of the gas layers in the winding.

Mercury vapor, sodium vapor, and fluorescent lamps came on the market in the 1930s. Before World War II it had already been noticed by experimenters that a visible glow of light was made possible by discharging electrical current through certain gases and vapors contained in glass tubes or bulbs. The first was the mercury vapor lamp, which revolutionized lighting with its higher output and longer life than incandescents. These forms, however, were used primarily in the industries because of their unusual color rendering. Orange sodium vapor lights (primarily a low-pressure type) were second in line and were used only outdoors, mainly on the roads of Europe and in some areas of the United States. Fluorescent lamps were third. In 1939 these lamps revolutionized the lighting industry of the world by producing a high amount of diffused, shadowless illumination of relatively better color and greater life from a linear source with very little energy. After the incandescents, this lighting was the only source that found use in interior installations. Light output was dependent primarily on the type of phosphor inserted inside the tube—this provided flexibility of fine tuning the color to taste for interior application. Because the light output was extremely sensitive to ambient temperature, its use was confined to interior applications and to the roads of the country's southern states. From the very beginning, its use steadily increased and even today it enjoys the same popularity. More than 80% of the lighting in the United States is presently provided by fluorescent lamps.

Although light was developed out of necessity and primarily for visibility, other purposes, especially those that are decorative, were recognized many years ago. For centuries before Christ some oriental countries used oil-wick lamps for celebrating the festival of light, a tradition still in practice. In 1780 the arena of a famous circus was lighted by 28 candelabras in which a total of 1200 float wicks burned in colored glass containers. In later years light was used for decorating the perimeters of buildings. In 1901 bare electric bulbs highlighted the Pan American Exposition in Buffalo.

Other uses of light developed gradually with prosperity and the development of additional sources. As the color rendition, distributing pattern, aesthetics, and controlling mechanisms (dimmers, strobing effect, etc.) improved, they spread into numerous applications that made them an indispensable part of modern living. Colored light is uniquely suited to theatrical and merchandising environments. The dimmers, which were bulky and used exclusively backstage, are now so small and compact that they have replaced the regular switches inside offices, churches, and homes. In the hands of creative manufacturers light today is a decorative object; in the hands of sensitive designers it is a source of creating environmental moods and impressions.

The physiological aspects of light have resulted in blessings and curses almost simultaneously. A certain type of ultraviolet ray (UVB flux, 285–320 nm) is suspected of being the main cause of skin cancer, whereas other ultraviolet rays, X rays, gamma rays, infrareds, and laser beams successfully implement medical treatment. Light in combination with objects of certain colors is often used for psychiatric treatments. Optic fibers are used as decorative objects, light transmitters, telecommunications and computers.

Despite the unique qualities of light, unfortunately only its "quantity" aspects have been given attention in the field of illumination. After the development of the fluorescent an abundance of light for little energy was made easily available. Cheap energy led to the concept that "more light is better light," which unfortunately became an industrial standard. In commercial interiors the general practice has been to fill the ceiling with evenly distributed, area-type luminaires, sometimes supplemented with incandescent downlights to cover the difficult areas. This practice continued unchallenged through the early seventies. Then, with the energy crunch at that time (and then again in the early eighties) a major change occurred in the style of lighting design. As energy costs skyrocketed, the flaws in "more light is better light" became painfully apparent. In a renewed form it was felt that merely reducing the level of light to save energy (which proved counterproductive) was not necessarily the answer. In the commercial atmosphere work is constantly regulated by many factors which include the visual, aesthetical, psychological, and physiological, to name a few. This dynamic work force cannot be effectively controlled by a static lighting level. The system must be flexible, with provisions for fine tuning to specific needs.

REFERENCES

Dunsheath, Percy. *A History of Electrical Power Engineering.* Cambridge, Massachusetts: The M.I.T. Press, 1962.

Maclaren, Malcolm. *The Rise of the Electrical Industry During the Nineteenth Century.* Princeton University, 1943.

T'Dea, W. O. *The Social History of Lighting.* Routledge, 1958.

2

Light and Vision

Light and vision are interdependent. We see with our eyes, but even a perfect pair is useless when there is no light. Light by itself is not visible; an object, as well as its color, is made visible when light falls on it.

THE EYE

The human eye is a highly delicate and precisely designed instrument whose operational characteristics are in many ways like those of a camera (see Figure 2-1). A description follows of the various parts of the eye and their similarities to a camera.

The *sclera* is the white, opaque covering that holds the eyeball in its proper position and shape. In a camera the sclera is comparable to the housing. Toward the front of the eye, however, it becomes transparent, thus allowing light to enter from the outside. This part, known as the *cornea*, acts to protect the lens.

The *choroid* consists of a layer of blood vessels that nourishes the coat of the eyeball and may be compared to the middle lining of a camera.

The *iris* is the front portion of the choroid, comparable to the diaphragm of a camera. In the human eye it is a colored diaphragm that automatically controls the amount of light that enters the eye in response to the intensity and direction of the ambient light.

The *pupil,* or the opening in the center of the iris, is dilated or contracted by the iris. Its operation is similar to that of the aperture in the shutter of a camera.

The *lens* is positioned immediately behind the pupil and held in place by its muscles. Its function is similar to that of the lens of a camera; that is, it focuses the light but its mechanism is very different. In a camera the lens has a fixed shape and focal length. Focusing is done by moving it forward and backward. In the human eye the biconvex lens is made of flexible, multilayer organic material. In response to optic nerve stimuli the supporting muscles automatically change their curvature, thereby altering the focal length to bring the object into focus. The lens in its natural stable state will normally focus objects 15 to 20 ft away. To view objects farther removed it becomes flatter

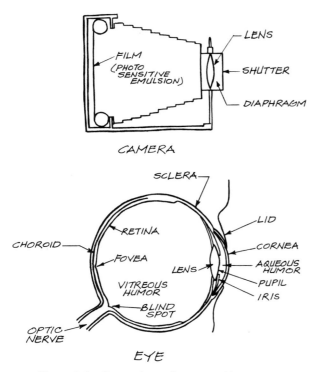

Figure 2-1. *Comparison of an eye with a camera.*

in a longer focal length. Closer viewing requires transformation to a more globular form. Prolonged maintenance of either form is conducive to eye fatigue.

The *retina* of the human eye is similar to the film in a camera. Light passing through the lens is focused on the retina; if, however, the lens is unable to focus precisely, blurred vision results. External help such as spectacles (glasses) or contact lenses are needed to correct the fault. The retina consists of nerve tissues with endings known as *cones* and *rods*. The retina also has two spots: the fovea centralis and the blind spot.

The *fovea*, also known as the yellow spot, is responsible for distinct vision. Millions of cones, which function in daylight, are packed near the fovea and are also responsible for distinguishing colors. Any malfunction results in color blindness. The rods, which are the other nerve endings, are scattered all the way from the fovea to the periphery of the retina and are responsible for the ability to see in early darkness and the only means of night vision. They cannot, however, detect color.

The *aqueous humor* is the watery solution between the cornea and iris.

The *vitreous humor* is the jellylike mass found in the entire space behind the lens. It refracts or bends light into the fovea, as necessary, to work in conjunction with the lens.

THE SEEING PROCESS (LIGHT-PERCEPTION)

Visible light lies between 380 and 780 nm (one nanometer or nm is equal to 10^{-9} m). All energy under 380 nm is ultraviolet (UV); above 780 nm it is infrared (IR): both areas are invisible to the eye. To be visible a ray of light passes through the cornea, the aqueous humor, and the pupil. The pupil expands or contracts to control the amount of light entering in response to optic nerve stimuli. Light then passes through the lens and vitreous humor to be focused on the retina. Electrochemical pulses are carried from the cones and rods to the optic nerve, which transmits them to the brain to be interpreted as light.

Rays of light in the form of photons fall on an object and are reflected from every point of its exposed surface. All reflected rays travel over the path described and converge to form an image on the retina. The image is upside down (Figure 2-2). By a process of adaptation practiced from birth the human eye interprets the inverted image as erect.

FIELD OF VISION

The field of vision of an average person extends approximately 180° in the horizontal plane and 130° in the vertical (see Figure 2-3a). Figure 2-3b is the binocular visual field. The white portion is the region seen by both eyes, the shaded portions, by each eye individually, and the dark portions, which extend from 60° above and 70° below the horizontal, are not seen. It is interesting to note that the two curved lines that separate the white and shaded portions are the cutoff line of the nose, as observed by the eye of the opposite side. The contour of the dark portions represents the cutoff formed by the eyebrows, cheeks, and nose. As a general rule, this field, which is encompassed by a circle of all points 30° from the optical axis, is considered to be the most effective for vision.

PHYSIOLOGICAL EFFECTS

Elasticity of the lens muscles begins to decrease at the age of 40 or older. Inability to focus precisely on the

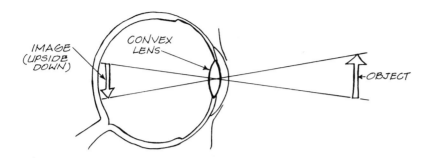

Figure 2-2. *The formed upside down image follows the characteristics of a convex lens. By a process of adaptation from birth the eye learns to interpret the inverted image as erect.*

retina results in myopia (nearsightedness) and hypermetropia (farsightedness) (Figure 2-4). In nearsightedness everything nearby is clearly seen but distant objects are not because in this condition the focal point lies in front of the retina. In farsightedness distant objects are clear but the closer objects are not clearly visible because the focal point lies beyond the retina. These defects can be corrected surgically or with the help of glasses or contact lenses. Astigmatism, another structural defect, occurs when irregularities develop in the curvature of the cornea and lens. A person affected by this disease is unable to focus vertical and horizontal surfaces simultaneously because the focal length inside the eye varies in two perpendicular planes. This condition, too, can be corrected by glasses, contact lenses, or surgery.

FACTORS INVOLVED IN THE VISIBILITY OF A TASK

So far we have discussed eye defects that are responsible for faulty vision. Yet a number of external factors also affect visibility:

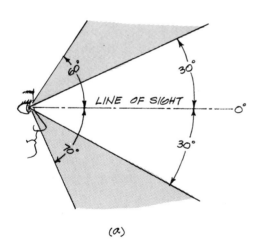

(a)

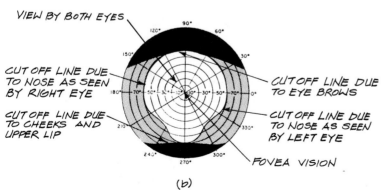

(b)

Figure 2-3. *(a) Field of view extends approximately 180° in the horizontal plane and 130° in the vertical. The most effective (seen by both eyes) is the portion encompassed by a circle of all points 30° from the optical axis. (b) The binocular visual field. Because a person with normal vision sees objects with both eyes simultaneously, the field of vision of the two eyes intermeshes in a perimeter bounded by the nose, eyebrows, cheeks, and lips.*

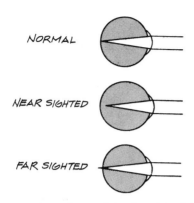

Figure 2-4. *Normal, nearsighted, and farsighted eyes.*

1. *Amount of Light.* For a specific task there must be enough light to allow the work to be done safely and efficiently. It must, however, be satisfactory as well in terms of quality. For exteriors daylight is predominantly the source of light (except at night when artificial light is required); artificial light is the main interior source. A mixture of daylight and artificial light is often a good source of illumination and a means of saving energy. A substantial difference in the illumination levels is required for exterior daylight and interior activities. All exterior daytime activities such as sports, lawn maintenance, and driving are totally dependent on widely varying natural light; for example, sunlight at noon on an open field may measure 7000 to 10,000 fc, but in shadow under a tree, only 1000. Cloudy days and late afternoons may register as low as 200 fc. Indoor activities, on the other hand, the illumina-

tion levels drop toward the bottom of the scale to a fraction of daylight levels. Normal office work such as reading and writing may need 100 fc; a storage pile in a warehouse may need no more than five. The levels of illumination required for indoor activities vary substantially, depending on the type of task, age of the viewer, and so on.

2. *Size of Task.* The task must be large and close enough to the eyes to be visible; for example, from a distance "3" can easily be mistaken for "8"; "I" for "1"; and "c" for "o." (see Figure 2-5).

3. *Duration.* To read a book faster and to avoid mistakes more light is needed.

4. *Contrast.* The contrast between the visual task and its background must be high; for example, if the lines in this book were printed in light gray instead of black it would certainly be more difficult to see or read. Research shows that for each 1% loss in contrast between visual task and background, there must be 15% more light to maintain the same degree of visibility.

5. *Brightness or Luminance.* In the world of lighting two types of brightness are a major consideration. The first is the direct glare from the luminaires and the second, the indirect or reflected glare from the task. From the standpoint of visibility the reflected glare is more of a problem than the direct. Luminaires located in offending zones provide light rays that reflect on shiny surfaces (e.g., a glossy picture or the

Figure 2-5. *Distinguishing features become increasingly difficult to comprehend as the letters or numbers become smaller.*

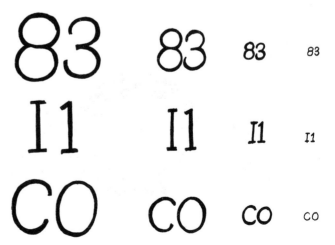

lines in a book) and direct toward the eyes, thus creating a "veil" over the task. This reduces contrast and makes it difficult to see. Brightness, or luminance, is measured in footlamberts.

EFFECT OF NATURAL OR ARTIFICIAL LIGHT ON SKIN

The effect of light on the human body is a controversial issue. From the very beginning and even today "sun worshiping" has been a large part of light in most of the world. In eastern countries, particularly the Soviet Union, children are exposed to artificial sunlight during school breaks to make up for the lack of natural sunlight. In the United States more than 100 million people per year spend their holidays following the sun. In India the sun is worshiped by many by facing it in the early hours of each day.

Scientific findings, however, hold overexposure to certain ultraviolet (UV) rays in sunlight (and artificial light) responsible for skin cancer. Based on current cohort data, without regard to changes in the ozone layer, an increase in skin-cancer mortality rates from 26.3 per million in 1971–1975 to 28.7 in 1976–1980 to 33.5 in 1981–1985 has been recorded among the white population alone.

The use of light with certain chemicals to treat disease has, however, been of great interest for decades. Niels R. Finsen received a Nobel Prize for his discovery of the efficacy of ultraviolet light on the treatment of tuberculosis. In 1925 ultraviolet light therapy (UVB) was introduced to fight ailments like psoriasis.

REFERENCES

Adler, F. H. *Physiology of the Eye.* St. Louis: Mosby, 1965.

Fitzpatrick, T. B. "The Trends and Future of Photobiology: Medical Aspects." *Trends in Photobiology.* New York: Plenum, 1984, pp. 391–395.

Kaufman, John E. *IES Lighting Handbook,* 1981, Reference Volume. New York: Illuminating Engineering Society, 1981, pp. 3-1–3-5.

3

Seeing Color

So far we have discussed how we observe light. Now we move on to color and how our eyes see it.

Although color is no more than an integral part of physical objects, from an artistic standpoint its scientific explanation is totally different. Scientists give us two separate theories to explain light and color: electromagnetic wave and quantum. Although science has proved neither one, the electromagnetic wave theory provides the more comprehensible explanation of the phenomenon. Electromagnetic energy is one of the many forms of energy such as the chemical, atomic, electrical, and thermal and is often referred to as radiant. This energy has a broad spectrum, all of which travels at an extremely high speed $(3 \times 10^8$ m/s, or 186,000 mps) in the air or a vacuum. At one end it has the cosmic rays and at the other, the electrical power waves (see Figure 3-1). In between are other rays such as the gamma, X ray, ultraviolet, infrared, microwaves, television, and radio. The energy in between the UV and IR is the only portion of the complete electromagnetic energy that is visible to the eye, known as "visible spectrum" or "light." Each type of ray is identified by a range of frequencies (number of wave cycles per second). Cosmic rays have the shortest cycles (maximum frequency) of radiant energy; each wavelength is 0.00001 nm and the electric power wavelength on the other end is as large as 5 million m (3100 miles). Light energy fits between UV and IR rays, whose wavelengths range from approximately 380 to 780 nm (1 in. = 25.4 million nm). Other wavelengths below or above these numbers are not visible to the eye and are considered the dark areas.

COLOR SPECTRUM FROM A WHITE LIGHT

A ray of light that contains the balanced radiant energy of all visible wavelengths appears as "white" to the eye. Isaac Newton passed a ray of white light through a prism to show that it consisted of many colors in a range of violet through red—the colors of a rainbow (see Figure 3-2). The normal eye immediately discerns three distinct colors: violet, green, and red in broad bands; the others lie in smaller bands and blend with the three that are distinctly visible. Thus each color can be identified not only by name, but by its range of wavelength; for example, blue lies between 440 and 500 nm, green between 525 and 550, and so on. A source of white light, whether it be the sun or an electric lamp, also produces some UV

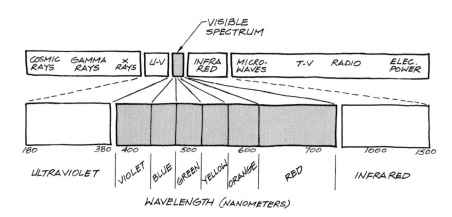

Figure 3-1. *Electromagnetic spectrum. The visible spectrum lies between 380 and 780 nm; 1 nm is equal to 10⁻⁹ m. (The angstrom unit of wavelength is equal to 10⁻¹⁰ m.)*

and IR energy that, as stated earlier, is not seen by the eye. It is interesting to note that a prism not only separates the colors in a white light but the UV and IR energy as well, which is useful for certain types of medical application.

Color has qualitative and quantitative characteristics. The qualitative refer to the wavelengths present; the quantitative measure their amount. Spectrum analysis will identify the "dominant wavelength," which indicates which of them appears to be most abundant, whereas the quantitative reveal the amount of energy that is a measure of luminance (photometric brightness). A white light is known as pure when its wavelengths are balanced. If there is an imbalance, purity may be described as the percentage of color to the percentage of white in the light.

WHAT IS COLOR IN AN OBJECT?

Color in an object is the result of waves of radiant energy that reach our eyes after they have been modified or filtered by the object; for example, an apple

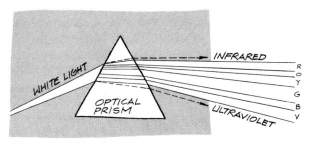

Figure 3-2. *When a ray of white light is passed through an optical prism, it bends shorter wavelengths more than longer wavelengths and separates them into distinctly identifiable bands of color.*

appears to be red because it absorbs all other colors of the incident light and reflects only the red wavelengths. The same phenomenon applies to artificially colored objects. Whether single- or multicolored, incident light falls on the object and all its colors, except for those that have the wavelengths for the designated colors, are absorbed. Thus it is evident that no color is visible without light and its true rendition is dependent primarily on the purity of the incident light. A pure white light that consists of balanced wavelengths of all colors will produce the true color of the object, as opposed to a light that has unbalanced chromaticity; that is, if the same apple were seen under a green light, it would appear to be gray.

Although the use of color for decoration or illustration goes back to the walls of the early caves, colored lighting is a recent development. Unlike white sources, colored light emits light in predetermined wavelength bands and their use must be carefully implemented to avoid unsatisfactory results as in the foregoing example of a red apple under a green light. Although white light is defined as having a balanced spectrum of all visible wavelengths, some light sources in industry that are significantly deficient in certain wavelengths are still called a white source. Incandescent lights are termed "warm white" sources because they produce the warm tones (red and yellow). Fluorescent, mercury vapor, and metal halide are termed "cool white" because they produce the cool tones of color (green and blue); a high-pressure sodium source is often termed "golden-white" because of its general dominance in the yellow-orange wavelengths. Low-pressure sodium, on the other hand, is termed monochromatic—an orange source—because its only color lies strictly in the orange wavelength.

From the standpoint of the lighting designer it should be remembered that the use of colored light

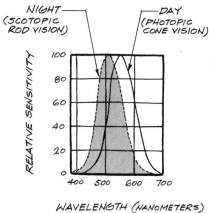

Figure 3-3. *Purkinje effect. The apparent brightness of colors shifts from day vision by cones to night vision by rods.*

can enhance the beauty of an ordinary piece of work as long as there is a wavelength for the designated object color. On the other hand, no matter how good the finish of an object may be, its true color will never be visible if the light source does not contain a matching wavelength.

VISION OF COLOR

Among the many explanations of the way that eyes see colors Young's three-component theory is the most comprehensible. This theory assumes that the cones of the eyes, which number approximately seven million in each eye and are concentrated in the fovea, can be divided into three types, each receptive to one of the primary colors of light: extreme spectrums of red, violet, and an imaginary green. These color-sensitive cones transform the received optical image pattern from radiant energy into chemical energy, which energizes the nerve endings. The optical is transmitted by electrical impulses through the optic nerves to the brain, where the signals are interpreted as the shape and color of the image. Cones are used mainly for color identification and daytime vision. At night the other light receptors (rods) take over the seeing process. These rods are receptive only to the quantity of light waves and cannot identify the color or fine details of the object.

PHYSIOLOGICAL EFFECTS

The degree of spectral sensitivity varies considerably between daytime (cones) and nightime (rods) vision. This was observed by Johannes Von Purkinje and is now known as the Purkinje effect (Figure 3-3). At dawn, while walking in a field, he observed that the blue flowers looked brighter than the red, just the opposite of what it seemed during the day. The apparent brightness (luminance) of different colors shifts from day vision by cones to night vision by rods. The Purkinje effect is generally used in measurements of light.

VISUAL DISABILITIES: COLOR BLINDNESS

Another form of visual disability, commonly known as color blindness or defective color-vision, is acquired by heredity or the process of aging and is usually untreatable. Various forms of color blindness, their visual capabilities, and percentage of occurrence are listed in Table 3-1.

The rarest (0.003% males, 0.002% females) and most serious kind of color blindness is rod monochromat, in which the person sees no color at all. The environment appears in various shades of gray, like watching a color program on a black and white TV. The spectral sensitivity function is scotopic. Persons with this type of vision defect are suspected of having a rod system and no cones. Dichromats are of three types: the protanopes lack sensitivity at the red end of the visual spectrum and cannot judge color above 520 nm; they have no trouble identifying blue. The denteranopes have normal spectral sensitivity but cannot judge color above 530 mm. The tritanopes have a spectral sensitivity curve but a slight difficulty in judging blue light; in addition they cannot distinguish colors between 445 and 480 nm wavelengths (blue to green).

There are three types of trichromat. Protanomalous are similar to dichromat protanope in spectral sensitivity functions but have reduced ability to judge from red to yellow-green wavelengths. The deuteranomalous, the most common (4.9% males and 0.38% females), see yellows and blues normally but have difficulty distinguishing greens from reds. The trianomalous trichromats have reduced judgment of green to blue.

Night blindness is another vision disability in which nothing can be seen after dark because of a total absence of rods.

PSYCHOLOGICAL EFFECTS OF LIGHT AND COLOR

This probably is the most important yet most ignored part of lighting design. It is important to remember

TABLE 3-1. DEFECTIVE COLOR VISION AND ITS PERCENTAGE OF OCCURRENCE[a]

Type	Monochromatic Wavelength Discrimination	Spectral Sensitivity Function and Wavelength of Peak Sensitivity	Percentage Frequency of Occurrence	
			Males	Females
Monochromat				
Rod monochromat	No discrimination	Scotopic (505 nm)	0.003	0.002
Dichromat				
Protanope	Absent above 520 nm	Insensitive to deep red light. Peak spectral sensitivity shifted (540 nm)	1.0	0.02
Deuteranope	Absent above 530 nm	Almost photopic (560 nm)	1.1	0.01
Tritanope	Absent from about 445 to 480 nm	Almost photopic (555 nm)	0.002	0.001
Trichromat				
Protanomalous	Reduced from red to yellowish green but varies considerably in different cases	Insensitive to deep red light, peak sensitivity wavelength shifted (540 nm)	1.0	0.02
Deuteranomalous		Almost photopic (560 nm)	4.9	0.38
Tritanomalous	Reduced for green to blue	—	—	—

[a] Reprinted from P. R. Boyce, *Human Factors in Lighting.* New York: Macmillan, 1981.

that light and color are inseparable and their existence is due to the concept that results from the interaction of physics, physiology, and psychology.

The interpretation by the brain of the impulses introduced by the optic nerves is probably the most mysterious part of the seeing process. Exactly how it takes place is still beyond human comprehension. Frequently the eye structure and the condition of the receptors in the eyes of those who are color blind are no different from others with normal vision. The reason for abnormality then points a finger at the malfunction of the impulse carrier (optic nerve) or at misinterpretation by the brain.

Psychological phenomena associated with lighting and color have for many years been a subject of interest. Since the early part of the twentieth century numerous researches have been conducted from which general conclusions can be made; for example, among all colored light sources yellow is the brightest and the most psychologically pleasing. In 1937 M. Luckiesh showed that yellow, on which the eyes focus easily, is most often selected as the brightest part of the color spectrum. C. E. Ferree and Gertrude Rand placed yellow light as the brightest and followed it with yellow-orange, yellow-green, green,

and then red, blue, and violet. Blue is difficult to focus on, which is obvious when we look at blue neon signs.

Color preferences in materials or objects seem to vary substantially with age. According to Faber Birren, infants are greatly attracted to yellow, white, pink, and red. As they grow older yellow gradually fades and is replaced by red and blue. At a mature age the order of preference starts with blue and green of shorter wavelengths (rather than red or yellow of longer wavelengths) and is followed by violet, orange, and yellow. Some experts claim that at very old age, when the eyes are feeble and the vision blurred, the order of preference returns to the bright colors for biological reasons.

In 1941, in extensive research that involved some 21,000 people, H. J. Eyseneck concluded that the order of preference among men is blue, red, green, violet, orange, and yellow and among woman, virtually the same, except that yellow is favored more than orange.

Extensive research conducted by many experts concludes in general that although people's reaction to color affects their individual preferences some colors have a universal effect. Red, for instance, a color universally selected for warmth and stimulation, tends to increase blood pressure, respiration, pulse rate, tension, and perspiration and may even excite brain waves. Blue, on the other hand, as the least exciting, has a cooling effect. Other colors with warmer tones, like orange and yellow, tend to react like red and the cooler tones, such as purple and violet, like blue, although less pronounced. Reaction to green is somewhat neutral. Colors may also be associated with various moods; for example red represents warmth and excitement, gold, luxury, purple, devotion and quietness, white, purity and cleanliness, and black, mourning and solemnity.

OPTICAL ILLUSIONS

Certain optical illusions that result from physiological and psychological reactions are of considerable interest; for example, warm colors (particularly red) appear to advance toward the eye, whereas cool colors (particularly blue) apparently recede. Based on this effect, selected colors can make a room seem larger or smaller than its actual size.

> *Dotted Fusion.* A lighter shade of the same color (e.g., red and pink or black and gray) can be created with the help of a pattern of dots (see Figure 3-4. The gray side is actually the product of minute black dots viewed through a magnifying glass. A variety of shades can be created by combining background and subject colors; for example, green dots on a yellow background will form a solid gray.

> *Disappearing Spots.* Focusing on any of the square blocks in Figure 3-5 produces imaginary spots "dancing" at the corners; try to focus on these spots; they quickly disappear.

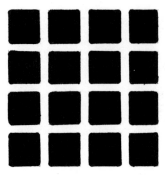

Figure 3-5.

Chameleon Effect. Colors of medium chroma will appear to change its intensity in the direction of its surrounding color. In Figure 3-6 the gray blocks between the white blocks appear to be lighter than those between black blocks even though they have exactly the same intensity.

Color Fatigue. Focus on a red object for a minute, turn away, and you will see a green image.

Contrast Induction. Response of one part of the retina is influenced by the response of another; this is made evident by the block in Figure 3-7. Hold a card vertically at the dividing edge of the black and white areas and examine the two sides of the block. Although its color has the same intensity, it appears to be lighter on the black background and darker on the white.

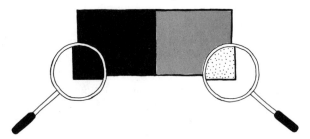

Figure 3-4. *A lighter shade is created with detached dots of the same color.*

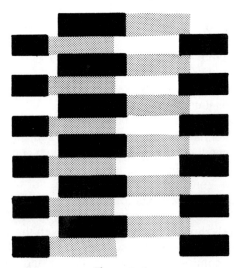

Figure 3-6.

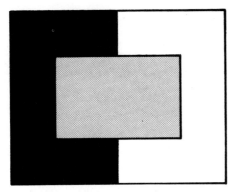

Figure 3-7.

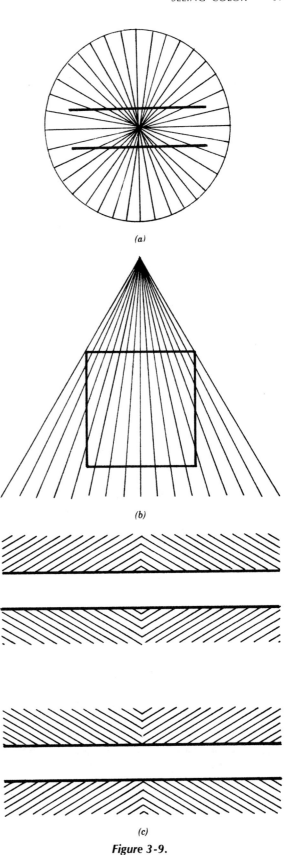

(a)

(b)

(c)

Figure 3-9.

Open and Close End Effect. The observer's perception is influenced by the inclusion of other parts in the whole pattern. In Figure 3-8 the upper horizontal line seems to be shorter than the lower (they are the same length) because of the influence of the direction of the arrowheads at the ends.

Background Effect. The shape of a figure may be altered by the background on which it is superimposed. Figure 3-9a shows two horizontal, straight, parallel lines which appear to be curved on a background with radiating lines. A similar phenomenon is shown in Figure 3-9b in which a perfect square appears to be distorted and becomes trapezoidal in shape. The horizontal lines in Figure 3-9c are actually straight and parallel to one another, but because they are combined with slanted lines they appear to be curved (bulging inward or outward in the middle). These visual illusions can be used for architectural treatment (columns, beams, etc.).

COLORIMETRY

The technique of measuring and systematically designating colors constitutes colorimetry, the importance of which is made apparent by the wide variety of

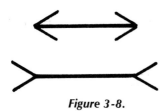

Figure 3-8.

colors that needs to be properly identified for selection and matching.

The primary colors of light (red, green, and blue) cannot be created by combining other colors. When added in different proportions, secondary colors of light are produced; that is, magenta (red plus blue), cyan (green plus blue), and yellow (red plus green). A proper combination of primary and secondary colors of light produces white light; for example, mixing magenta and green, yellow and blue, or cyan and red will produce white light. Each of these combinations is a complementary color of light. The secondary colors are made by mixing the primary colors; hence colors of light are also known as "additive."

In pigments (material color) the primary color is defined as one that subtracts or absorbs a primary color of light and reflects the remaining two. In pigments the primary colors are magenta, cyan, and yellow, which are the secondary colors of light. In pigments the primary colors are also known as subtractive. When a pigment primary color filter is placed over a white light, one of the primary colors of light is filtered and those remaining are transmitted; for example, if the filter is cyan, it will absorb the red and transmit only blue and green (the two primary colors of light that produced cyan). Similarly, a yellow filter will absorb blue and transmit green and red and magenta will absorb green and transmit red and blue. It is interesting to note that if two filters are used simultaneously all colors will be absorbed except one primary color of light; for example, if the filters are cyan and yellow, only green is transmitted, and for magenta and yellow red is transmitted. If all three are superimposed, all primary colors of light will be absorbed and the net transmission is no light (Figure 3-10). A variety of methods can be used to identify and organize color, all of which, however, recognize the use of white and black in creating a variation from its purest form. Among the various methods the Munsell color system provides the most comprehensive form. There are three variables in this system: hue, value, and chroma. Hue, the color as the eye sees it, is designated by the first letter(s) of the color or combination of colors; for example, red is R, blue is B, and yellow-green is YG. Value is the lightness or darkness of a color, achieved by adding white or black. Chroma is the purity or the saturation of the net color. The Munsell system of color notation is put together in an irregularly shaped globe; its vertical axis represents value, its outer surface, hue, and the horizontal axis, chroma. The color spectrum circles the outer surface in its purest form and is divided into

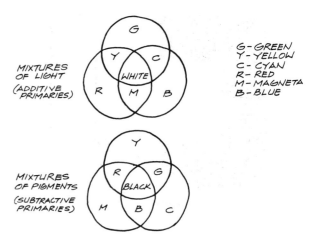

Figure 3-10. Additive and subtractive primaries (mixtures of light and mixtures of pigments).

20 basic hues, identified by the first letter of the color and a code number. The vertical axis, which represents value, is divided into 10 equal parts, its origin at the bottom (black) and maximum at the top (white). Chroma is designated by numbers starting at zero at the vertical axis and increasing gradually outward. A complete structure of a specific color resembles a vertical pie (Figure 3-11) that describes color in terms of hue, value, and chroma. To identify a particular color the hue code, written first, is followed by the value code, a slash, and the chroma code; for example, a very grayed blue would be identified by the notation 5B3/2.

COLOR TEMPERATURE

Color temperature refers to the absolute temperature in degrees kelvin of a theoretical blackbody or full radiator whose color appearance matches that of the source of light.

In 1900 Max Planck found that when an object is raised in temperature the color of the light emitted changes. This became the method of identifying or matching the color of a light source. To attain the same color at a certain temperature it is necessary that the reference be a blackbody radiator, which is theoretically a complete, perfect radiator. When a blackbody radiator is heated, it produces first red, then yellow white, and then bluish white as its temperature rises. Color temperature is not a measure of actual light-source temperature but is that of a blackbody heated to the same color (chromaticity); for example, an incandescent lamp is claimed to have a

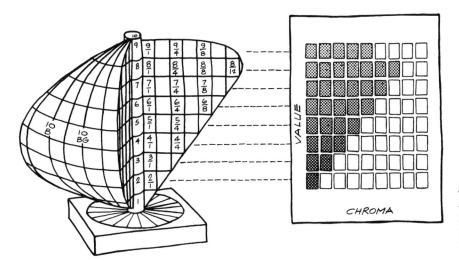

Figure 3-11. Munsell color solid system. A quarter of the solid is removed to show interior selection and color notation scales for hue, value, and chroma.

color temperature of 3000 K, which indicates that this is the matching color of a blackbody radiator heated to 3000 K.

SPECTRAL POWER DISTRIBUTION (SPD)

An additional requirement in the assignment of a color temperature to a light source is its spectral power distribution (SPD), which must match that of a blackbody radiator. An SPD curve shows the magnitude of the radiant power and the shapes of the colors (wavelengths) of the source. In reality an incandescent lamp is the only source that matches the chromaticity and SPD of a blackbody radiator; hence a color temperature can be assigned successfully to identify a specific color rendering. For a gaseous discharge source the assignment is made in terms of "correlated or apparent color temperature" because its chromaticity matches but its SPD does not.

COLOR RENDERING INDEX (CRI)

This index is another method of specifying the color rendering of light sources. The color rendering of the source of interest on a neutral surface is compared with that of a reference source (blackbody radiator, up to 5000 K; daylight, more than 5000 K). The com-parison is made by assigning the numbers 0 to 100. The higher the number, the closer the color to that of the reference source; for example, a CRI of 98 means that the color rendition of the source of interest is close to the color produced by the reference source on a neutral surface. A CRI of 100 indicates a perfect match. It is important to note that the same CRI values of two sources will not match in color rendering if their reference sources of comparison are different.

Although color temperature (degree K), spectral power distribution, and color rendering index are in-dividual measures of color rendering, for a true color identification of a source it may be necessary to spec-ify all three measures simultaneously.

REFERENCES

Birren, Faber. "Psychological Implication of Color and Illumina-tion." *Illuminating Engineering,* 64, 5, 397–401 (1969).

Birren, Faber. *Color and Human Response.* New York: Van Nos-trand-Reinhold, 1978.

Ferree, C. E. and Gertrude Rand, "Lighting and the Hygiene of the Eye." *Archives of Opthalmology* (July 1929).

General Electric, Light and Color, TP-119. Cleveland, Ohio: Nela Park, 1967.

Luckiesh, M. *The Science of Seeing.* New York: Van Nostrand, 1937.

Luckiesh, M. *Light Vision and Seeing.* New York: Van Nostrand, 1944.

ENGINEERING TOOLS

4

Light Sources and Accessories

INCANDESCENT LAMPS

Principles of Operation

Among all electrically operated light sources the operating principle of the incandescent is the simplest. A glass envelope houses a high-resistance metallic filament that becomes hot and intensely bright when electricity is passed through it. An electrical connection is made through its base, which is screwed into a socket. Figure 4-1 is a diagram of a typical incandescent lamp.

Filament

Tungsten is the most suitable filament because of its high melting point, low evaporation, high strength and ductility, and favorable radiation characteristics. Operating temperatures generally are more than 4000°F. These filaments come in different forms, designated by a letter-code: S = straight, C = coiled, CC = coiled coil, and R = flat or ribbon. Some typical examples are given in Figure 4-2. Most bulbs use a CC filament because it offers maximum efficiency. Because of the filament's lower cold resistance at

start, a large inrush of current (for a fraction of a second) occurs before a steady operating current is established. At this steady operating current the filament reaches the temperature of incandescence.

Enclosure

The enclosure is usually made of common lime glass, but for special applications bulbs are available in heat-resistant, low-expansion glasses. A variety of bulb shapes is designated by the following letters: A = standard; C = cone, F = flame, CA = donor, G = globular, GT = chimney, P = pear, PS = pear straight, T = tubular, PAR = parabolic reflector, and R = reflector (see Figure 4-3). In addition to the letter designation, a bulb bears a number to identify its maximum diameter. To determine the diameter in inches the number is divided by eight. A bulb designated by A-21 indicates a standard bulb with a maximum diameter of 21/8 or 2⅝ in.; PAR-38 indicates a parabolic reflector bulb with a maximum diameter of 38/8 or 4¾ in. (Figure 4-4).

Bulb finishes can be clear, acid-etched, frosted, silver-bowl, tinted, outside-spray, ceramic, glazing, or fused-on color filters. Standard lamps in the market

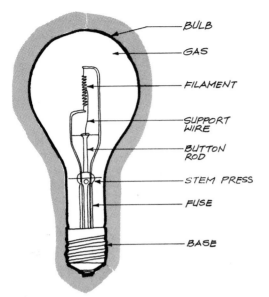

Figure 4-1. *Typical construction of an incandescent lamp.*

are clear or frosted. In clear lamps the intensely bright filament is directly visible. Lamps with acid-etched interiors give the impression of a glowing ball of light inside the bulb enclosure. Frosted lamps (also known as soft white light) are coated with silica powder that

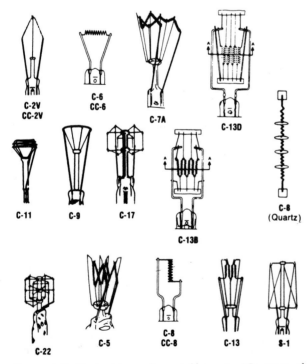

Figure 4-2. *Typical incandescent filaments. (Courtesy of General Electric.)*

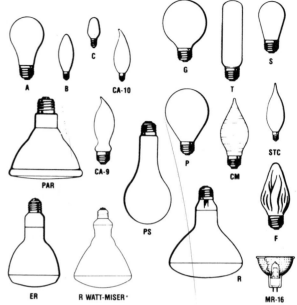

Figure 4-3. *Typical incandescent bulb shapes. (Courtesy of General Electric.)*

diffuses the intense brightness of the filament and gives the appearance of a uniformly illuminated bulb. This arrangement, however, reduces the lamp's light output by approximately 1% less than clear bulbs. Silver-bowl lamps are primarily A or P in shape but are installed with the base up. The lower half of the bulb is coated with a specular aluminum that prevents the filament from being directly visible from the bottom. The remaining finishes are for choice color rendition.

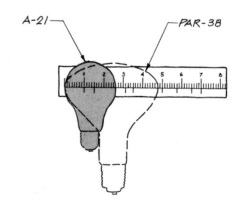

Figure 4-4. *Incandescent bulb size (its maximum diameter) is expressed in eighths of an inch (1/8); for example an A-21 bulb is 21 eighths of an inch or 2⅝ in. diameter. A PAR-38 is 4¾ in. diameter.*

Bases

The base of a bulb is made mainly of brass and is used for mounting and positioning and to provide an electrical connection with the filament. There is a variety of bases but most are of two types; screwbase and precise positioning bases. As the name implies, the first kind is screwed inside the socket for connection and is the most common. Screw-bases can be (a) mogul, which are used only for lamps of 300 W or more; (b) medium, for almost all other lamps in popular use; (c) candelabra, the narrowest base operating on 120-V, used for decorative, lantern, and mirror lights; and (d) minicandelabra, similar to candelabra but smaller (the socket is skirted); (e) screw with ring contacts used for special lamps with multifilaments (usually three-way) to operate one, two, or all three simultaneously. Some typical bases are shown in Figure 4-5. Screw-base lamps have one disadvantage; it is hard to determine from the outside whether the base has made proper contact with the socket. Improper contact may result in heat buildup inside the socket. Precise positioning bases eliminate this problem and, as the name suggests, provide a precise location of the filament for best light control. These can be (a) bipost with two cylindrical posts extending to the bottom of the base, (b) bayonet with two small prongs extending from the sides of the base, (c) prefocus which aligns the filament with flanges, and (d) disks mounted at the ends of a tubular incandescent lamp (lumiline).

Filling Gas

The filament partly evaporates each time the lamp is turned on. To minimize this condition 40-W and higher wattage lamps are filled with an inert gas, mainly argon and nitrogen, which allows the filament to operate at a higher temperature and offers higher efficacies and better longevity. Bulbs of fewer than 40 W are evacuated because their filaments operate at a much lower temperature and there is insignificant evaporation.

Tungsten-halogen lamps (described in a later section) are filled with a halogen gas (usually bromide or iodine). As the lamp reaches its operating temperature the halogen gas prevents the evaporated particles of the filament from depositing on the bulb's inner surface. When the bulb cools down, halogen combines with the free, evaporated tungsten particles and recirculates to the filament, a process that keeps the bulb clean and increases the lamp's efficacy and longevity.

Krypton gas, instead of argon-nitrogen, is used in some lamps to improve efficacy. Krypton has a lower heat conductivity than argon or nitrogen that contributes to the system's operating efficiency and lowers power consumption. These lamps are used mainly to replace conventional lamps of 40 to 150 W with extended life.

Types of Lamp

There are hundreds of different types of incandescent lamp: a complete coverage is beyond the scope of this book. We discuss only those lamps in frequent use for commercial purposes. They are categorized by their use or by the names commonly referred to.

General Service

A and PS types, clear or frosted, are general service lamps and the most economical. Their first cost is the lowest and 750 to 1000 h of life are typical.

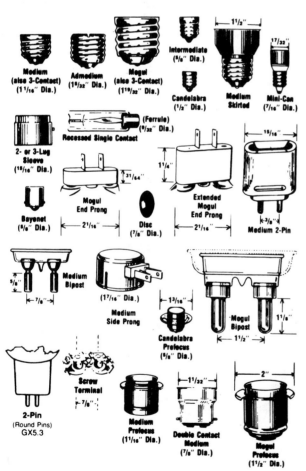

Figure 4-5. *Typical incandescent lamp bases. (Courtesy of General Electric.)*

Rough Service

These modified versions of general service lamps have additional filament-holding supports for use in areas with physical shock or vibration. Additional supports increase the overall resistance of the filament and reduce efficacy.

Silver and White Bowl

These are modified general service and G-type lamps with reflective coatings on the globular part of the bulb. The white bowls are treated with a translucent coating and silver bowls with opaque silver. They are used mainly for indirect and decorative purposes; their light output is much lower than that of general service lamps.

ER, R, and PAR (Standard Voltage)

Elliptical reflector (ER), reflector (R), and parabolic reflector (PAR) lamps are manufactured with built-in reflectors to direct the light. They are available with plain or prismatic lenses and a wide variety of beam spreads. Wide-beam (flood) lamps are suitable for general or wall-wash lighting purposes and to provide a uniform amount of light without "hot spots." Lamps with narrow beam spreads are known as "spot lamps" and are used primarily when a concentrated amount of light is required to illuminate a specific object. In general, PAR lamps are more precise in light control than R and ER lamps. The greatest ad-

vantage of all these lamps is that they have long life, and, when replaced, the complete optical system, including the reflector, is renewed. These lamps cost approximately three to four times more than general service lamps of the same wattage.

Elliptical reflector lamps may successfully replace R or A lamps in some luminaires to produce the same amount of light with lower wattage. A good portion of the light emitted by A or R lamps is trapped and wasted inside the cylindrical luminaire; ER lamps designed on the basic principles of elliptical reflectors with two focal points eliminate this problem. The filament is precisely located on the first focal point and all reflected light rays emit through the second. When installed inside a luminaire, the light rays avoid contact with the cylinder and end in a pool of light that is emitted through a small opening (Figure 4-6). This principle is also used for "pinhole" luminaires.

PAR (Low Voltage)

Low voltage lamps, generally available in 12 and 5.5 V, use a much smaller filament that offers better optical control. Superior light control, longer life, and somewhat higher amounts of light per watt have made them more desirable than their standard voltage counterparts wherever precision in light control and economy are simultaneously important. An additional benefit is that the low voltage is much safer to work with than 120 V. This feature alone makes these

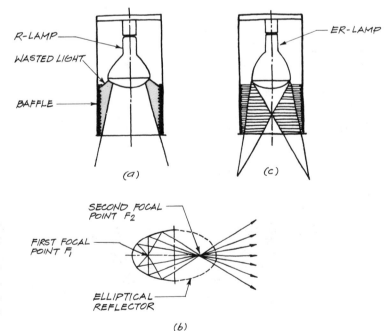

Figure 4-6. (a) A good portion of light is wasted when an R or A lamp is used inside cylindrical luminaires. (b) When a point source is placed in the first focal point of an elliptical reflector, all reflected rays merge through the second focal point. (c) An ER-lamp, working on the principle of an elliptical reflector, produces a pool of light from small openings.

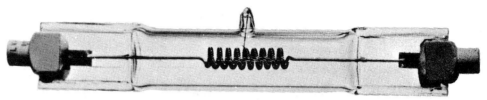

Figure 4-7. A typical tungsten-halogen lamp. (Courtesy of GTE Sylvania Incorporated.)

lamps ideally suited to exterior ground lighting and inside or near water. The wiring needs neither special insulation nor conduits.

The main disadvantages are their high initial cost, maintenance requirements for the low-voltage transformer, and heavier wire sizes to carry greater amounts of current. These lamps must be installed as close as possible to the transformer to avoid voltage drop.

Tungsten-Halogen

Tungsten-halogen lamps (also known as quartz iodine or simply, quartz; Figure 4-7) produced a major breakthrough in preventing evaporated tungsten from depositing on the bulb's inner surface (lamp blackening). It utilizes a halogen such as iodine or bromide as the fill gas. The bulb is a narrow cylinder of quartz that generates and operates at high temperatures. At high temperatures the evaporated tungsten combines with a halogen molecule and is returned to the hot filament, where the halogen is freed and the cycle is repeated. This constant action of cleaning minimizes bulb-wall blackening to retain almost all of the initial lumen output throughout the life of the lamp (Figure 4-8).

Perhaps the main disadvantage of a tungsten-halogen lamp is its high operating temperature which may cause trouble if installed in a compact luminaire. Its linear configuration (primarily cylindrical) may not be the ideal shape of a source of light control. The other disadvantage is that in a dimmed condition the operating temperature falls too low to continue the cleaning cycle. The inner bulb wall begins to blacken at this stage. When the lamp is brought back to its normal, high-operating temperature, source particles are recycled.

MR-16 (Low Voltage)

This is a compact, 12-V lamp (2 in. in diameter) with a tiny filament in a miniature tungsten-halogen capsule positioned for optical accuracy in a dichroic-coated, multimirrored, reflector. An abundance of light with an even beam and accurate optical control is achieved with excellent color rendering. It varies from 20 to 75 W and its life ranges from 2000 to 3500 h.

Extended Service

These lamps offer more than twice the life span of the conventional and are useful in areas in which it is difficult to reach the luminaires for lamp changing. Lumen efficacy is lower than that of standard lamps.

Tubular

Tubular lamps are long and cylindrical and come in two models. The "showcase" has a single screwbase at one end, the "lumiline" has one disk at each end. Both are available in different sizes and wattages. The lumilines resemble small fluorescent lamps that can be used in areas in which linear light sources are

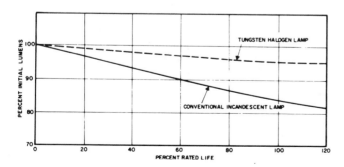

Figure 4-8. At high temperatures in tungsten-halogen lamps, evaporated tungsten combines with a halogen molecule and is returned to the hot filament. This improves its lumen maintenance.

needed to emit more favorable light color than fluorescents.

Electrical Characteristics

Incandescent lamps are sensitive to voltage variation. In general, the light output is direct and longevity is inversely proportional to voltage variation. As the voltage is increased the light output increases but with loss of life. When operated at lower than its rated voltage, its reduced light output produces significant improvement.

Dimming

Dimming of incandescent lamps is done mainly for aesthetics purposes and "mood" creation. Additional benefits are energy saving and lamp longevity. In the past rheostats and autotransformers which were bulky and resulted in certain loss of power were the only dimmers used. The new solid-state dimmers which eliminate these problems are compact, available from 600 to 2000 W, and can be wall-mounted. A relation between the performance of light output and life can be seen in Figure 4-9 as the input power is varied. A saving in power is not in the same proportion as the light level; for example, at 75% input power only 52% light is achieved, but this is not quite so bad as it sounds in terms of visual acuity because the eyes can accommodate relatively wide variations in lumen levels. Also note that at 75% input power with 25% energy savings the life of the bulb shows an increment of 11.3 times the normal.

Dimming has some disadvantages, however.

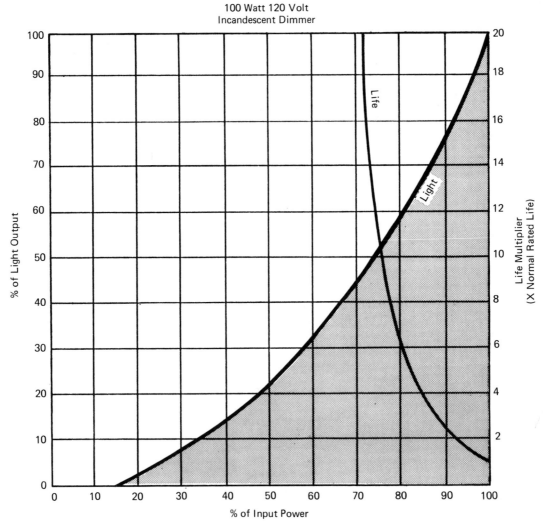

Figure 4-9. Effect of light output and life with a change in input power for incandescent lamps.

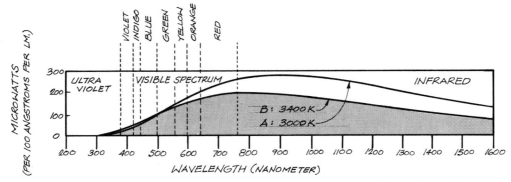

Figure 4-10. *SPD of incandescents. Curve A represents a conventional incandescent lamp. Maximum energy lies in the warm tones and in the infra red zone. The result is a "yellow white color". Curve B represents a tungsten-halogen lamp. With substantially less energy at infrared and slightly more in ultraviolet zones, the color is white.*

Some lamps produce "filament ringing" caused by radio frequency (RF) noise created by a distorted sine-wave of solid-state dimming. Many manufacturers provide RF suppression and chokes that will minimize filament ringing. Dimming reduces filament temperature, which also reduces the effectiveness of tungsten-halogen's automatic cleaning feature.

Color Characteristics

Incandescent sources are predominantly the thermal emission type in which a majority of the energy lies in the infrared zone (long wavelength) and the least in the ultraviolet zone (short wavelength), as shown in the Figure 4-10. Approximately 10% of its total energy lies in the wavelengths that produce visible radiation. The appreciation order of the colors by the sources can be determined by observing the magnitude of their radiant power in the visible spectrum; for example, the conventional incandescent lamps (curve A) and tungsten-halogen lamps (curve B) appreciate red the most and then gradually diminish to orange, yellow, green, blue, and indigo, with the least at violet. Also note that curve B has slightly more radiant power at the ultraviolet range and much less

at the deep-red range when compared with those of curve A. This results in a visible "white" effect for the tungsten-halogen and "yellow-white" for the incandescents when observed on a neutral surface. The effects of the colors of conventional and tungsten halogen incandescents are listed in Table 4-1.

Efficacy

Efficacy (lumen per watt) improves as the wattage rises; for example, up to 500 W efficacy varies from 17 to 23 lm/W; for higher wattage lamps (e.g., 1000 to 10,000 W) it varies from 23 to 33 lm/W. Tungsten filament incandescents appear to have a practical efficacy limit of 40 lm/W.

Mortality

A mortality curve is drawn, based on the fact that although many inherent reasons make it impossible to predict the life of a particular lamp many fail in a predictable manner. The rated life of a lamp is designated when 50% of a given number burns out. In lighting design, in the determination of the light-loss factor, it is necessary to know when the lamps will

TABLE 4-1. INCANDESCENT LAMP SELECTION BY COLOR[a]

Lamp Type	Visible Effect on Neutral Surface	Effect on Atmosphere	Color Strengthened	Color Grayed	Effect on Complexion
Incandescent filament	Yellowish white	Warm	Red, orange, yellow	Blue	Ruddy
Tungsten-halogen	White	Warm	Red, orange, yellow	Blue	Ruddy

[a] Courtesy of General Electric.

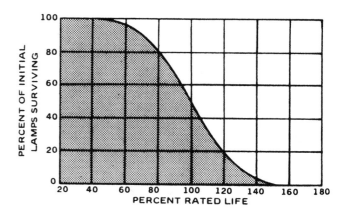

Figure 4-11. *Mortality curve of incandescent lamps. (Courtesy of GTE Sylvania Incorporated.)*

start to burn out and at what stage they will be replaced. A mortality curve helps to determine the number or burnouts before the time of planned replacement is reached (Figure 4-11). In use the life of the lamps is seldom so long as predicted by the mortality curve because of field factors such as physical shock and vibration that affect life performance.

Effect of Burning Position and Depreciation

When incandescent lamps are burned over a period of time, the filaments evaporate and become smaller. This evaporation increases their resistance and reduces the ampere watt, and lumen output. Figure 4-12 shows the effect of lumen output, the wattage, and the efficacy of general-purpose lamps for their rated life.

Lumen reduction is also caused by lamp blackening (deposits of evaporated tungsten on the bulb). In vacuum lamps this blackening is uniform; in gas-filled lamps the evaporated tungsten particles are carried by convection currents to the upper part of the bulb.

In gas-filled bulbs the base-up position lamps offer

more useful lumens over the base-down or horizontal types because most of the blackening occurs in the neck area, where part of it is intercepted by the base (see Figure 4-13). This may affect the selection of a luminaire (Figure 4-14).

FLUORESCENT LAMPS

Principles of Operation

The Illuminating Engineering Society of North America (IES) defines the fluorescent lamp as a "low-pressure mercury electric-discharge lamp in which a fluorescent coating (phosphor) transforms some of the ultraviolet energy generated by the discharge into light."

As the switch of the lamp is turned on the heated electrodes at each end expel electrons. When sufficient voltage is applied, electrons from one electrode to the other travel at high speed to create an electrical discharge. The filling gases ionize and allow mercury to vaporize and current to flow. Collision between the traveling electrons and the atoms of the mercury

Figure 4-12. *Typical effect on lumen output, wattage, and efficacy of general-purpose incandescent lamps for their rated life.*

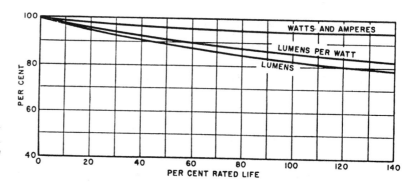

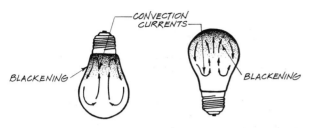

Figure 4-13. *Lamp blackening due to convection currents within a gas-filled bulb.*

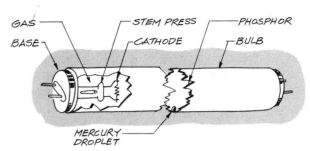

Figure 4-15. *Typical construction of a fluorescent lamp.*

vapor releases ultraviolet radiation at a specific wavelength of 253.7 nm on the electromagnetic spectrum. They are then absorbed by the phosphor crystals on the inside wall of the tube and reradiated as visible light (see Figures 4-15 and 4-16).

It is interesting to note that the quantity of UV radiation is dependent largely on the mercury vapor pressure, which is regulated by the bulb-operating temperature. Light output may vary substantially if the bulb-wall temperature is subjected to ambient temperature variation.

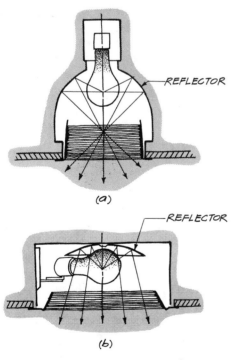

Figure 4-14. *(a) When lamps are in base-up position, blackening occurs in the neck area. Light distribution is not affected. (b) With horizontal lamps, blackening occurs on the top. This may reduce light output and affect light distribution.*

Bulbs

The bulbs are mostly straight glass tubes; others are U-shaped, circular, or dented tubular (see Figure 4-17). These tubes are available in a number of lengths, diameters, and other dimensions. The straight tubes may range from 8 in. to 8 ft in length with diameters varying from 5/8 to 2 1/8 in. Light output is distributed uniformly throughout the bulb, except for the two ends which are darkened by the cathodes and bases. Most common fluorescent lamps are 4 ft long and placed inside 4-ft luminaires of varying widths. The 2 × 2 ft luminaires may be fitted with U-shaped bulbs or 2-ft straight bulbs. From the standpoint of light output, energy-use, and longevity the U-shaped bulbs outperform the straight variety. Their legs can be 3 or 6 in. apart. The circline bulbs can be 8 1/4, 12, or 16 in. outside diameter (OD) and are used mainly indoors with circular luminaires. Light from a circline bulb is uniform all around except for the ends where the cathodes are connected to the base.

All lamp designations contain the wattage (or length), shape, diameter in eighths of an inch, color,

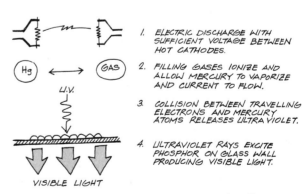

Figure 4-16. *Many cycles of operation inside a fluorescent lamp.*

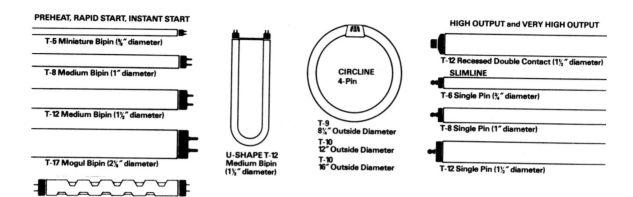

Figure 4-17. Fluorescent lamp shapes.

and type of lamp circuiting, for example, F40T12/CW/RS indicates a fluorescent lamp of 40 nominal watts (F40), a tubular bulb of 12 ÷ 8 = 1½ in. diameter (T12), cool white (CW) color rendition, and rapid start (RS) circuiting.

Bases

Bases are produced in three different types: (a) single-pin, (b) bi-pin, and (c) recessed double-contact and are available in all sizes. The bi-pin bases, which are the most common, come in miniature (T5), medium (T8, T12), and mogul (T17). The single-pin bases provide single contact, and the bi-pins, double contact at each end of the lamp. Recessed double-contact bases, used mainly for lamps with high light output, have a safer contact for higher voltage starting (Figure 4-18).

Electrodes

An electrode (also known as hot cathode) is placed at each end of a fluorescent lamp. It is a coiled coil, triple coil, or stick coil made of tungsten and is similar to the filament of an incandescent lamp. It does not glow but has an electric arc for starting and continuous electrons for lamp current. It is sometimes coated with an alkaline earth oxide to emit electrons when heated.

Filling Gas and Mercury

The tube holds a small quantity of pure argon or a combination of argon and neon. Some have krypton. In addition, the tube contains a few drops of liquid mercury.

Phosphor

Phosphor is coated on the entire inside wall of the tube. This fluorescent material is responsible for producing visible light. A wide variation in color is made by the application of different types of phosphor, e.g. cadmium borate, pink; calcium halophosphate, white; calcium silicate, orange; calcium tungstate, blue; magnesium germanate, red; magnesium tungstate, bluish white, zinc silicate, green.

Fluorescent Lamps by Type of Circuit

Because fluorescent lamps cannot produce light by direct connection to the power source, they need auxilliary circuits and devices to get started and stay lighted. The auxiliary circuit is contained inside an enclosure known as the ballast. Fluorescent lamps

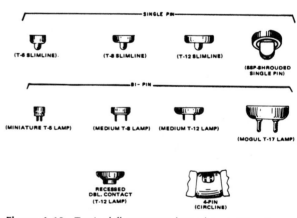

Figure 4-18. Typical fluorescent lamp bases. (Courtesy of GTE Sylvania Incorporated.)

can be further divided into three types based on the circuiting used for their starting operation:

1. *Preheat.* These lamps require a starting circuit for preheating the cathodes to aid in starting (see Figure 4-19a).

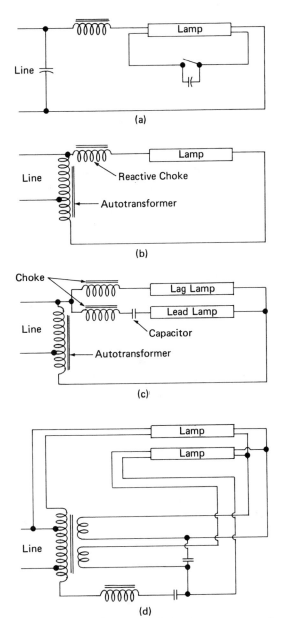

Figure 4-19. (a) Preheat type of circuit starter across lamp can be automatic or manual. (b) Instant-start type of circuit. Reactive choke coil and autotransformer constitute the ballast components. (c) Two-lamps slimline lead-lag (split-phase) type of circuit. Capacitor, choke coils, and autotransformer constitute ballast components. (d) Two-lamp rapid-start-series type of circuit.

2. *Instant Start and Slimline.* These lamps have a single pin at each end but do not need the starter and starting circuit. A ballast provides a high starting voltage, thus eliminating the starter circuit. Standard lamps operate at 425 mA. (see Figure 4-19b). Slimline fluorescents function on the same starting principles and accommodate single-pin lamps (Figure 4-19c). Special lampholders which open the primary circuit when a lamp is removed are used in instant-start circuits with slimline lamps to safeguard against the higher circuit voltage.

3. *Rapid Start.* These are the lamps most commonly used for commercial purposes. The principles of preheat and instant-start circuits are applied but starters are not required. (see Figure 4-19d). The preheating is supplied by a built-in, low-voltage transformer coil in the ballast. These lamps are the only kind that can be dimmed or flashed in the complete fluorescent family and are available in four different types of loading:

   (a) *Standard Loading.* These lamps are most often used in offices and schools in 4 foot long luminaires. They operate at 430 mA on medium bipin bases.

   (b) *High Output.* These lamps operate at 800 mA on recessed double-contact (RDC) bases.

   (c) *Very High Output.* These lamps operate at 1500 mA on recessed double-contact bases.

   (d) *Circline.* These lamps operate at 390, 420, and 430 mA.

4. *Trigger Start.* This is a combination of a preheat lamp and a special ballast with a cathode heating coil that eliminates the use of a starter. It has higher preheating voltage for starting than the rapid-start ballasts and is typically used only for lamps of less than 40 W.

More about fluorescent ballasts is discussed elsewhere in this chapter.

Color Characteristics

The color of a fluorescent lamp depends strictly on the phosphor used in the bulb. The spectral power distribution (SPD) of fluorescence has two components: a continuous smooth curve and a line or bar spectrum, which represent the two types of light sources inside the lamp. The smooth portion occurs because of the excitement of the phosphor and the bar portion results from the arc inside the lamp.

Fluorescent lamps are commonly manufactured in six standard colors: cool white, deluxe cool white, warm white, deluxe warm white, white, and daylight. These and a few others are shown in Figure 4-20. Cool white, warm white, white, and daylight lamps are weak in red. The deluxe cool white and deluxe warm white are improved in red but at the expense of reduced efficacy. Table 4-2 lists the color characteristics of different types of fluorescent lamp.

In general, cool color schemes should be considered in areas in which a high amount of light is required. Warm sources in these applications may appear to be overpowering. Conversely, for areas with low light-level requirements warm sources may be preferred.

Efficacy

Efficacy usually improves with the length of the lamp. Fluorescent ballasts are designed to operate one to three lamps. Efficacy of the system also increases with the larger number of lamps per ballast. In general, the efficacy of a fluorescent lamp is two to three times that of incandescents.

Effect of Temperature

Light output and operating power are affected simultaneously by ambient temperature. Figure 4-21 describes the performance characteristics of a typical indoor fluorescent lamp. As mentioned earlier, a fluorescent lamp is dependent primarily on mercury vapor pressure for its operation. This pressure, in turn, is dependent on the bulb wall temperature. In general, most indoor fluorescent lamps are designed to allow

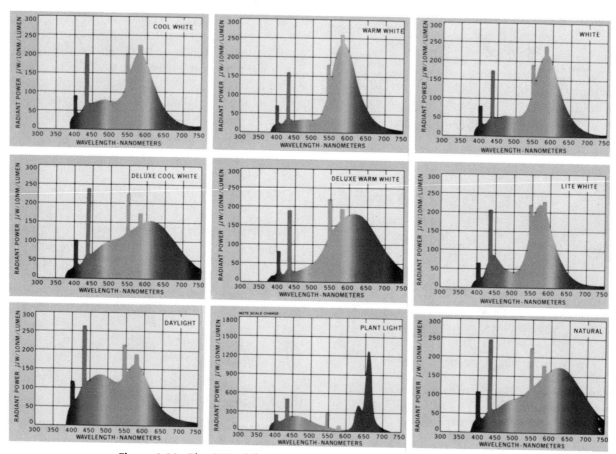

Figure 4-20. *The SPD of fluorescent lamps. (Courtesy of General Electric.)*

TABLE 4-2. FLUORESCENT LAMP CHARACTERISTICS BY COLOR

Lamp Type	Visible Effect on Neutral Surface	Effect on Atmosphere	Color Strengthened	Color Grayed	Effect on Complexion	Remark
Cool white	White	Neutral to moderately cool	Orange, yellow, blue	Red	Pale pink	Blends with natural daylight; good color acceptance
Deluxe cool white	White	Neutral to moderately cool	Nearly all colors	None appreciably	Most, natural	Best overall color rendition; simulates neutral daylight
Warm white	Yellowish white	Warm	Orange, yellow	Red, green, blue	Sallow	Blends with incandescent light; poor color acceptance
Deluxe warm white	Yellowish white	Warm	Red, orange, yellow, green	Blue	Ruddy	Good color rendition simulates incandescent light
Daylight	Bluish white	Very cool	Green, blue	Red, orange	Greyed	Usually replaceable with cool white
White	Pale yellowish white	Moderately warm	Orange, yellow	Red, green, blue	Pale	Usually replaceable with cool white or warm white

their light output to peak at 100°F bulb wall temperature, which occurs at an ambient room temperature of approximately 77°F. A substantial change in ambient temperature would alter the bulb wall temperature and affect the lamp's performance. Referring to Figure 4-21, note that light output and operating power reduce simultaneously as the bulb wall temperature exceeds 100°F. At lower temperatures, however, light output decreases more drastically than power.

It must be noted that lamp performance data and the input power of different lamp-ballast combinations, available from manufacturers' catalogs, are actually the result of a series of bench tests performed according to predetermined fixed parameters. Although these bench tests meet accepted national standards, their results are true only to the extent of the parameters by which they were tested. When lamps are inserted in luminaires installed in the ceiling, the performance of the lamps and ballasts differs substantially from their bench-test values, hence affect the overall efficiency. As a rule of thumb, it can

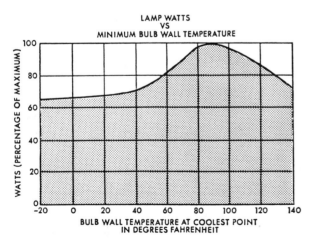
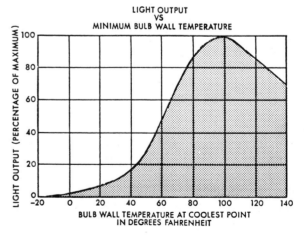

Figure 4-21. *Typical fluorescent-bulb wall-temperature characteristics. Light output drops more drastically in the lower temperatures than in the upper, but the power does not drop by the same proportion. This results in drastic efficacy reduction at lower temperatures.*

be said that there will be 1% loss in light for every 2°F that the ambient temperature around the lamp exceeds 77°F. All standard fluorescent lamps, when operated at normal-rated voltage and with approved auxiliaries, will produce satisfactory results, even at a temperature as low as 50°F. For ambient temperatures lower than 50°F lamps must have some form of thermal protection, such as sleeves or enclosed inside housing, to reach optimum efficacy.

Effect of Humidity

Moisture and humid air surrounding the outside of the glass tube build up an electrostatic charge that results in a higher voltage requirement for starting. The effect on rapid-start lamps is particularly noticeable if the humidity level is 65% or higher. The problem is minimized by a coating of silicon on the tube, applied during manufacture.

Mortality and Lumen Depreciation

The life of a fluorescent lamp is significantly dependent on the number of hours it is burned per start. Every time a lamp is started electron emission material on the electrodes sputters off and reduces the lamp life. The electrodes of a preheated fluorescent lamp take a much more severe shock in the starting period than in the actual burning period. Therefore the longer the lamp is burned at a noninterrupted stretch, the longer its life. The average rated lamp values supplied in tabular form by manufacturers are based on burning cycles of 3 h per start. The most commonly used lamps, such as the 4-ft rapid start, are rated at 20,000 h, based on 3 h of burning per start. For other burning-hour frequencies the multiplication factors are the following:

For 6 h, burning per start	1.25
For 12 h, burning per start	1.60
For continuous burning	2.50 or more

As the lamp ages, general darkening along the length of the tube is caused by mercury streaking. The blackening starts at each end when material emitted by the electrodes (cathodes) indicates that the end of the lamp life is near. Figure 4-22 shows lumen depreciation over lamp life.

Ballast

The principal functions of a ballast are the following:

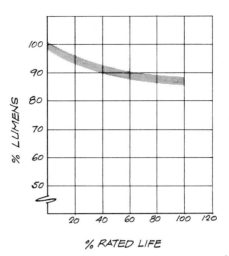

Figure 4-22. *Approximate lumen maintenance of various types of cool white fluorescent lamps.*

1. Limits the Current. A fluorescent lamp is a low-pressure, arc-discharge device. The more current in the arc, the lower the resistance.

2. It provides sufficient voltage to light the lamp.

3. It provides power-factor correction to offset in part the coil's inductive reactance and to help maintain the efficiency of the electrical distribution system.

4. It provides a coil for cathode heating for rapid-start and trigger-start lamps.

5. It provides radio interference suppression.

No specific voltage is associated with fluorescent lamps because they are not directly connected to the power source. The ballasts, however, are rated for specific voltages and must be used with the proper lamp types.

The starting reliability, life, and light output of a fluorescent lamp depend on the design of the ballast. To be assured that the ballast will operate within prescribed standards, the following should be observed:

CBM certified   The ballast must display a certified ballast manufacturer's (CBM) emblem. A CBM certifies that the performance of the ballast conforms to the standards set by the American National Standard Institute (ANSI). Its certificate bears the statement, "CBM Certified by ETL." Electrical Testing Laboratories (ETL) is an independent testing agency by which the tests are carried out.

UL This label states that the ballasts were tested and listed by Underwriter's Laboratories (UL), a nonprofit organization that "by scientific investigation, study, experiment, and test does its part in helping to prevent the loss of life and property from the hazards of fire, casualty and crime."

Class P This is a National Electric Code (NEC) requirement for all ballasts used indoors. The class P ballast has a built-in, thermal device to disconnect power when internal temperature exceeds a safe limit.

Life of a Ballast

According to CBM reports, a properly constructed ballast operated under normal conditions and at a ballast-case temperature not exceeding 90°C should have a life expectancy of 12 years. As a rule of thumb, a 10°C rise above that level will reduce ballast longevity by half. A 10°C decrease, on the other hand, will increase the ballast life twofold. For proper operation of a ballast to attain normal life the following should be observed:

1. Select luminaires that provide proper ventilation to remove ballast heat.

2. Ballast should be operated at its rated voltage. Tolerance should not exceed +5 to 7½% of rated voltage.

3. Watch for an environmental (ambient) temperature rise.

4. Remove burned-out lamps immediately, (especially in preheat and instant-start types) to avoid overheating the ballast.

Ballast Hum

Every ballast produces a certain degree of humming noise that is due to the expansion and collapse of magnetic field in its laminated core. The sound is sometimes amplified by improper mounting on the metallic housing of the luminaire. Some manufacturers rate ballasts on the basis of their sound; for instance, ballasts rated A are quieter than ballasts rated

B, and B is quieter than C. For applications in which there must be absolutely no external sound the ballasts may be remotely installed in an adjacent room, where the humming of the ballasts will not be bothersome. The designer must be aware of the heat produced by the ballasts. It is often required that a ventilation system be installed to remove the heat constantly from such a room.

Power Factor

A ballast may have a high or a low power factor (pf). By definition, the power factor is the ratio of electric power (watts) delivered at the lamps to the product of voltage and current (voltampere). When this ratio is greater than 0.9 (90%), it is known to have a high pf.

Ballasts with low pf draw more current than those with high pf. A low pf will then mean larger conductors and circuit protection not only for the designer's circuit but also those of the utility company.

The designer should always use high pf ballasts to keep the wiring cost low and to utilize more luminaires per circuit.

Let us demonstrate with some examples:

Luminaire 1   200 W, 0.8 pf (low), 277 V

$$\text{current} = \frac{\text{watt}}{\text{volt} \times \text{power factor}}$$

$$= \frac{200}{277 \times 0.8}$$

$$= 0.90 \text{ A}$$

Luminaire 2   200 W, 0.95 pf (high), 277 V

$$\text{current} = \frac{200}{277 \times 0.95}$$

$$= 0.76 \text{ A}$$

Therefore in a 20-A, 1-pole, 277-V branch circuit, in which NEC restricts loading to 80%, the number of luminaires are:

$$\text{luminaire 1} = \frac{20 \times 0.80}{0.90} \approx 18$$

$$\text{luminaire 2} = \frac{20 \times 0.80}{0.76} \approx 21$$

Ballasts for Single or Multilamp Operation

Ballasts are designed to operate one to three lamps at a time. In general, a ballast designed to operate multi-

lamps consumes less power than the total power of the same number of lamps connected by individual ballasts; for example, a single-lamp ballast connected to a standard lamp 4 ft long consumes 45 W whereas a double-lamp ballast connected to two standard lamps consumes 78 W, and a three-lamp ballast connected to three standard lamps consumes 102 W. Therefore to light six lamps the single-lamp ballasts will take 6 × 45 = 270 W, double-lamp ballasts, 3 × 78 = 234 W, and three-lamp ballasts, 2 × 102 = 204 W.

Some ballasts are designed to produce two or three levels of light. Two-level ballasts produce 55 and 100% light outputs, whereas three-level ballasts produce 38, 55, and 100% outputs. The variation in light output is obtained by the method of connecting the lamps. These methods are handy to use in areas in which the task types are varied and need different illuminance levels.

Stroboscopic Effect of Fluorescent Lamps

When any light source is connected to alternating current (ac), its input power varies with the sinewave. Theoretically, for a 60-Hz system the power is off 120 times, thereby turning the light off and on 120 times. For an incandescent light this goes undetected because the filament gets too little time to cool off during an off period. For a fluorescent light, however, this is not true. Although not fully turned off, the excited phosphor gets enough time to decay in light output during each off period and to cause a flickering or stroboscopic effect on moving objects. These effects can be eliminated by operating the lamps in a direct current (dc) circuit or by using two lamps in a "series sequence" or "lead-lag" circuits on ac. The circuiting of a series sequence or lead-lag ensures that one of the two lamps is always on while the other is off.

Dimming

The basic concepts for fluorescent dimming are quite different from those for incandescents, which require a special dimming ballast, different electronic dimmer (not interchangeable with the incandescent dimmers discussed earlier), different circuitry, and special lamp holders. A conventional "wall-box" type of fluorescent dimmer can operate up to 30 lamps of 40 W each, whereas a "dimming module" can operate as many as 80. Figure 4-23 shows the effect on lighting output with input power variation.

The dimming effect of fluorescents can be aesthetically pleasing as well as energy saving, but there are some noted disadvantages. First of all only the rapid-start lamps can be dimmed and, second, compared with incandescents, this can be 15 to 20 times more expensive.

Energy-Saving Products

The oil embargo of the early seventies produced a surge of energy-saving lighting products. Although most were suitable only for retrofits, others were good for new installations. The first cost of most units is quite high and all aspects (performance, energy use, life, and cost) should be analyzed before a decision is made to use any of them.

Compact Screw-In Adaptor Lamps

Available as circline or straight, these lamps are equipped with a medium screwbase and designed to replace incandescent lamps (see Figure 4-24). The circlines are available in diameters of 8 and 10 in. and consume 22 and 44 W to replace 60- to 100-W incandescent lamps, respectively. A compact ballast-cum-adaptor is suspended in the center of the lamp, which has a medium screwbase for direct connection to the sockets of table lamps and swag and ceiling-mounted luminaires.

The twin lamps of the straight versions are available in three sizes: 5.25, 6.5, and 7.4 in. These lamps consume 7, 9, and 13 W and produce light to replace 40-, 60-, and 75-W incandescents. A compact screw-in adapter is available for the 7- and 9-W twin tubes. This allows for a smaller overall length. The 13-W twin tube needs a separate compact ballast and is used for wall-mounted, ceiling-recessed, or surface-mounted luminaires.

With color-corrected phosphors approaching incandescent color rendering and long life (7500 to 12,000 h), fluorescents are excellent replacements for incandescents. The main drawback is their initial cost, which is approximately 10 to 15 times higher than their incandescent counterparts.

Krypton and High-Efficiency Phosphor Lamps

Krypton lamps use krypton gas instead of the conventional argon as their fill gas. The higher molecular weight of this gas reduces voltage drop across the lamp, thus reducing the power consumption anywhere from 10 to 20%, depending on the type of

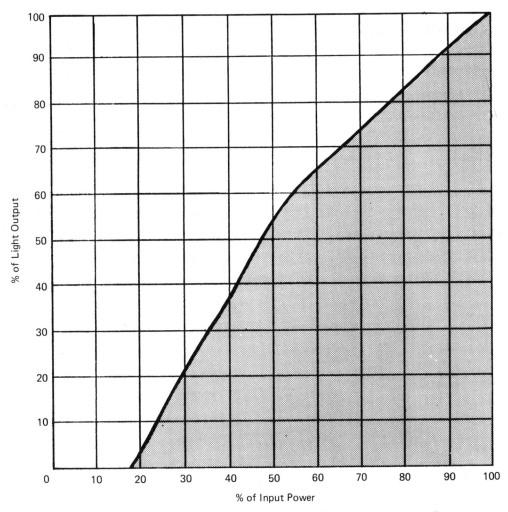

Figure 4-23. *Light output versus input power of a 40-W, 120-V rapid start fluorescent dimmer.*

lamp, at the expense of light reduction of about the same proportion. With no reduction in life rating, these lamps normally offer somewhat better service than standard lamps, but because of the lower light output per lamp and higher initial cost they should be considered only for retrofit application. These lamps are available in all standard colors: cool white, warm white, deluxe cool white, deluxe warm white, daylight, and white.

High-efficacy phosphor lamps are argon or krypton-filled but use a special phosphor to improve light output. A combination of low wattage and high lumen output results in the best luminous efficacy of the whole family of fluorescent lamps. Depending on the type, these lamps save between 14 and 20% of power consumption at the expense of only 3 to 12%

of light output when compared with their conventional counterpart. For 4-ft rapid-start lamps, which are the most popular, the loss in light output is only 3%. They are available only in "lite-white," which is well balanced in all wavelengths except red in which it is somewhat low.

Dummy Tubes

When a reduction in light level is necessary, removal of some of the lamps is often the simplest solution. However, because each pair of lamps is usually connected in series with a common ballast, removal of one lamp would cause the other to go out. The problem can be controlled with the use of a dummy tube, which is made of a glass (or plastic) tube similar to that of a conventional fluorescent lamp, with a tuned

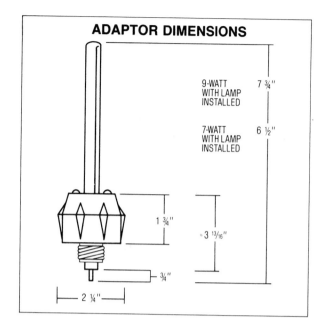

ADAPTOR DIMENSIONS

9-WATT WITH LAMP INSTALLED 7 ¾"

7-WATT WITH LAMP INSTALLED 6 ½"

1 ¾"

3 ¹³/₁₆"

¾"

2 ¼"

A compact screw-in adaptor is available for the 7- and 9-watt twin tubes. With its unique circular ballast (which allows for a shorter overall length and smaller diameter than most comparable systems) it can be used in almost any incandescent socket. The screw-in adaptor comes with a lamp and a screw-in socket-ballast. An optional retaining collar and two screws are also included for base-up operation where vibration exists.

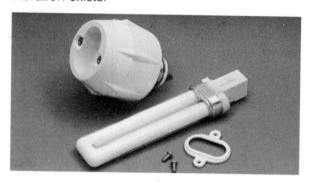

Circlite® lamps

- Circlite, a circular fluorescent lamp designed for incandescent sockets

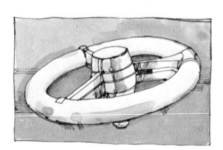

Figure 4-24. Compact fluorescent lamps. (Courtesy of General Electric.)

capacitor inside. The tube does not produce any light, but when used to replace a lamp, it completes the series circuit allowing the other remaining lamp to operate without its pair at a reduced light output (66%). Dummy tubes should be considered when operating costs and light levels are given priority over aesthetics.

Low-Power-Consuming Ballasts

A variety of low-power-consuming ballasts can be had in the market. Some are designed to operate with standard or conventional lamps; others are strictly for matching "energy saving" lamps. In selecting a product, the designer should consult its manufacturer's specification since a wild combination may produce

disastrous results such as premature ballast failure and drastically shortened lamp life.

MERCURY VAPOR LAMPS

Principle of Operation

Like fluorescents, mercury vapor lamps produce light by establishing an arc between two electrodes; however, the electrodes are only a few inches apart, enclosed in opposite ends of a small, sealed, translucent, or transparent arc tube (see Figure 4-25a).

The nitrogen-filled outer bulb encloses the inner arc tube, which contains high-purity mercury and ar-

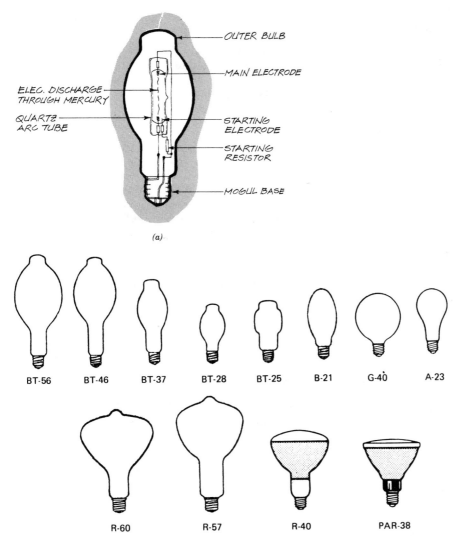

(a)

BT-56   BT-46   BT-37   BT-28   BT-25   B-21   G-40   A-23

R-60   R-57   R-40   PAR-38

(b)

Figure 4-25. (a) *Typical construction of a mercury vapor lamp.* (b) *Standard mercury vapor lamp shapes. (Courtesy of GTE Sylvania Incorporated.)*

gon gas. As the circuit is energized, the starting voltage provided across the starting electrode and adjacent main electrode creates an argon arc, which increases the heat and vaporizes the mercury. The ionized mercury atoms decrease the resistance across the main electrodes and cause the main arc to strike.

Bulb and Base

The outer bulb is made of lime glass, either clear or phosphor-coated, and acts as a UV filter. All bulb shapes are limited to the following (see Fig. 4-25b): A, arbitrary or artistic, BT, bulged-tubular, E, elliptical, T, tubular, R, reflector, PS, pear-shaped, and PAR, parabolic aluminized reflector.

Mercury vapor lamps are available in 40 to 1000 W; all have mogul screwbases except 40- to 100-W lamps which are equipped with medium screw bases.

Mercury vapor lamps are designated by code letters and numbers but, unlike incandescents or fluorescents do not follow a set rule. Except for the letter H (for mercury), the remaining are arbitrary and inconsistent and vary from one manufacturer to another.

Color Characteristics

The three different colors of mercury vapor lamps are clear, deluxe white, and warm deluxe white. Figure 4-26 displays their SPD curves.

The clear lamps have predominantly blue-green color characteristics, mainly because of the arc, shown by the line spectrum. The other lamps are coated with phosphor to improve the quantity and the color of the light. The deluxe white lamp, for instance, offers the maximum amount of light with improvement in color but still remains low in the rendi-

tion of red. The warm deluxe white lamps use a heavier coating of the same type of phosphor which improves overall color rendition but shows a substantial loss in light output (sometimes lower than clear lamps). Unfortunately all phosphor-coated mercury vapor lamps gradually become cooler in color as the phosphor slowly wears out with age.

Warm-Up and Restriking Time

Mercury vapor lamps take about 5 to 7 min to warm up, depending on ambient temperature. When a momentary interruption occurs, the mercury atoms in the arc tube are deionized and radiation stops. The lamp is unable to reionize the argon and mercury gases because in the hot condition it needs much higher starting voltage than the ballast can supply. This requires the arc tube to cool and pressure to drop to a level at which the available voltage can restrike. This period lasts about 3 to 6 min, depending on the wattage, temperature characteristics, and operating conditions of the lamp.

Effects of Temperature

Because of the insulating effect between the outer bulb and arc tube, mercury vapor lamps, unlike fluorescents, are not critically affected by changes in ambient temperature. Abnormally low temperatures may develop a vapor-pressure condition in the arc tube that prevents striking at the rated voltage or the lamp from warming up to its fullest brightness. The user should always follow the lamp manufacturer's instructions and operate the lamp for optimum usage within the specified temperature range. It is recommended, in general, that mercury vapor lamps be operated between −20 and 104°F for best performance.

Burning Position

Although all mercury vapor lamps may operate in any position, their lumen output, hence efficacy, and life are substantially reduced when operated horizontally. This is due primarily to the thermal changes within the arc tube that cause the arc to bow upward by convection effect.

Efficacy

Among all high-intensity discharge (HID) sources mercury vapor has the worst efficacy. Ranging from 22 to 60 lm/W, they are only better than incandescents. The efficacies increase with lamp wattage.

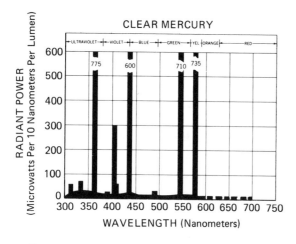

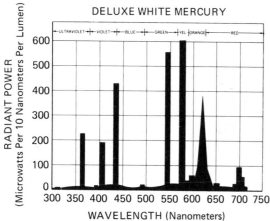

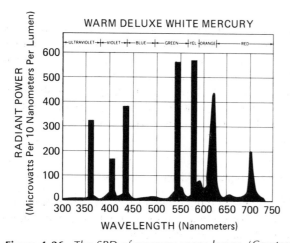

Figure 4-26. The SPD of mercury vapor lamps. (Courtesy of General Electric.)

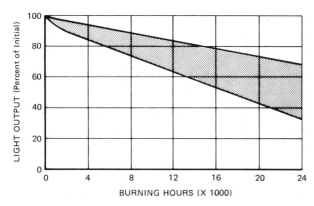

Figure 4-27. *Lumen depreciation of mercury vapor lamps with various ballasts. (Courtesy of General Electric.)*

Lumen Maintenance and Depreciation

The depreciation in light output is usually the result of the combined effects of physical changes inside the arc tube and the deposition of light-absorbing particles of electrodes or their coatings on the tube that are sputtered off from the prolonged impact of arc particles. Figure 4-27 shows lumen depreciation of different mercury vapor lamps as they age.

Mortality

For any lighting source the average rated life of a lamp is normally designated when 50% of the lamps in a group still operate. For mercury vapor lamps, however, at the end of their rated life of 24,000 h as much as 67% of the group still remains active (see Figure 4-28). 24,000 h was accepted as the rated life, because the lumen output beyond that time is very

low. In manufacturers' catalogs the life of some mercury vapor lamps is ended with a plus sign, which indicates that its 50% burnout occurs in excess of the rated 24,000 h.

Ballast

The purpose of a ballast in any HID lamp is similar to that in a fluorescent lamp. In addition, lamp voltage and current are adjusted to the requirements of the lamp as it ages.

Inductive or Reactor Ballast

This ballast is the least expensive, the lightest, and the simplest type in the whole family. It is merely a coil wound on an iron core connected in series with the lamp, which serves to limit the current. Unless an across-the-line capacitor is connected, this highly inductive circuit produces a low power factor, as low as 50%. Ballast losses are low. The main disadvantage is that a ±5% change in line volts will result in a ±10% variation in lamp watts and should not be used wherever the line voltage may fluctuate at ±5% or more.

Lag Ballast

This ballast includes an autotransformer and reactor combined on a single structure. Unless a capacitor is used its inherent power factor is very low, as in a reactor ballast. It has all the good features of a reactor ballast and adjusts in line voltage to provide lamp-operating voltage. The main disadvantage is that it is slightly larger and more expensive than the reactor ballast and with greater ballast loses, somewhat less efficient. It is to be used primarily on a 120-V circuit.

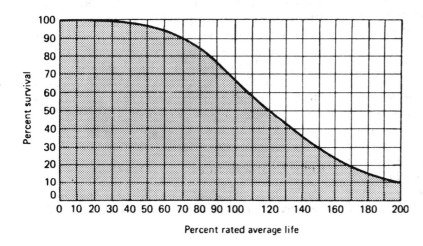

Figure 4-28. *Typical mercury vapor lamp mortality. (Courtesy of General Electric.)*

Regulator Ballast

The main advantage of this ballast is its ability to operate at wide variations of input voltage. The regulator circuit is such that, with a line voltage variation as high as ±13%, the change in lamp-operating power is only ±3%. It has a high power factor and is suitable for use with any lamp of any wattage at any line voltage.

The biggest disadvantage is its initial cost, which is quite high.

Autoregulator Ballast

This ballast combines the autotransformer and the regulator circuit. The degree of regulation depends on the amount of primary voltage coupled into secondary. Being a trade-off between the regulator and the lag ballasts, it includes the most popular ballasts in new installations. In addition to being smaller, lighter, and less expensive it has all the advantages of a regulator ballast. One disadvantage is that with a line voltage change of ±10% the lamp wattage variation is about ±5%, which is slightly more than the regulator ballasts.

Self-Ballasted Mercury Vapor Lamps

These special lamps are not equipped with separate ballasts but the ballast circuits are an integral part of the filaments. They use medium-skirted mogul bases and screw-in sockets just like incandescents. In general, self-ballasted mercury lamps are less efficient than standard mercury vapor lamps but more efficient than incandescents. Depending on the type of lamp and wattage, their life ratings are as much as 8 to 20 times longer than those of their incandescent counterparts. The combined quality of easy installation, higher efficacy, and longer life make them ideally suitable to replace the incandescents located in high-ceiling areas. They are also sometimes effective in areas in which a high amount of light is required but installation of separately mounted ballasts is impractical. The cost of these lamps tends to be excessive.

Dimming

The dimming system of HID uses the principle of sinewave phase control, in which the peak voltage that must be retained to maintain the arc is supplied in full magnitude but for a shorter or longer period of time. This lowers or increases the operating power and results in a dimming or increment in light output.

Unfortunately, the time required for the lamp to attain a desired light level may not match the time of command because it must merge with the operating-lamp temperature. In addition, a smooth variation is possible only for a specific range, beyond which the lamp will extinguish; for example, for a 100-W mercury vapor the minimum light level may be reduced to 8%; below that the light will go off (Figure 4-29).

Dimming systems can be controlled manually or automatically with the help of a timer, computer, or light sensor. The main advantage is that, when dimmed, less power is used; hence an energy saving is possible. The disadvantage is the initial cost of the dimming module and the dimming ballast, which can be very expensive. Color shift is also a problem in HID dimming; for mercury vapors, however, phosphor-coated lamps minimize this problem.

METAL HALIDE LAMPS

The operating principles of a metal halide lamp (Figure 4-30) are similar to those of a mercury vapor except that the metal halide contains some metallic additives (sodium iodide and scandium iodide or sodium iodide, thallium iodide, and indium iodide) in addition to argon and mercury in the arc tube, which partially vaporize to produce color rendering in the overall light output. The other main difference is that the arc tubes in metal halide lamps are usually much smaller than those in the mercury lamps of the same wattage and the starting voltage is much higher.

Bulb and Base

Metal halide lamps, available in 175 to 1500 W, use mogul screwbases for all wattage. The bulb shapes (Figure 4-31) are E (elliptical) or BT (bulged-tubular). All lamps, except for the 1500-W, are available in base-up and base-down designs. Some lamps are specifically designed to be operated horizontally. The lamps may be clear or phosphor-coated.

A special breed, known as "compact metal halide lamps," was introduced to the market at the time of writing this book. These lamps are available in 70 to 400 W, and have double-ended, narrow, cylindrical-quartz envelopes with recessed single- or blade-type bases. More about them is discussed later of this section.

Color Characteristics

The main advantage of a metal halide lamp over a mercury vapor is its energy at all wavelengths across

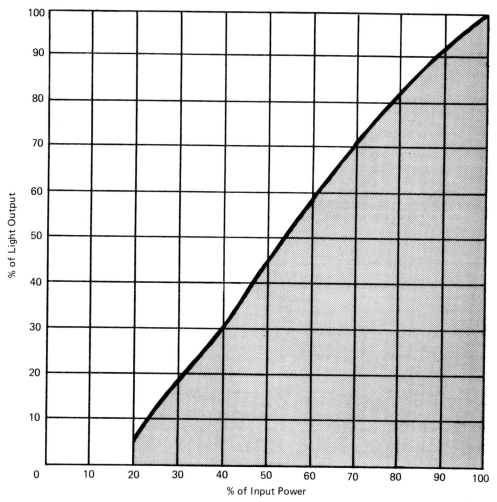

Figure 4-29. Light intensity versus input power of a 100-W, 120-V, mercury vapor dimmer.

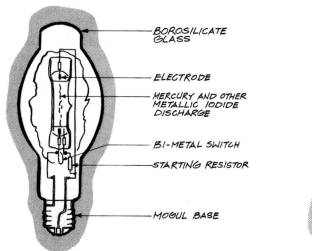

Figure 4-30. A typical metal halide lamp.

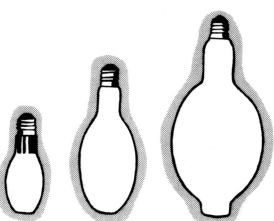

Figure 4-31. Typical metal halide bulb shapes.

CLEAR

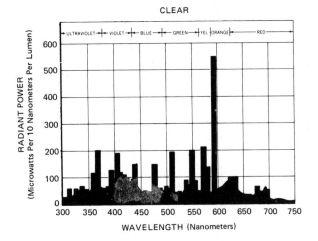

PHOSPHOR COATED

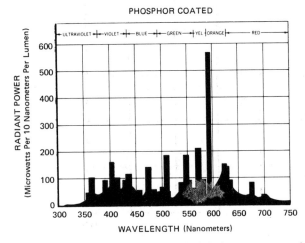

Figure 4-32. The SPD of metal halide lamps. In metal halide lamps phosphor coating does not improve light color but diffuses the source significantly.

the visible spectrum, which creates well-balanced color rendering (see Figure 4-32). A phosphor coating is not necessary for color improvement because the excellent color rendering is directly available from the arc itself. A phosphor coating helps to diffuse the source and should be considered for low-ceiling applications. Some luminaires are specifically designed to work with phosphor-coated lamps. The use of a clear lamp may create a "dark hole" directly under the luminaire.

Unfortunately color rendition of metal halide varies from lamp to lamp and throughout the life cycle. Initially a metal halide lamp is slightly bluish white, then white, and then pinkish white as it ages. Inconsistency in the type and proportion of metal additives, supply voltage, and ballast are some of the other rea-sons for its color variation. When color consistency is critical, lamps should be replaced in groups (all purchased from the same manufacturer) rather than on a spot burnout basis.

Warm-Up and Restriking Time

Because of the additional metallic additives, the starting voltage is normally higher than the mercury vapor lamps. Approximately 2 to 4 min to warm-up and between 10 and 15 min to restrike are needed.

Effects of Temperature

As in mercury vapor lamps, metal hallide is not critically affected by changes in ambient temperature. The recommended minimum starting temperature is −20°F for single-lamp ballasts and 0°F for twin-lamp ballasts. The maximum operating ambient temperature is 130°F.

Burning Position

Metal halide lamps are sensitive to their burning positions; each lamp is designed to be operated in a particular position. These vertically operated lamps have two separate designs, one to burn with base up, the other with base down. When operated horizontally, as much as 15% light may be lost in addition to a change in color. When the burning position of a metal halide is changed, as many as 6 h may be required before the lamp color, lumen output, and other electrical characteristics stabilize. Some lamps may shatter if not operated in the recommended position, thus releasing ultraviolet rays and causing bodily injury. The curved arc-tube lamps are specially designed with arc tubes that match the contour of the arcs when the lamps are operated horizontally. With this development the temperature around the arc tube is uniformly maintained and a much higher lumen output is produced than by the vertically operated. The main thing to remember is that these lamps must be installed horizontally with the bulge upward.

Efficacy

Perhaps the greatest advantage of metal halide lamps over mercury vapor lamps is their substantially higher efficacy. The efficacy range of metal halide lamps may vary from 66 to 100 l/W, compared with only 22 to 60 l/W for mercury, including ballast losses.

Lumen Maintenance and Depreciation

In the whole family of HID lamps the metal halides lose their light output most rapidly; for example, a 400-W lamp that produces 34,000 lms drops down to as little as 70% of its initial value after only 10,000 h of burning, compared with 80% for mercury lamps of the same wattage.

Mortality

The main disadvantage of the metal halide lamps is perhaps their relatively short life. The 175- and 250-W lamps are rated at 7500 h; the 400-W at 20,000 h (at best); 1000 W at 10,000 h and 1500 W at only 3000 h.

Dimming

Like mercury vapors, metal halides can be dimmed smoothly for a limited range, beyond which the lamps will extinguish; for example, for a 250-W metal halide lamp light can be dimmed to 20%; below that it will turn off.

Color-shift during dimming can be considerably greater in metal halides than in mercury vapors. Dimming should be considered only when color consistency is not a concern; flexibility in light output and energy saving are the priorities.

Ballast

Because of the metallic additives and their ionization phenomenon, a metal halide lamp requires a much higher starting and reignition voltage than a mercury vapor. For this reason mercury vapor ballasts may not be used for all metal halide lamps.

A metal halide lamp uses a lead-peaked ballast that adopts the circuiting of an autoregulator mercury ballast but provides the higher voltage requirements. Ballast losses are compatible with those of mercury regulator ballasts and are suitable for all metal halide lamps, operating at any voltage. It is interesting to note that although no mercury vapor ballasts can be operated with metal halide lamps all metal halide lead-peak ballasts can be used to operate mercury vapor lamps of the same wattage and similar characteristics.

Special Metal Halide Lamps for Mercury Vapor Ballasts

Some manufacturers offer special metal halide lamps to replace existing mercury vapor lamps of the same

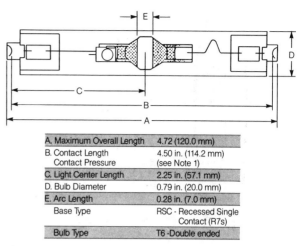

A. Maximum Overall Length	4.72 (120.0 mm)
B. Contact Length Contact Pressure	4.50 in. (114.2 mm) (see Note 1)
C. Light Center Length	2.25 in. (57.1 mm)
D. Bulb Diameter	0.79 in. (20.0 mm)
E. Arc Length	0.28 in. (7.0 mm)
Base Type	RSC - Recessed Single Contact (R7s)
Bulb Type	T6 -Double ended

Figure 4-33. *Cross section of a 70-W compact metal halide lamp. (Courtesy of Osram Corporation.)*

wattage without replacing the ballasts. With these lamps the light output increases as much as 180% but shows a substantial loss in life rating (as low as 50%).

Compact Metal Halide Lamps

These lamps have double-ended quartz envelopes and are available in 70-, 150-, 250-, and 400-W sizes. The bulb is a narrow cylinder and has recessed single- or blade-type press-in bases (see Figure 4-33). With the maximum overall length varying from 4.72 to 8.18 in., and the diameter, from 0.79 to 1.25 in., these lamps are so compact that they can be used in many applications in which, because of the shortage of mounting space, conventional metal halide lamps cannot. With good efficacy (approx. 70 l/w), excellent color rendition (CRT, 85) and long life (15,000 h), the additional benefit is the excellent light control that results from the compactness of the arc tube. The 70-W lamps are particularly suited to many indoor areas in which conventional metal halide lamps, whose minimum size is 175 W, are too big to be used.

HIGH-PRESSURE SODIUM LAMPS

Principles of Operation

High-pressure sodium lamps need high temperatures to operate. The arc tube has a smaller diameter than the tubes in mercury vapor or metal halide lamps to

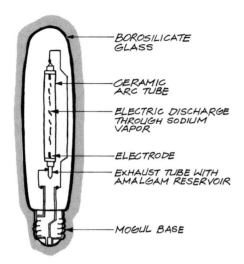

Figure 4-34. A typical HPS lamp.

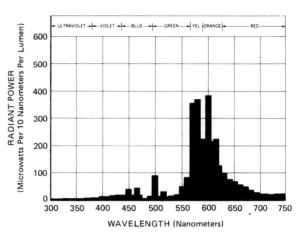

Figure 4-36. *The SPD of HPS lamps. (Courtesy of General Electric.)*

maintain these temperatures, but because of the narrow profile, there is no starting electrode inside the arc tube. It does, however, contain a special starting circuiting that vaporizes xenon gas mixed with a small quantity of sodium-mercury amalgam. To withstand the heat the arc tube is made of a ceramic, translucent aluminum oxide that tolerates up to 2372°F, and the outer envelope is borosilicate glass that withstands 750°F (Figure 4-34).

Bulb Shapes and Base

High-pressure sodium bulb shapes can be E (elliptical) BT, (bulge-tubular), and T (tubular) (see Figure 4-35). Some manufacturers have produced R (reflector) shaped bulbs in lower wattages. All lamps rated at 50 to 150 W use medium or mogul bases, 35-W use medium, and all others to 1000 W use mogul only.

Color Characteristics

Figure 4-36 shows the SPD curves of HPS lamps. These lamps produce energy at all wavelengths, but the major portion is concentrated in the yellow-orange section of the spectrum. Because of this color characteristic, red objects appear to be orange and blue or green objects look gray. Color consistency from lamp to lamp is better than in metal halide lamps, although some color shift can occur because of different ballast characteristics and input voltage variation. A comparison of color characteristics of HID lamps is made in Table 4-3.

Warm-Up and Restriking Time

HPS takes 3 to 4 min to start. Because the operating pressure of an HPS lamp is lower than that of a mercury vapor lamp, the restriking time is much shorter—about 1 min.

Effects of Temperature

Like other HID lamps, the HPS is virtually unaffected by external temperature variation. HPS lamps will start at ambient temperatures as low as −22°F.

Burning Position

The diameter of the arc tube is so small that when a lamp is operated horizontally it has insignificant convection effect. All HPS lamps can be operated in any position.

Figure 4-35. Typical HPS bulb shapes.

TABLE 4-3. HIGH-INTENSITY DISCHARGE LAMP SELECTION BY COLOR

	Clear Mercury	White Mercury	Deluxe White Mercury	Metal Halide	High-Pressure Sodium
Efficacy	Low	Low	Low	Medium	High
Effect on neutral surface	Greenish blue-white	Greenish white	Purplish white	Greenish white	Yellowish
Effect on atmosphere	Very cool, greenish	Moderately cool, greenish	Warm, purplish	Moderately cool, greenish	Warm, yellowish
Colors strengthened	Yellow, green, blue	Yellow, green, blue	Red, yellow, blue	Yellow, green, blue	Yellow, orange, green
Colors grayed	Red, orange	Red, orange	Green	Red	Red, blue
Effects on complexions	Greenish	Very pale	Ruddy	Greyed	Yellowish
Remarks	Very poor color rendering	Moderate color rendering	Color acceptance similar to C.W. fluor.	Color acceptance similar to C.W. fluor.	Color acceptance similar to W.W. fluor.

Efficacy

The main advantage of HPS lamps is their outstanding efficacy (lumen output per watt). HPS lamps are available in 35 to 1000-W sizes and their efficacy ranges from 50 to 127 l/W, ballast losses included. The efficacy, however, slightly decreases as the lamps get older. This is primarily because they need increasingly higher operating voltage as they age.

Lumen Maintenance and Depreciation

Figure 4-37 describes the lumen maintenance curves of all HPS lamps. The mean for all lamps occurs at approximately 91% of the initial outputs and terminates at 67% of initial outputs at the end of rated life (24,000 h).

Mortality

HPS lamps have extremely long life (24,000 h for most), which is another of their main attractions. As mentioned earlier, the lamp needs increasingly higher operating voltage as it gets older. When the ballast can no longer produce this voltage, the lamp's life ends (Figure 4-38).

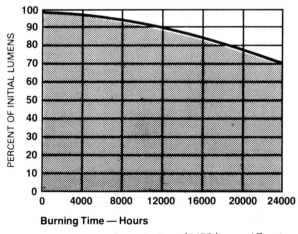

Figure 4-37. Lumen depreciation of HPS lamps. (Courtesy of GTE Sylvania Incorporated.)

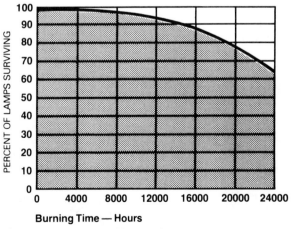

Figure 4-38. A typical mortality curve of HPS lamps. (Courtesy of GTE Sylvania Incorporated.)

Ballast

The HPS lamp has two unique problems for which the ballast must be specially designed: (a) the starting voltage is substantially higher (approx. 3000 V), (b) lamp voltage increases as the lamp gets older.

Reactor Ballast

The reactor ballast is similar in design to that used in mercury vapor lamps except that it has an additional starting aid and a lamp-voltage correcting circuiting. It is the least expensive, lightest, and simplest type of ballast in the family. Ballast losses are similar to mercury regulators and can be used when the system voltage is appropriate for operation. When operated with an autotransformer, the reactor ballast will work with any lamp at any operating voltage.

Magnetic Regulator Ballast

The magnetic regulator compensates for the line and lamp voltage needs. With this device the lamp watts are controlled more precisely than by the reactor. A variation in ±10% line voltage causes a deviation of approximately ±3% in lamp wattage.

Autoregulator Ballast

This ballast resembles the regular mercury autoregulator ballast, but with the help of special core slots and leakage reactance it meets the special starting and lamp-operating voltages of an HPS lamp.

Electronic Regulator Ballast

This is a recent development for lamps of 50 to 400 W. It has many advantages: (a) because of the use of solid-state components, it is much lighter; (b) it has excellent control (at ±10% variation in input line voltage its lamp voltage fluctuates less than ±1% in wattage); (3) its lumen output is fairly constant throughout the lamp life; (4) it has lower power consumption. The main disadvantages are (a) its high cost and (b) its power factor lies between 85 and 90%.

HPS Lamps for Mercury Vapor Retrofits

Some manufacturers offer these lamps as replacements for mercury vapor lamps, using the existing ballasts. Although in most cases the light output is increased by more than 60% and considerable savings in power are realized, it must be remembered that there are some disadvantages as well. The life of these lamps is only about half of all others (12,000 h), the color rendition is dramatically different, the first cost tends to be high, and their light output and life is much lower when compared with their counterparts. They should be used only for retrofits.

Dimming

Like the mercury vapors or metal halides, HPS lamps also have a limited range wherever light can be smoothly varied. For a 250-W HPS lamp the light level can be brought down to 18%; below that it will go off. Also like metal halides, the HPS shifts in color during the dimming mode. It may be considered when color of light is of no importance and a variance in light level and energy saving is required.

OTHER LIGHT SOURCES

Low-Pressure Sodium Lamps

The light-producing element in a low-pressure sodium (LPS) is a U-shaped arc tube enclosed in an outer jacket borate glass. The starting gas is neon, with small amounts of xenon, argon, or helium. The lamps are available from 9 to 180 W and need a ballast to start and operate.

The low-pressure sodium has maximum efficacy (lumen per watt) in the whole family of gaseous discharge light source, but, despite its high efficacy, its application indoors is limited because of its poor color rendition (monochromatic yellow). The starting time to full brightness is about 7 to 15 min and the restriking time may vary between 1 and 30 s. Lamps ranging up to 55 W are recommended for both vertical and horizontal operation; the higher wattage lamps, however, are recommended for horizontal use only; LPS lamps have long life (18,000 h). As the lamp ages its light output remains fairly constant but it consumes increasing power.

Cold Cathode Lamps

Cold cathode lamps operate primarily like an instant-start fluorescent lamp. It varies only in the diameter of its glass, which is narrower, and the tube is handmade to conform to any shape. The filling gas is argon or a mixture of argon and neon. The bulb (tube) also carries a few droplets of mercury. As in fluorescent lamps, high voltage is applied to the cold-cathode electrodes at the two ends. Ultraviolet is produced by the interaction of mercury vapors with the ionized argon, which excites phosphor on the inside of the tube. When neon is used with argon, it pro-

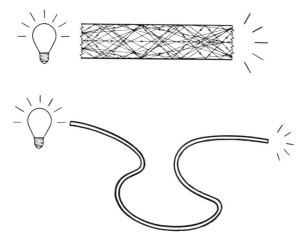

Figure 4-39. *Operating principles of fiber optics.*

duces a reddish color. A variety of colors is created with the help of special types of phosphor.

Neon Light

Neon has become the generic name for all types of gaseous discharge, thin-tube lighting. It is used primarily for display. Its operating principle is similar to that of cold-cathode lamps except that the tube diameter is much narrower (typically 8 to 15 mm) and the light is produced by the ionization of the gas itself without the help of phosphor. Neon produces a reddish hue. Other gases (primarily inert family) produce a variety of color of multipurpose light.

A neon lamp produces a low amount of uniformly distributed light throughout its length and has a very long life. It needs a special ballast for starting at high voltage and staying alight. Its ballasts are usually noisy but can be remote-mounted or concealed in a suitable area.

Although neon lamps have been used almost totally for commercial purposes, they have endless potential for creative interior lighting. The bulbs can be shaped to fit any unusual contour and the low-discharged, uniformly emitted light of numerous

color possibilities can be used successfully for visual effects, decoration, highlighting, dramatization, and lighting sculptures.

The ballast for a neon or cold-cathode light is 1.5 to 2 times the size of a fluorescent ballast and may weigh as much as 20 lb. The operating voltage varies from 2000 to 15,000 V, depending on the length of the tube. As a rule of thumb, a 500-VA ballast, rated at 15 kV/30 mA secondary, is used for a 15-mm diameter tube no longer than 70 ft. If the tube needs to be longer, additional ballasts can be used. Use of neon or cold-cathode light is limited by the user's imagination, but the initial cost can be quite high.

Fiber Optics

Fiber optics is a term given to the optical science associated with thin, solid, cylindrical glass or plastic fibers. The fibers do not produce light by themselves, but when a ray of light is passed through one end it emerges from the other after a total internal reflection (Figure 4-39). Typically, a large number of fibers (50 to 1,000,000) is grouped together inside an opaque, flexible cover for practical application. To minimize light loss each fiber is insulated with a glass (or plastic) coating of refractive index lower than that of the material of the fiber itself; the ends of the bundle are bonded together, grounded, and highly polished. There are two major types of fiber bundle: coherent and noncoherent. The coherent types are used for transmitting images and the noncoherent, for transmitting light from the source to areas of investigation in which a conventional light source cannot be installed.

Electroluminescent Lamps

Electroluminescence is achieved by exciting phosphor under a pulsating electrical field. An electroluminescent lamp is a thin area source in which phosphor is sandwiched between two conductive layers, one (or both) of which is translucent. Additional transparent material is provided to protect it from external abuse (Figure 4-40). Electricity (usually 120-V

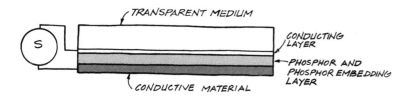

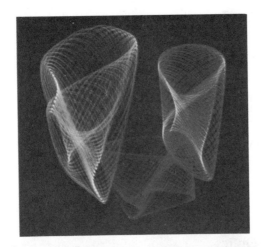

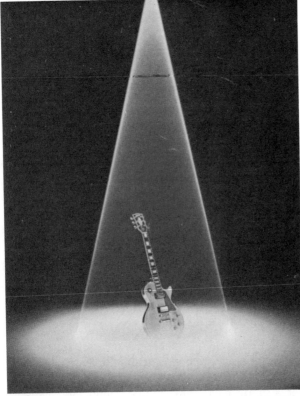

Figure 4-41. Three-dimensional images created by laser beam; (a) on screen, and (b) in space. (Courtesy of Laser Rays Art Productions Inc.)

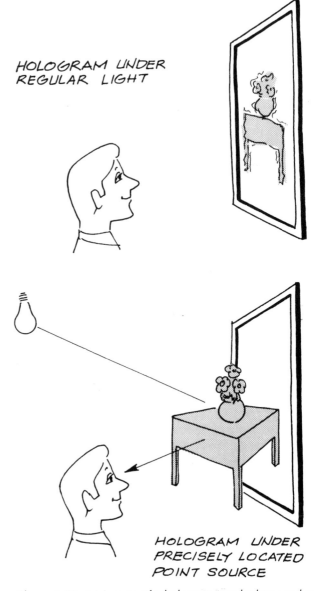

HOLOGRAM UNDER REGULAR LIGHT

HOLOGRAM UNDER PRECISELY LOCATED POINT SOURCE

Figure 4-42. (a) Images of a hologram may be hazy under regular light. (b) When placed under a point source at a predetermined angle, the reflected image is a three-dimensional object identical to the original.

ac) is passed through the lamp to create an electrostatic field that excites phosphor producing light in green, blue, yellow, or white, depending on the type of phosphor; its intensity varies with applied voltage, frequency, and temperature. Green phosphor has the highest luminance. These lamps are available in ce-

ramic and plastic form, flexible or stiff, with or without sticky-back, and are easily fabricated into shapes and sizes to meet needs that range from decorative to general, low-level illumination.

Laser Beam and Holography

The word laser refers to "light amplification by stimulated emission of radiation." It produces a monochromatic, coherent light in which light waves are in phase with space and time.

Although laser beams can be injurious to the body (contact with high-power beam can burn the skin; staring at the source of even a low-power source can damage the retina of the eye), with precaution they can be used effectively in special architectural and theatrical lighting. In addition to creating a search-light effect, they can produce moving, three-dimensional figures in space and on-screen with the help of a computer or mechanical action (Figure 4-41).

Holography is photography developed under laser light in which the image of the picture appears to project from the hologram in three-dimensional representation (Figure 4-42). It is a two-step process by which (a) an object illuminated by laser light is made to produce interference fringes in a photosensitive medium, such as a photosensitive emulsion, and (b) reillumination of the developed interference pattern reconstructs a three-dimensional image of the original object. For best effect the hologram should be observed under a point source.

Phosphor Tube-Light

Phosphor tube-light itself does not produce light but glows in brilliant colors similar to neon under long-wave UV light sources. The tubes are made of highly flexible PVC coated with phosphor through which a wire can be inserted to give it shape. The diameter of the tube usually varies from 2 to 12 mm. Its greatest advantage is that the tube does not need electricity; it can be cut to any length and shaped into almost any form imaginable.

REFERENCES

General Electric Company, Ballasts for High Intensity Discharge Lamps, Rating and Data, GEA-8928C, December, 1977.

IES. "Light Sources." *IES Lighting Handbook,* 5th ed. New York: Illuminating Engineering Society, 1972, pp. 8-1–8-44.

Osram Corporation, New Technology for a New Era of Lighting. Mississauga, Ontario, Canada, 1984.

Sorcar, Prafulla C. *Energy Saving Lighting Systems.* New York: Van Nostrand-Reinhold, 1982.

Sylvania. Mercury Lamps, Engineering Bulletin 0-346. Danvers, Massachusetts, 1972.

Sylvania. Metalarc Lamps, Engineering Bulletin 0-344. Danvers, Massachusetts (no date).

5

Photometrics: Measurement of Light

Photometrics is the state of the art that analyses the light sources or luminaires from an operational standpoint and helps the lighting designer to make a selection. Photometrics of each type of luminaire are available from the manufacturer and are prepared in the format recommended by the Illuminating Engineering Society of North America (IES).

For the purpose of clarification let us consider a commonly used luminaire that may cover most of the questions applicable to almost all indoor luminaires. Figure 5-1 is a typical photometric report of a 2 × 4 ft fluorescent troffer that contains four lamps and a plastic lens. For convenience, each item discussed in the photometric report has been labeled alphabetically.

A. LUMINAIRE IDENTIFICATION AND GENERAL DESCRIPTION

This section of the report identifies the luminaire with its manufacturer's name and product number (catalog number); it illustrates with a cross-sectional diagram its physical dimensions and general description and provides the number and type of lamps used with the rated number of lumens produced per lamp. In this

example the luminaire has an acrylic prismatic lens, 0.125 in. thick; cool white, 3200-lumen rapid-start lamps 4 ft long; and two premium ballasts. A photometric report can be based on one-, three-, or five- or more plane analyses. In this example the photometric is based on three planes, hence is called three-plane photometry.

B. CANDLEPOWER DISTRIBUTION CURVE

The candlepower distribution curve is drawn on a polar (or rectilinear) coordinate system to illustrate the luminous intensity distribution. To determine the curve the luminaire is placed at the center of an imaginary sphere with a radius equal to the test distance. The mathematics involved in the determination of the candlepower readings uses the inverse square law method (explained in Chapter 6), which requires the luminaire to be a perfect point source. Clear bulbs with small filaments or arc tubes are closer examples of a point source than area sources. For area sources (like those in the example) and linear sources the test distance must be five or more times the maximum

Photometric Report for Sorcar Lighting Co., Product Catalog No. XYZ

Three-Plane Photometry

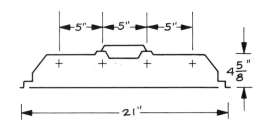

Ⓐ ⟶ Luminaire. Metal troffer, synthetic enamel
Clear prismatic plasic lens No. 12,
acrylic

Lamps. Four F40T12/CW, 3200 lm each

Reflectance. 0.87

CANDLEPOWER

Angle	Along	45·	Across
0	3500	3500	3500
5	3468	3478	3484
15	3387	3434	3478
25	3220	3347	3473
35	2696	2956	3122
45	1949	2100	2388
55	1183	950	1335
65	568	376	600
75	291	210	254
85	88	132	86
90	0	0	0	⟵ Ⓒ

ZONAL LUMEN SUMMARY

Zone	Lumens	% Lamp	% Fixture
0–30	2850	22.3	34.8
30–60	4464	34.8	54.5
60–90	876	6.9	10.7
0–90	8190	64.0	100.0
90–180	0	0	0
0–180	8190	64	100

Ⓓ

Ⓔ ⟶ Efficiency. 64%

Ⓖ ⟶ CIE-IES type. Direct

Ⓗ ⟶ Shielding angle. across 90°
along 90°

Ⓘ ⟶ SC. 1.4 (⊥), 1.35 (∥)

Ⓑ ⟶

LUMINANCE SUMMARY ⟵ Ⓕ

Degree	Average (f-L) Parallel	Average (f-L) Normal	Maximum (f-L) Parallel	Maximum (f-L) Normal	Footlambert Ratio Parallel	Footlambert Ratio Normal
0	1682	1682	2855	2855	1.7	1.7
45	1324	1623	1884	2296	1.4	1.4
55	991	1118	1354	1737	1.4	1.6
65	646	682	736	942	1.1	1.4
75	539	472	559	677	1.0	1.4
85	487	473	589	559	1.2	1.2

COEFFICIENTS OF UTILIZATION: ZONAL CAVITY

Pfc				20%									
Pcc	80%				70%				50%			30%		
Pw	70%	50%	30%	10%	70%	50%	30%	10%	50%	30%	10%	50%	30%	10%
1	71	68	66	64	69	67	65	63	64	63	61	62	61	59
2	66	62	58	55	64	60	57	54	58	56	53	51	48	46
3	61	56	51	48	60	55	51	47	53	49	47	51	48	46
4	57	50	45	42	55	49	45	42	48	44	41	46	43	40
5	52	45	40	36	51	45	40	36	43	39	36	42	38	36
6	49	41	36	32	47	40	36	32	39	35	32	38	34	32
7	45	37	32	28	44	37	32	28	36	31	28	35	31	28
8	41	33	28	25	41	33	28	25	32	28	25	31	27	24
9	38	30	25	22	37	30	25	22	29	25	21	28	24	21
10	35	27	22	19	35	27	22	19	26	22	19	26	22	19

Ⓙ ⟶ (row 3)

Figure 5-1. A photometric report.

dimension of the luminaire so that the luminaire can be considered a point source. Luminous intensity is then plotted at each angle on the polar coordinate; its contour represents the candlepower distribution curve. (Section B of Figure 5-1 is the candlepower diagram of this example.) In the polar coordinate the reference axis is at 0°, which is at the bottom (nadir), and 180° at the top. The readings are normally taken at intervals of 5°. If the distribution is symmetrical and the curve is smooth, reading intervals of 10 to 15° are not uncommon. For a nonuniform, unpredictable distribution readings may be taken in smaller increments.

Rectilinear coordinates (as opposed to polar) are sometimes used if the light intensity of the source changes drastically within a small angular area. Figure 5-2 is a typical example. To save space sometimes the plot is confined to the angles at which it varies. For sources with symmetrical light distribution only half the plot is shown because the other half is a mirror image.

The candlepower distribution curves for a symmetrical luminaire will always be identical at any vertical plane (see Figure 5-3). For an asymmetrical luminaire distribution curves are plotted for a minimum of three vertical planes (0, 45, and 90°) shown in the example. If further accuracy is required, curves are plotted at 22.5 and 67.5° as well.

C. CANDLEPOWER SUMMARY

This section of the photometric report serves two purposes. First, it tabulates all candlepower readings for each angle measured at vertical planes; second, with the help of these figures the zonal lumens or zonal flux is determined. The first column represents the angles at which the candlepower readings were

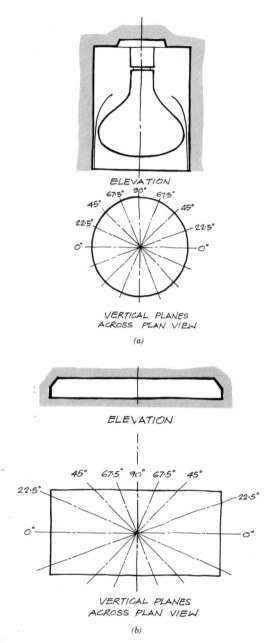

Figure 5-3. (a) A typical elevation of a symmetrical luminaire with a round reflector and a vertically mounted lamp. At vertical planes (perpendicular to the page) the candlepower distribution curves are the same. (b) Vertical planes (perpendicular to the page) across the luminaire of the example in Figure 5-1.

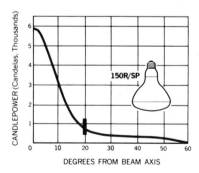

Figure 5-2. A candlepower distribution curve on a rectangular coordinate.

taken. In this example the readings are taken at intervals of 10°. The second, third, and fourth columns represent the candlepower (luminous intensity) values in candelas (cd) for 0, 45, and 90° vertical planes, respectively.

D. ZONAL LUMEN SUMMARY

This portion of the report provides the lumen concentration summary at a key zone. Light emitted at 0 to 45° is usually called the direct light zone because it falls onto the task without causing any direct glare to the viewer. The 45 to 90° zone is known as the direct glare zone. The degree of brightness caused by the luminaire is usually dependent on the candela values at those angles. Total lumens at the 90 to 180° zone represents light in the upper hemisphere and that at 0 to 90° represents the lower hemisphere. Finally, the lumens at the 0 to 180° zone represent the total output of the luminaire. In section D of Figure 5-1 the first column lists the key zones, the second column shows the total lumens at these zones, and the third and fourth columns give the lumen percentage compared with the total output of bare lamps and the total output of the luminaire.

E. EFFICIENCY

The efficiency of a luminaire is the ratio of the total number of lumens emitted by the luminaire to the total number of lumens produced by the bare lamps. Thus the third column in section D of the photometric, which compares the percentage of lumens in the 0 to 180° zone with the bare-lamp lumens, represents the luminaire's efficiency. In the example given the efficiency is

$$\frac{8190 \times 100}{(4 \times 3200)} = 64\%$$

F. LUMINANCE (MEASURED BRIGHTNESS) SUMMARY

This section of the photometric report will help the designer to select a luminaire with regard to the amount of discomforting glare it produces when observed at certain angles. Average luminance at a certain angle is a calculated value based on the luminous intensity and projected area at that angle. The maximum luminance of a luminaire, listed in the fourth and fifth columns of section F (Figure 5-1), is a measured quantity. In its determination a photometer with a circular aperture of 1 in.^{2} is used to search the surface of the lens or louvers for the maximum luminance at the glare angles. These values are different for vertical angles and are tabulated as shown in our example.

G. CIE-IES LUMINAIRE CLASSIFICATION

The CIE-IES classification system identifies a luminaire by the percentage of light in the upper and lower hemispheres of the candlepower distribution curve. There are six categories in the CIE-IES classification: (a) direct, (b) semidirect, (c) direct-indirect, (d) general diffuse, (e) semiindirect, and (f) indirect. The percentage of light shared by the two hemispheres is given in Figure 5-4. To determine the classification the percentage of total output in the upper and lower hemispheres must be calculated:

$$\% \text{ total output} = \frac{\text{lumen produced in upper and lower hemispheres} \times 100}{\text{total lumens produced at 0 to 180}°}$$

H. SHIELDING ANGLE

The shielding angle is measured from a horizontal line drawn at the bottom of the luminaire to the line of first sight of the source. It is at this angle that the source is concealed from direct viewing. For an evenly illuminated source like frosted incandescent,

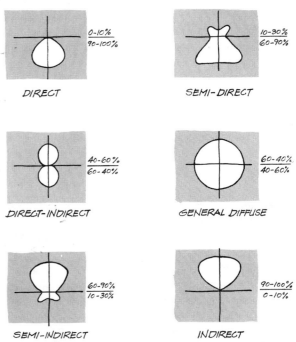

Figure 5-4. *The CIE-IES classification system of luminaires according to their candlepower distribution.*

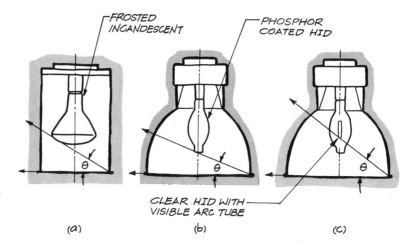

Figure 5-5. A shielding angle with (a) frosted incandescent, (b) phosphor-coated HID, and (c) clear HID with a visible arc tube.

phosphor-coated HID, or fluorescent lamps the shielding angle is measured between the horizontal line and the bottom of the bulb (Figure 5-5). For sources with visible filaments the angle is measured between the horizontal line and the filament. For a clear HID source this angle is measured between the horizontal line and the bottom of the arc tube.

For most indoor luminaires with incandescent, mercury vapor, metal halide, or high-pressure sodium lamps and no diffusing media the shielding angle is typically 45° or more. When the luminaire has a diffusing medium, the light source may not be directly visible from any angle but a maximum glare may be obtained at certain angles. For area sources like the one in the example this angle is 90° (viewed directly from beneath the luminaire).

I. SPACING CRITERION

The spacing criterion (SC) represents a numerical value that, when multiplied by the luminaire mounting height from the work plane, provides a luminaire spacing number that may be used to achieve an even illuminance. The concept of SC, shown in the IES Lighting Handbook, Reference Volume, 1981, replaces the previously accepted terminology "spacing to mounting height ratio," or S/MH. Its main purpose was to erase the conventional assumption that the quality of lighting distribution would remain the same, regardless of luminaire spacing, as long as it did not exceed the S/MH of the luminaire.

In our example the luminaire's SC in the direction across the lamps is 1.4 and that in the direction along

the lamps is 1.35. If these luminaires were mounted 8 ft above the floor and a certain amount of uniform lighting was required on the floor, the luminaires could be spaced 1.4 × 8 = 11.2 ft apart sideways and 1.35 × 8 = 10.8 ft apart in the other direction (Figure 5-6). Note that if the task level is above the floor the mounting height of the luminaires above that level should be considered; for example, if the task level were 2.5 ft above the floor the spacings would change to 1.4 × (8−2.5) = 7.7 ft sideways and 1.35 × (8−2.5) = 7.42 ft in the other direction.

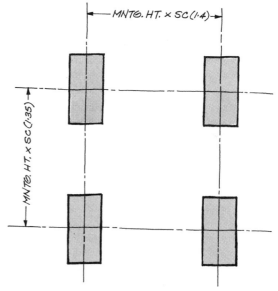

Figure 5-6. Luminaire spacings can be determined by multiplying the mounting height by the spacing criterion.

J. COEFFICIENT OF UTILIZATION

When a luminaire is turned on, its light is produced in various directions, but only a certain portion of this light will arrive at the level of interest. The coefficient of utilization (CU) represents the portion of the total light that would fall on the work plane (the level of interest). In general, light appearing on the work plane, which represents the CU, is accumulated from two kinds of ray. The first is the direct ray and the second, the ray that hits the room surfaces, bounces back and forth, and finally reaches the work place. Their determination then depends on the candle-power distribution of the luminaire, its mounting height above the work plane, room proportions, and surface reflectances. Item J in Figure 5-1 represents the CU table of our example. For a specific application only one value in this table is applicable. Once the CU is determined it is used in the mathematical formulas for lighting calculations. The technique of determining the required CU value (zonal cavity method) is discussed in Chapter 6.

OTHER REPORTS ON PHOTOMETRICS

On request luminaire manufacturers will include supplementary information on their products.

Visual Comfort Probability

Visual comfort probability (VCP) is a method of measuring the discomfort glare of a lighting system currently accepted by the IES. It represents a statistical prediction of the percentage of the people who will be expected to find a lighting system acceptable in terms of discomforting glare. Based on the format and procedure of the IES, VCP data are available for most area-type luminaires (e.g., the 2 × 4 ft fluorescent troffers in our example), usually free of cost from manufacturers. Their values, as expected, vary for different room sizes, the type of light distribution of the luminaires, and the height of luminaire mounting planes. For example, in Table 5-1, which lists VCP for the example, for a room 30 ft long and 30 ft wide,

TABLE 5-1. VCP VALUES OF THE EXAMPLE GIVEN

Room Dimensions		VCP Lengthwise Mounting Height (ft)				VCP Crosswise Mounting Height (ft)			
W	L	8.5	10.0	13.0	16.0	8.5	10.0	13.0	16.0
20	20	67	71	75	79	65	68	71	75
20	30	59	63	68	71	59	62	65	67
20	40	55	58	62	65	56	58	61	62
20	60	52	55	58	60	53	56	58	59
30	20	68	72	76	78	67	70	73	75
30	30	59	64	68	70	59	63	66	67
30	40	54	58	62	64	55	58	61	62
30	60	51	54	56	58	51	54	56	58
30	80	48	52	53	55	49	53	54	56
40	20	70	73	77	78	69	72	75	77
40	30	60	65	69	71	60	65	67	68
40	40	55	59	62	65	55	58	61	63
40	60	51	54	56	58	51	54	56	58
40	80	48	51	53	55	49	52	53	55
40	100	47	50	51	53	48	51	52	54
60	30	61	65	70	72	61	65	68	70
60	40	55	59	63	65	55	59	62	64
60	60	50	53	56	59	50	54	56	58
60	80	47	50	52	54	48	51	53	55
60	100	47	49	50	52	47	50	51	53
100	40	57	61	64	67	58	61	64	66
100	60	52	55	57	60	52	55	57	60
100	80	49	51	52	56	49	51	53	56
100	100	47	49	50	52	48	49	50	53

with a luminaire mounting height 10 ft above the floor we go to the sixth line of the table (under $W = 30$, $L = 30$) and read 64 and 63 under the mounting height = 10 for VCP lengthwise and VCP crosswise, respectively. If the room dimensions or the mounting height under consideration are different from those shown in the table, the VCP data can be interpolated.

A number of reasons may limit the use of VCP in practice; for example, it is good only for preliminary study. The method is applicable to spaces with uniformly distributed direct-type luminaires; its values are not suited to nonuniform layout or to uniformly distributed indirect lighting.

Equivalent Sphere Illumination

By definition, equivalent sphere illumination (ESI) is "the level of sphere illumination which would produce task visibility equivalent to that produced by a specific lighting environment." A sphere is used as the reference mainly because it is easily reproducible, and experiments show that a proper placement of the task within an evenly illuminated spherical surface produces good task contract. A high ESI value would mean good task contrast and less veiling reflection, hence better visibility.

Unfortunately, determining ESI for an application is a complex process because of the number of variables to be accounted for; for example, the angle and direction of view, luminaire type and locations, type of task, its ink and background contrast, all are contributing factors. If a change occurs in any of these variables (which happens in practice), the ESI values will change significantly. ESI is a good tool to analyze a situation or compare luminaires, but it should never be used as the only criterion for final decision. More discussion on ESI occurs in Chapter 18.

REFERENCES

DiLaura, D. L. "On the Computation of Equivalent Sphere Illumination." *Journal of the Illuminating Engineering Society*, **4**, 129 (1975).

Faucett, R. E. and J. R. Judge, "An Improved Method for S/MH Ratings of Luminaires with Direct Symmetrical Distributors." *Illuminating Engineering*, 37 (January 1971).

General Electric. Light Measurement and Control, TP-118. Cleveland: Nela Park, 1965.

IES, Design Practice Committee. "Classification of Interior Luminaires by Distribution: Luminaire Spacing Criteria." *Lighting Design & Application*, 20–21 (August 1977).

Sorcar, Prafulla C. *Energy Saving Lighting Systems*. New York: Van Nostrand-Reinhold, 1982.

6

Lighting Calculations

Although lighting calculations can be complex, those that are required for an architectural lighting design are fairly easy. They deal primarily with the determination of quantity.

Two basic design techniques are the point-by-point and lumen methods.

POINT-BY-POINT METHOD

This method is based on the inverse-square law, which states that the illuminance at a point on a surface perpendicular to the light ray is equal to the luminous intensity of the source at that point, divided by the square of the distance between the source and the point of interest (see Figure 6-1a):

$$E = \frac{I}{D^2}$$

where E = illuminance in footcandles
I = luminous intensity in candelas (in the direction of the point of interest)
D = distance in feet between the source and the point of interest

If the surface is not perpendicular to the light ray, the appropriate trigonometrical functions must be applied to account for the deviation; for example (referring to Figure 6-1b), if the ray of light arrives at an angle θ, then the formula must be multiplied by cos θ, which will represent its component perpendicular to the horizontal surface. This modifies the basic formula:

$$E(h) = \frac{I_\theta \cos \theta}{D^2}$$

Similarly, the formula must be multiplied by sin θ if the point of interest lies on a vertical plane (Figure 6-1c).

$$E(v) = \frac{I_\theta \sin \theta}{D^2}$$

Note that I_θ is the luminous intensity aimed at angle θ and that its value for a luminaire may not be the same at all angles. Let us illustrate with an example. If the distance in each case is $D = 15$ ft and the candlepower distribution curve of the luminaire is as shown in Figure 6-2, then for the situation in Figure 6-1a the

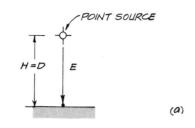

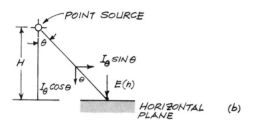

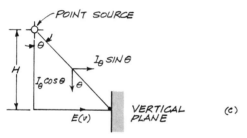

Figure 6-1. *Illumination at a point: (a) directly below the luminaire, (b) on a horizontal plane, (c) on a vertical plane.*

illuminance is

$$E = \frac{I}{D^2} = \frac{22,500}{15^2} = 100 \text{ fc}$$

Similarly, illuminance for the point on a horizontal plane (Figure 6-1b) with angle $\theta = 30°$ is

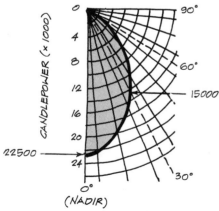

Figure 6-2. *Candlepower distribution of the luminaire in the example.*

$$E(h) = \frac{I_\theta \cos \theta}{D^2} = \frac{15,000 \times \cos 30°}{15^2} = 57.7 \text{ fc}$$

and that for the point on a vertical plane (Figure 6-1c) with angle $\theta = 30°$ is

$$E(v) = \frac{I_\theta \sin \theta}{D^2} = \frac{15,000 \times \sin 30°}{15^2} = 33.3 \text{ fc}$$

When several luminaires contribute light to the point of interest, they must be calculated separately and then added together for the net illuminance level.

Advantages and Disadvantages of Point-by-Point Method

The point-by-point method of calculation is easily applicable to areas in which point sources (incandescents, HID) are involved and no surface reflectances, accounted for; for example, exterior lighting in parking lots, spot or flood lighting, or in interiors in which few luminaires are required and surface reflectances are negligible. This method, however, cannot be used for area sources (such as fluorescent troffers) unless some modifications are made; for example, (1) the luminaires must be mounted high enough to act as point sources or (2) they must be divided into small clusters, each of which is treated as a point source. To account for the room surface reflectances a number of separate calculations must be made by first evaluating the luminances and then treating them as groups of small sources.

LUMEN METHOD

The lumen method eliminates these problems and offers a simplified way of calculating an average lighting level on an interior plane, taking into account the room surface reflectances. It is developed from the basic definition of a footcandle, which states that "a footcandle is the illuminance on a surface of one square foot in area having a uniformly distributed flux of one lumen." Mathematically,

$$E = \frac{\phi}{A}$$

where E = average illuminance in footcandles
  ϕ = total flux in lumen on the area
  A = area in square feet

If the area is in square meters, the illuminance is in lux.

In reality, it must be noted that a number of factors, such as the luminaire candlepower distribution, efficiency, room size and shape, surface reflectances, and luminaire mounting height, will affect the total number of lamp lumens that reach the work plane. Therefore the formula must be multiplied by a coefficient of utilization (CU) which takes them into consideration. Thus

$$E = \frac{\phi \times CU}{A}$$

This, however, is the initial illuminance level. In time luminaires and lamps will accumulate dirt and the lamps will depreciate in lumen output. To obtain a maintained illuminance level the formula must now be multiplied by a light-loss factor (LLF) to account for this loss. Thus

$$E = \frac{\phi \times CU \times LLF}{A}$$

Now by replacing ϕ with the total number of lumens produced by all luminaires the formula can be modified as follows:

$$E = \frac{(L \times N) \times CU \times LLF}{A}$$

where L = total initial lumens per luminaire
N = number of luminaires

To express the formula in a more useful form,

$$N = \frac{A \times E}{L \times CU \times LLF}$$

DETERMINATION OF A CU BY ZONAL CAVITY METHOD

In this method the space to be lighted is divided into three cavities (see figure 6-3). The space between the luminaire mounting plane and the ceiling is known as the ceiling cavity and the distance is h_{cc} or the height of the ceiling cavity; the space between the work plane and the luminaire mounting plane is the room cavity and this distance is h_{rc} or the height of room cavity. The space between the work plane and the floor is the floor cavity and the distance is h_{fc} or the height of floor cavity.

Cavity ratios represent the geometric proportions of the ceiling, room, and floor cavities and can be

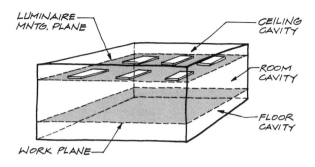

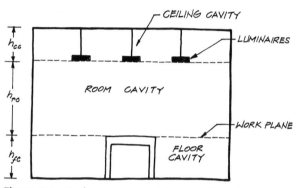

Figure 6-3. *Ceiling, room, and floor cavities of a space to be illuminated.*

determined by the following formula:

$$\text{cavity ratio} = \frac{5h \text{ (room length + room width)}}{\text{room length} \times \text{room width}}$$

where $h = h_{cc}$, h_{rc} or h_{fc}

Cavity ratios can also be found by consulting Table 6-1, which is derived from this formula.

Note that the formula is applicable to all rectangular or square-shaped rooms with flat ceilings only. For nonrectangular or nonsquare rooms the following general formula can be used:

$$\text{cavity ratio} = \frac{2.5h \text{ (perimeter of room)}}{\text{area of cavity base}}$$

We apply this formula to some irregularly shapes:

(a) For an L-shaped room (Figure 6-4a)

$$\text{cavity ratio} = \frac{2.5h \times 2(W + L)}{(WL - XY)}$$

TABLE 6-1. CAVITY RATIO TABLE[a]

Room Dimensions		Cavity Depth																			
Width	Length	1	1.5	2	2.5	3	3.5	4	5	6	7	8	9	10	11	12	14	16	20	25	30
8	8	1.2	1.9	2.5	3.1	3.7	4.4	5.0	6.2	7.5	8.8	10.0	11.2	12.5	—	—	—	—	—	—	—
	10	1.1	1.7	2.2	2.8	3.4	3.9	4.5	5.6	6.7	7.9	9.0	10.1	11.3	12.4	—	—	—	—	—	—
	14	1.0	1.5	2.0	2.5	3.0	3.4	3.9	4.9	5.9	6.9	7.8	8.8	9.7	10.7	11.7	—	—	—	—	—
	20	0.9	1.3	1.7	2.2	2.6	3.1	3.5	4.4	5.2	6.1	7.0	7.9	8.8	9.6	10.5	12.2	—	—	—	—
	30	0.8	1.2	1.6	2.0	2.4	2.8	3.2	4.0	4.7	5.5	6.3	7.1	7.9	8.7	9.5	11.0	—	—	—	—
	40	0.7	1.1	1.5	1.9	2.3	2.6	3.0	3.7	4.5	5.3	5.9	6.5	7.4	8.1	8.8	10.3	11.8	—	—	—
10	10	1.0	1.5	2.0	2.5	3.0	3.5	4.0	5.0	6.0	7.0	8.0	9.0	10.0	11.0	12.0	—	—	—	—	—
	14	0.9	1.3	1.7	2.1	2.6	3.0	3.4	4.3	5.1	6.0	6.9	7.8	8.6	9.5	10.4	12.0	—	—	—	—
	20	0.7	1.1	1.5	1.9	2.3	2.6	3.0	3.7	4.5	5.3	6.0	6.8	7.5	8.3	9.0	10.5	12.0	—	—	—
	30	0.7	1.0	1.3	1.7	2.0	2.3	2.7	3.3	4.0	4.7	5.3	6.0	6.6	7.3	8.0	9.4	10.6	—	—	—
	40	0.6	0.9	1.2	1.6	1.9	2.2	2.5	3.1	3.7	4.4	5.0	5.6	6.2	6.9	7.5	8.7	10.0	12.5	—	—
	60	0.6	0.9	1.2	1.5	1.7	2.0	2.3	2.9	3.5	4.1	4.7	5.3	5.9	6.5	7.1	8.2	9.4	11.7	—	—
12	12	0.8	1.2	1.7	2.1	2.5	2.9	3.3	4.2	5.0	5.8	6.7	7.5	8.4	9.2	10.0	11.7	—	—	—	—
	16	0.7	1.1	1.5	1.8	2.2	2.5	2.9	3.6	4.4	5.1	5.8	6.5	7.2	8.0	8.7	10.2	11.6	—	—	—
	24	0.6	0.9	1.2	1.6	1.9	2.2	2.5	3.1	3.7	4.4	5.0	5.6	6.2	6.9	7.5	8.7	10.0	12.5	—	—
	36	0.6	0.8	1.1	1.4	1.7	1.9	2.2	2.8	3.3	3.9	4.4	5.0	5.5	6.0	6.6	7.8	8.8	11.0	—	—
	50	0.5	0.8	1.0	1.3	1.5	1.8	2.1	2.6	3.1	3.6	4.1	4.6	5.1	5.6	6.2	7.2	8.2	10.2	—	—
	70	0.5	0.7	1.0	1.2	1.5	1.7	2.0	2.4	2.9	3.4	3.9	4.4	4.9	5.4	5.8	6.8	7.8	9.7	12.2	—
14	14	0.7	1.1	1.4	1.8	2.1	2.5	2.9	3.6	4.3	5.0	5.7	6.4	7.1	7.8	8.5	10.0	11.4	—	—	—
	20	0.6	0.9	1.2	1.5	1.8	2.1	2.4	3.0	3.6	4.2	4.9	5.5	6.1	6.7	7.3	8.6	9.8	12.3	—	—
	30	0.5	0.8	1.0	1.3	1.6	1.8	2.1	2.6	3.1	3.7	4.2	4.7	5.2	5.8	6.3	7.3	8.4	10.5	—	—
	42	0.5	0.7	1.0	1.2	1.4	1.7	1.9	2.4	2.9	3.3	3.8	4.3	4.7	5.2	5.7	6.7	7.6	9.5	11.9	—
	60	0.4	0.7	0.9	1.1	1.3	1.5	1.8	2.2	2.6	3.1	3.5	3.9	4.4	4.8	5.2	6.1	7.0	8.8	10.9	—
	90	0.4	0.6	0.8	1.0	1.2	1.4	1.6	2.0	2.5	2.9	3.3	3.7	4.1	4.5	5.0	5.8	6.6	8.3	10.3	12.4
17	17	0.6	0.9	1.2	1.5	1.8	2.1	2.3	2.9	3.5	4.1	4.7	5.3	5.9	6.5	7.0	8.2	9.4	11.7	—	—
	25	0.5	0.7	1.0	1.2	1.5	1.7	2.0	2.5	3.0	3.5	4.0	4.5	5.0	5.5	6.0	7.0	8.0	10.0	12.5	—
	35	0.4	0.7	0.9	1.1	1.3	1.5	1.7	2.2	2.6	3.1	3.5	3.9	4.4	4.8	5.2	6.1	7.0	8.7	10.9	—
	50	0.4	0.6	0.8	1.0	1.2	1.4	1.6	2.0	2.4	2.8	3.1	3.5	3.9	4.3	4.5	5.4	6.2	7.7	9.7	11.6
	80	0.4	0.5	0.7	0.9	1.1	1.2	1.4	1.8	2.1	2.5	2.9	3.3	3.6	4.0	4.3	5.1	5.8	7.2	9.0	10.9
	120	0.3	0.5	0.7	0.8	1.0	1.2	1.3	1.7	2.0	2.3	2.7	3.0	3.4	3.7	4.0	4.7	5.4	6.7	8.4	10.1
20	20	0.5	0.7	1.0	1.2	1.5	1.7	2.0	2.5	3.0	3.5	4.0	4.5	5.0	5.5	6.0	7.0	8.0	10.0	12.5	—
	30	0.4	0.6	0.8	1.0	1.2	1.5	1.7	2.1	2.5	2.9	3.3	3.7	4.1	4.5	4.9	5.8	6.6	8.2	10.3	12.4
	45	0.4	0.5	0.7	0.9	1.1	1.3	1.4	1.8	2.2	2.5	2.9	3.3	3.6	4.0	4.3	5.1	5.8	7.2	9.1	10.9
	60	0.3	0.5	0.7	0.8	1.0	1.2	1.3	1.7	2.0	2.3	2.7	3.0	3.4	3.7	4.0	4.7	5.4	6.7	8.4	10.1
	90	0.3	0.5	0.6	0.8	0.9	1.1	1.2	1.5	1.8	2.1	2.4	2.7	3.0	3.3	3.6	4.2	4.8	6.0	7.5	9.0
	150	0.3	0.4	0.6	0.7	0.8	1.0	1.1	1.4	1.7	2.0	2.3	2.6	2.9	3.2	3.4	4.0	4.6	5.7	7.2	8.6
24	24	0.4	0.6	0.8	1.0	1.2	1.5	1.7	2.1	2.5	2.9	3.3	3.7	4.1	4.5	5.0	5.8	6.7	8.2	10.3	12.4
	32	0.4	0.5	0.7	0.9	1.1	1.3	1.5	1.8	2.2	2.6	2.9	3.3	3.6	4.0	4.3	5.1	5.8	7.2	9.0	11.0
	50	0.3	0.5	0.6	0.8	0.9	1.1	1.2	1.5	1.8	2.2	2.5	2.8	3.1	3.4	3.7	4.4	5.0	6.2	7.8	9.4
	70	0.3	0.4	0.6	0.7	0.8	1.0	1.1	1.4	1.7	2.0	2.2	2.5	2.8	3.0	3.3	3.8	4.4	5.5	6.9	8.2
	100	0.3	0.4	0.5	0.6	0.8	0.9	1.0	1.3	1.6	1.8	2.1	2.4	2.6	2.9	3.1	3.7	4.2	5.2	6.5	7.9
	160	0.2	0.4	0.5	0.6	0.7	0.8	1.0	1.2	1.4	1.7	1.9	2.1	2.4	2.6	2.8	3.3	3.8	4.7	5.9	7.1
30	30	0.3	0.5	0.7	0.8	1.0	1.2	1.3	1.7	2.0	2.3	2.7	3.0	3.3	3.7	4.0	4.7	5.4	6.7	8.4	10.0
	45	0.3	0.4	0.6	0.7	0.8	1.0	1.1	1.4	1.7	1.9	2.2	2.5	2.7	3.0	3.3	3.8	4.4	5.5	6.9	8.2
	60	0.3	0.4	0.5	0.6	0.7	0.9	1.0	1.2	1.5	1.7	2.0	2.2	2.5	2.7	3.0	3.5	4.0	5.0	6.2	7.4
	90	0.2	0.3	0.4	0.6	0.7	0.8	0.9	1.1	1.3	1.6	1.8	2.0	2.2	2.5	2.7	3.1	3.6	4.5	5.6	6.7
	150	0.2	0.3	0.4	0.5	0.6	0.7	0.8	1.0	1.2	1.4	1.6	1.8	2.0	2.2	2.4	2.8	3.2	4.0	5.0	5.9
	200	0.2	0.3	0.4	0.5	0.6	0.7	0.8	1.0	1.1	1.3	1.5	1.7	1.9	2.0	2.2	2.6	3.0	3.7	4.7	5.6
36	36	0.3	0.4	0.6	0.7	0.8	1.0	1.1	1.4	1.7	1.9	2.2	2.5	2.8	3.0	3.3	3.9	4.4	5.5	6.9	8.3
	50	0.2	0.4	0.5	0.6	0.7	0.8	·1.2	1.4	1.4	1.7	1.9	2.1	2.5	2.6	2.9	3.3	3.8	4.8	5.9	7.2
	75	0.2	0.3	0.4	0.5	0.6	0.7	0.8	1.0	1.2	1.4	1.6	1.8	2.0	2.3	2.5	2.9	3.3	4.1	5.1	6.1
	100	0.2	0.3	0.4	0.5	0.6	0.7	0.8	0.9	1.1	1.3	1.5	1.7	1.9	2.1	2.3	2.6	3.0	3.8	4.7	5.7
	150	0.2	0.3	0.3	0.4	0.5	0.6	0.7	0.9	1.0	1.2	1.4	1.6	1.7	1.9	2.1	2.4	2.8	3.5	4.3	5.2
	200	0.2	0.2	0.3	0.4	0.5	0.6	0.7	0.8	1.0	1.1	1.3	1.5	1.6	1.8	2.0	2.3	2.6	3.3	4.1	4.9
42	42	0.2	0.4	0.5	0.6	0.7	0.8	1.0	1.2	1.4	1.6	1.9	2.1	2.4	2.6	2.8	3.3	3.8	4.7	5.9	7.1
	60	0.2	0.3	0.4	0.5	0.6	0.7	0.8	1.0	1.2	1.4	1.6	1.8	2.0	2.2	2.4	2.8	3.2	4.0	5.0	6.0
	90	0.2	0.3	0.3	0.4	0.5	0.6	0.7	0.9	1.0	1.2	1.4	1.6	1.7	1.9	2.1	2.4	2.8	3.5	4.4	5.2
	140	0.2	0.2	0.3	0.4	0.4	0.5	0.6	0.8	0.9	1.1	1.2	1.4	1.5	1.7	1.9	2.2	2.5	3.1	3.9	4.6
	200	0.1	0.2	0.3	0.4	0.4	0.5	0.6	0.7	0.9	1.0	1.1	1.3	1.4	1.6	1.7	2.0	2.3	2.9	3.6	4.3
	300	0.1	0.2	0.3	0.3	0.4	0.5	0.5	0.7	0.8	0.9	1.1	1.3	1.4	1.5	1.7	1.9	2.2	2.8	3.5	4.2

[a] Reprinted with permission from the *IES Lighting Handbook*, 5th ed.

Continued on next page.

TABLE 6-1. (Continued)

Room Dimensions		Cavity Depth																			
Width	Length	1	1.5	2	2.5	3	3.5	4	5	6	7	8	9	10	11	12	14	16	20	25	30
50	50	0.2	0.3	0.4	0.5	0.6	0.7	0.8	1.0	1.2	1.4	1.6	1.8	2.0	2.2	2.4	2.8	3.2	4.0	5.0	6.0
	70	0.2	0.3	0.3	0.4	0.5	0.6	0.7	0.9	1.0	1.2	1.4	1.5	1.7	1.9	2.0	2.4	2.7	3.4	4.3	5.1
	100	0.1	0.2	0.3	0.4	0.4	0.5	0.6	0.7	0.9	1.0	1.2	1.3	1.5	1.6	1.8	2.1	2.4	3.0	3.7	4.5
	150	0.1	0.2	0.3	0.3	0.4	0.5	0.5	0.7	0.8	0.9	1.1	1.2	1.3	1.5	1.6	1.9	2.1	2.7	3.3	4.0
	300	0.1	0.2	0.2	0.3	0.3	0.4	0.5	0.6	0.7	0.8	0.9	1.0	1.1	1.3	1.4	1.6	1.9	2.3	2.9	3.5
60	60	0.2	0.2	0.3	0.4	0.5	0.6	0.7	0.8	1.0	1.2	1.3	1.5	1.7	1.8	2.0	2.3	2.7	3.3	4.2	5.0
	100	0.1	0.2	0.3	0.3	0.4	0.5	0.5	0.7	0.8	0.9	1.1	1.2	1.3	1.5	1.6	1.9	2.1	2.7	3.3	4.0
	150	0.1	0.2	0.2	0.3	0.3	0.4	0.5	0.6	0.7	0.8	0.9	1.0	1.2	1.3	1.4	1.6	1.9	2.3	2.9	3.5
	300	0.1	0.1	0.2	0.2	0.3	0.3	0.4	0.5	0.6	0.7	0.8	0.9	1.0	1.1	1.2	1.4	1.6	2.0	2.5	3.0
75	75	0.1	0.2	0.3	0.3	0.4	0.5	0.5	0.7	0.8	0.9	1.1	1.2	1.3	1.5	1.6	1.9	2.1	2.7	3.3	4.0
	120	0.1	0.2	0.2	0.3	0.3	0.4	0.4	0.5	0.6	0.8	0.9	1.0	1.1	1.2	1.3	1.5	1.7	2.2	2.7	3.3
	200	0.1	0.1	0.2	0.2	0.3	0.3	0.4	0.5	0.5	0.6	0.7	0.8	0.9	1.0	1.1	1.3	1.5	1.8	2.3	2.7
	300	0.1	0.1	0.2	0.2	0.2	0.3	0.3	0.4	0.5	0.6	0.7	0.7	0.8	0.9	1.0	1.2	1.3	1.7	2.1	2.5
100	100	0.1	0.1	0.2	0.2	0.3	0.3	0.4	0.5	0.6	0.7	0.8	0.9	1.0	1.1	1.2	1.4	1.6	2.0	2.5	3.0
	200	0.1	0.1	0.1	0.2	0.2	0.3	0.3	0.4	0.4	0.5	0.6	0.7	0.7	0.8	0.9	1.0	1.2	1.5	1.9	2.2
	300	0.1	0.1	0.1	0.2	0.2	0.2	0.3	0.3	0.4	0.5	0.5	0.6	0.7	0.7	0.8	0.9	1.1	1.3	1.7	2.0
150	150	0.1	0.1	0.1	0.2	0.2	0.2	0.3	0.3	0.4	0.5	0.5	0.6	0.7	0.7	0.8	0.9	1.1	1.3	1.7	2.0
	300	—	0.1	0.1	0.1	0.1	0.2	0.2	0.2	0.3	0.3	0.4	0.5	0.5	0.6	0.6	0.7	0.8	1.0	1.2	1.5
200	200	—	0.1	0.1	0.1	0.1	0.2	0.2	0.2	0.3	0.3	0.4	0.5	0.5	0.6	0.6	0.7	0.8	1.0	1.2	1.5
	300	—	0.1	0.1	0.1	0.1	0.1	0.2	0.2	0.2	0.3	0.3	0.4	0.4	0.5	0.5	0.6	0.7	0.8	1.0	1.2
300	300	—	—	0.1	0.1	0.1	0.1	0.1	0.2	0.2	0.2	0.3	0.3	0.3	0.4	0.4	0.5	0.5	0.6	0.7	0.8
500	500	—	—	—	—	0.1	0.1	0.1	0.1	0.1	0.1	0.2	0.2	0.2	0.2	0.2	0.3	0.3	0.4	0.5	0.6

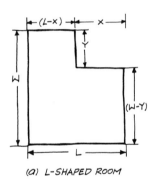

(a) L-SHAPED ROOM

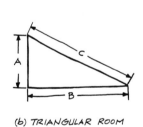

(b) TRIANGULAR ROOM

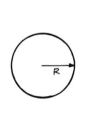

(c) CIRCULAR ROOM

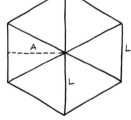

(d) HEXAGONAL ROOM

Figure 6-4. *Irregular shaped rooms: (a) L-shaped room, (b) triangular room, (c) circular room, (d) hexagonal room.*

(b) For a triangular room (Figure 6-4b)

$$\text{cavity ratio} = \frac{2.5h \times (A + B + C)}{1/2\,BC}$$

(c) For a circular room (Figure 6-4c)

$$\text{cavity ratio} = \frac{2.5h \times (2R)}{R^2}$$

$$= \frac{5h}{R}$$

(d) For a hexagonal room (Figure 6-4d)

$$\text{cavity ratio} = \frac{2.5h \times 6L}{(1/2\,LA)6}$$

$$= \frac{2.5h \times 6L}{(1/2\,L^2 \times 0.866)6}$$

$$= \frac{5.76h}{L}$$

SAMPLE PROBLEMS

6-1 Determine the ceiling cavity ratio (CCR), room cavity ratio (RCR), and the floor cavity ratio (FCR) for a rectangular room of length $L = 40$ ft, width, $W = 30$ ft, and height, $H = 10$ ft. The luminaire mounting plane is 2 ft below the ceiling and the work plane is 2.5 ft above the floor.

Solution

By referring to Figure 6-5 and using the formula for the cavity ratio, for $h = h_{cc} = 2$ ft

$$CCR = \frac{5 \times 2(40 + 30)}{40 \times 30}$$

$$= 0.58$$

Similarly, for $h = h_{rc} = (10 - 2.5 - 2) = 5.5$

$$RCR = \frac{5 \times 5.5(40 + 30)}{40 \times 30}$$

$$= 1.6$$

and for $h = h_{fc} = 2.5$

$$FCR = \frac{5 \times 2.5(40 + 30)}{40 \times 30}$$

$$= 0.72$$

6-2   In the preceding example (Problem 6-1) a part of the room (15 × 10 ft; see Figure 6-6) is used for a different purpose than the remaining area and requires a different illumination level. Determine the cavity ratios.

Solution

In applications in which more than one type of task is performed in a single room with separate illuminance level requirements the areas should be treated as two separate rooms.

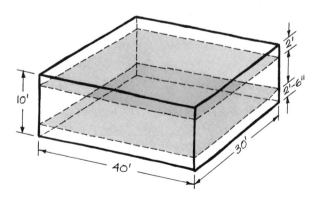

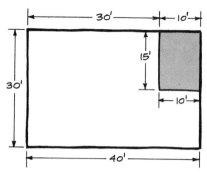

Figure 6-6.

Figure 6-6 for the shaded room gives

$$\text{cavity ratio} = \frac{5h\,(10 + 15)}{10 \times 15}$$

$$= \frac{5h}{6}$$

and for the L-shaped room

$$\text{cavity ratio} = \frac{2.5h \times 2(L + W)}{WL - XY}$$

$$= \frac{2.5 \times h \times 2(40 + 30)}{(40 \times 30) - (15 \times 10)}$$

$$= \frac{h}{3}$$

Now by substituting the values of h_{cc}, h_{rc}, and h_{fc} the CCR, RCR, and FCR can be determined for each room.

ROOM SURFACE REFLECTANCES AND EFFECTIVE CAVITY REFLECTANCES

Coefficient of utilization values are almost totally dependent on reflecting surfaces. In general, higher reflectances of ceiling, walls, and floor would mean higher CU values. Thus to evaluate the correct CU of a luminaire we must know the true surface reflectances. These reflectances vary largely with the type of work performed. An industrial facility, in which fumes, smoke, and a dirty environment are commonplace would obviously have lower reflectances than an well maintained office that is usually located in a clean environment. The other difficulty in evaluating true reflectance develops when a surface has several colors or finishes of varying reflectances, in which

case a weighted average must be taken. The formula
to be used is

$$\rho = \frac{\rho_1 A_1 + \rho_2 A_2 + \rho_3 A_3 + \cdots}{A_1 + A_2 + A_3 + \cdots}$$

where
ρ = the weighted average reflectance

$A_1, A_2, A_3 \cdots$ = areas of different surfaces

$\rho_1, \rho_2, \rho_3 \cdots$ = surface reflectances of $A_1, A_2, A_3 \cdots$

6-3 A specific wall of a room has 90 ft² of white paint (80% reflectance), 160 ft² of dark wood paneling (20% reflectance), 40 ft² of wallpaper (50% reflectance), and 30 ft² of bookshelves of approximately 15% reflectance. Find the weighted average reflectance of the wall.

Solution

By applying the formula for weighted average reflectance

TABLE 6-2. APPROXIMATE SURFACE REFLECTANCE OF TYPICAL BUILDING INTERIOR FINISHES

Building Finishes	App. Reflectance (%)
Ceilings	
White paint (plain plaster surface)	80
White paint on acoustic tile	70
White paint on smooth concrete	60
White paint on rough concrete	50
Walls	
White paint on plaster tiles	80
Medium blue-gray, yellow-gray	50
Light gray concrete	40
Bricks (other than rough gray)	30
Unfinished cement, rough tile	25
Wood panel (light)	25
Wood panel (dark)	20
Rough brick	15
Floors	
Light wood	35
Medium wood	25
Dark wood	20
Light tile	30
Dark tile	20
Light carpet (gray, orange, medium-blue)	20
Dark carpet (dark gray, brown)	15

$$\rho = \frac{\substack{(0.80 \times 90) + (0.20 \times 160) \\ + (0.5 \times 40) + (0.15 \times 30)}}{90 + 160 + 40 + 30}$$

$$= 40.1\%$$

In the next step we find the effective reflectances of the ceiling and floor, which take into account the fact that because of their depth the total overall reflectances of the ceiling and floor cavities are different from the direct surface reflectances. Obviously the deeper the cavity, the poorer light reflected. In addition, some of this reflected light at the ceiling or floor is actually bounced off the walls. Thus the determination of the effective ceiling and floor cavity reflectances would be dependent on their cavity depths, surface reflectances, and cavity ratios. Table 6-3 supplies predetermined effective reflectances for ceiling or floor cavities. Problem 6-4 shows how to use it.

6-4 A room has 80, 50, and 30% ceiling, wall, and floor surface reflectances, respectively; CCR and FCR of the room are 1.6 and 0.5, respectively. Determine the effective ceiling and floor cavity reflectances (ρ_{cc} and ρ_{fc}) by referring to Table 6-3.

Solution

To determine ρ_{cc} we select the column with 80% ceiling reflectance and 50% wall reflectance at the top of the table and read ρ_{cc} = 60% at CCR = 1.6. Similarly, for ρ_{fc} we select the column with 30% floor reflectance and 50% wall reflectance at the top of the table and read ρ_{fc} = 28% at FCR = 0.5.

EFFECTIVE CAVITY REFLECTANCES FOR NONHORIZONTAL CEILINGS

The effective ceiling reflectance (ρ_{cc}) of a nonhorizontal ceiling can be calculated by using the following formula and solved in the usual manner:

$$\rho_{cc} = \frac{\rho_c A_o}{A_S - \rho_c A_S + \rho_c A_o}$$

where A_o = the area of the ceiling opening

A_S = the area of the ceiling surface

ρ_c = the reflectance of the ceiling surface

6-5 Determine the effective ceiling cavity reflectance of a hemispherical dome with a 10-ft radius. The surface reflectance of the dome is 80%.

TABLE 6-3. PERCENT EFFECTIVE CEILING AND FLOOR REFLECTANCES FOR VARIOUS REFLECTANCE COMBINATIONS[a]

Per Cent Base* Reflectance	90										80										70										60										50									
Per Cent Wall Reflectance / Cavity Ratio	90	80	70	60	50	40	30	20	10	0	90	80	70	60	50	40	30	20	10	0	90	80	70	60	50	40	30	20	10	0	90	80	70	60	50	40	30	20	10	0	90	80	70	60	50	40	30	20	10	0
0.2	89	88	88	87	86	86	85	85	84	82	79	78	78	77	77	76	76	75	74	72	70	69	69	68	68	67	67	66	65	64	60	59	59	58	58	57	56	56	55	53	50	50	49	49	48	48	47	47	46	44
0.4	88	87	86	85	84	83	81	80	79	77	77	77	76	75	74	73	72	71	70	68	69	68	68	66	65	64	63	62	61	58	60	59	58	57	55	55	54	53	51	50	50	49	48	47	47	46	45	45	44	42
0.6	87	86	84	82	81	80	77	76	74	73	78	76	75	73	71	71	68	67	65	62	69	67	65	64	63	61	59	58	56	54	60	58	57	55	54	53	52	51	50	46	50	49	48	47	46	45	44	43	42	41
0.8	87	85	82	80	79	77	75	73	69	67	78	75	73	71	69	68	65	63	61	57	68	66	64	62	60	58	56	54	53	50	59	58	56	54	52	51	48	47	45	44	50	48	47	46	45	44	43	42	40	38
1.0	86	83	80	77	75	72	69	66	64	62	77	74	72	69	67	65	62	60	58	55	68	65	62	60	58	55	53	52	49	47	59	57	55	53	51	48	47	44	43	41	50	48	46	44	43	41	40	38	36	34
1.2	85	82	78	75	72	69	66	63	60	57	76	73	70	67	64	61	58	55	53	51	67	64	61	59	57	54	50	48	46	44	59	56	52	49	46	43	40	38	36	34	50	47	45	43	41	39	36	35	33	31
1.4	85	80	77	73	69	65	62	59	57	52	76	72	68	65	62	59	55	53	50	48	67	63	60	58	55	51	47	45	43	41	58	55	50	47	44	41	38	35	33	30	50	47	43	41	39	36	34	32	30	27
1.6	84	79	75	71	67	63	59	56	53	50	75	71	67	63	60	56	53	50	48	44	67	62	59	56	53	50	45	43	41	38	58	54	49	45	42	39	36	33	31	28	50	46	42	40	38	35	33	31	28	26
1.8	83	78	73	69	64	60	56	53	50	48	75	71	66	62	58	54	50	47	44	41	66	61	58	54	51	47	44	40	38	35	58	53	48	44	40	37	34	31	28	26	50	46	41	39	37	34	33	31	28	25
2.0	83	77	72	67	62	56	53	50	47	43	74	69	64	60	56	52	48	45	42	38	66	60	56	52	49	45	42	38	36	33	58	53	47	43	39	35	32	30	27	24	50	46	40	37	34	32	30	28	26	24
2.2	82	76	70	65	59	54	50	47	44	40	74	68	63	58	54	49	45	42	38	35	66	60	55	51	48	43	38	36	34	32	57	52	46	41	37	33	31	28	25	23	49	46	41	37	33	30	28	26	24	22
2.4	82	75	69	64	58	53	48	45	41	37	73	67	61	56	52	47	43	40	36	33	65	60	54	50	46	41	37	35	32	30	57	51	45	40	36	32	30	27	24	21	49	45	40	36	32	29	27	25	23	21
2.6	81	74	67	62	56	51	46	42	38	35	73	66	60	55	50	46	41	37	34	31	65	59	54	49	45	40	35	33	30	28	57	50	44	39	35	31	28	25	22	20	49	45	40	35	31	28	25	23	21	20
2.8	81	73	66	60	54	49	44	40	36	34	73	66	59	53	48	44	39	36	32	29	65	59	53	48	43	38	33	32	28	26	57	50	43	38	33	30	27	24	21	18	49	44	39	34	30	27	24	22	20	18
3.0	80	72	64	58	52	47	42	38	34	30	72	65	58	52	47	42	37	34	30	27	64	58	52	47	42	37	32	31	27	24	57	49	42	37	32	28	25	23	20	17	48	44	38	33	29	26	23	21	19	17
3.2	79	71	63	56	50	45	40	36	32	28	72	65	57	51	45	40	35	33	28	25	64	58	51	46	40	36	31	28	25	23	56	49	41	36	31	27	24	22	19	16	48	43	38	32	28	25	22	20	18	16
3.4	79	70	62	54	48	43	38	34	30	27	71	64	56	49	44	39	34	32	27	24	64	57	50	45	39	35	29	27	24	22	56	48	40	35	30	26	23	20	18	15	48	43	37	31	27	24	21	19	17	15
3.6	78	69	61	53	47	42	36	32	28	25	71	63	54	48	43	38	32	30	25	23	63	56	49	44	38	33	28	25	22	20	56	48	39	34	29	25	22	19	17	14	48	42	36	31	26	23	20	18	16	14
3.8	78	69	60	51	45	40	35	31	27	23	70	62	53	47	41	37	31	28	24	22	63	56	49	43	37	32	27	24	21	19	56	47	39	33	28	24	21	18	16	13	47	42	36	30	26	22	19	17	15	13
4.0	77	69	58	51	44	39	33	29	25	22	70	61	53	46	40	35	30	27	23	20	63	55	48	42	36	31	26	23	20	17	56	47	38	32	27	24	20	18	15	12	47	41	35	30	25	21	18	16	14	12
4.2	77	62	57	50	43	37	32	28	24	21	69	60	52	45	39	34	29	25	21	18	62	55	47	41	35	30	25	22	19	16	55	46	37	32	27	22	19	16	14	11	47	41	34	29	24	21	18	15	13	12
4.4	76	61	56	49	42	36	31	27	23	20	69	60	51	44	38	33	28	24	21	17	62	54	46	40	34	29	24	21	18	15	55	46	37	31	26	22	19	16	13	11	47	40	34	29	24	20	17	15	12	11
4.6	76	60	55	47	40	35	30	26	22	19	69	59	50	43	37	32	27	23	19	15	62	53	45	39	33	28	24	21	17	14	55	45	36	31	26	21	18	15	13	10	46	40	33	28	23	19	16	14	12	10
4.8	75	59	54	46	39	34	28	25	21	18	68	58	49	42	36	31	26	22	18	14	62	53	45	38	32	27	23	20	16	13	55	45	36	30	25	21	17	15	12	09	46	39	33	27	22	19	16	13	11	09
5.0	75	59	53	45	38	33	28	24	20	16	68	58	48	41	35	30	25	21	18	14	61	52	44	36	31	26	22	19	16	12	55	45	35	30	25	21	17	14	12	09	46	39	32	27	22	18	15	13	11	09
6.0	73	61	49	41	34	29	24	20	16	11	66	55	44	38	31	27	22	19	15	10	60	51	41	35	28	24	19	16	13	09	55	43	35	29	23	19	15	13	10	06	45	37	30	24	19	15	13	10	08	06
7.0	70	58	45	38	30	27	21	18	14	08	64	53	41	35	28	24	19	16	12	08	58	48	38	32	26	22	17	14	11	06	54	43	33	27	21	17	14	11	08	05	43	35	27	22	17	14	12	09	07	05
8.0	68	55	42	35	27	23	18	15	12	06	62	50	38	32	25	21	17	14	11	06	57	46	35	30	24	19	15	13	10	05	53	42	31	26	19	16	12	10	07	03	42	33	25	20	16	13	10	08	07	03
9.0	66	52	38	31	25	21	16	14	11	05	61	49	36	30	23	19	15	11	10	05	56	45	33	27	21	16	13	11	09	04	52	40	29	24	18	15	11	09	07	03	41	31	24	19	15	11	09	07	06	03
10.0	65	51	36	29	22	19	15	11	09	04	59	46	33	27	21	18	14	11	08	03	55	43	31	25	19	16	12	10	08	03	51	39	29	24	18	15	11	08	06	02	40	29	22	17	14	11	08	06	05	02

* Ceiling, floor or floor of cavity.

[a] Reprinted with permission from the *IES Lighting Handbook*, 1981 Reference Volume.

Per Cent Base* Reflectance / Per Cent Wall Reflectance

Cavity Ratio	40										30										20										10										0									
	90	80	70	60	50	40	30	20	10	0	90	80	70	60	50	40	30	20	10	0	90	80	70	60	50	40	30	20	10	0	90	80	70	60	50	40	30	20	10	0	90	80	70	60	50	40	30	20	10	0
0.2	40	40	39	38	39	38	38	37	37	36	31	31	30	30	30	29	29	28	28	27	21	20	20	20	20	20	19	19	19	17	11	11	11	10	10	10	10	09	09	09	02	02	02	01	01	01	01	00	00	0
0.4	41	40	39	39	38	37	36	35	35	34	31	31	30	30	29	28	28	26	26	25	22	21	21	20	20	19	19	18	17	16	12	11	11	11	10	10	09	09	09	08	04	03	03	02	02	02	01	01	00	0
0.6	41	40	40	39	38	36	36	34	34	32	32	31	30	29	28	27	26	25	25	23	23	21	21	20	19	18	18	17	17	15	13	13	12	11	11	11	10	09	08	08	05	05	04	03	03	02	02	01	01	0
0.8	41	40	38	38	37	36	34	33	32	31	33	31	29	28	28	26	25	24	23	22	24	22	21	19	19	18	17	16	16	14	15	14	13	12	11	11	10	10	08	08	07	06	05	04	03	03	02	02	01	0
1.0	42	40	38	37	36	35	33	32	31	27	33	32	30	29	27	25	24	22	22	20	25	23	22	20	19	18	17	15	15	13	16	14	13	12	12	11	10	09	08	07	08	07	06	05	04	03	03	02	01	0
1.2	42	40	38	36	35	34	32	30	29	25	33	32	30	28	27	25	23	22	21	19	25	23	22	20	19	17	16	14	14	12	17	15	14	13	12	11	10	09	07	06	10	08	07	06	05	04	03	02	01	0
1.4	42	39	37	35	34	33	31	29	27	23	34	32	30	28	26	24	22	21	19	18	26	24	22	20	18	17	15	14	13	11	18	16	14	13	13	11	09	08	07	06	11	09	08	07	06	04	04	03	02	0
1.6	42	37	37	35	32	30	29	27	25	22	34	33	29	27	25	23	21	20	18	17	26	24	22	20	18	16	15	13	12	10	19	17	15	14	12	11	09	08	07	06	12	10	09	07	06	05	04	03	02	0
1.8	42	39	36	34	31	29	28	26	24	21	35	33	29	27	25	23	21	19	17	16	27	25	23	20	18	16	15	13	11	09	19	17	15	14	13	11	09	08	06	05	13	11	09	08	07	05	04	03	03	0
2.0	42	39	36	34	31	28	26	25	23	19	35	33	29	26	24	22	20	18	16	14	28	25	23	20	18	16	14	13	11	09	20	18	16	14	13	11	09	08	06	05	14	12	10	09	07	05	04	03	03	0
2.2	42	39	36	33	30	27	24	24	22	18	36	32	29	26	24	22	19	17	15	13	28	25	23	20	18	16	14	12	10	09	21	19	16	14	13	11	09	07	06	05	15	13	11	09	08	06	04	03	03	01
2.4	43	39	35	33	29	27	24	23	21	17	36	32	29	26	24	21	19	16	14	12	29	26	23	20	18	16	14	12	10	08	22	19	17	15	13	11	09	07	06	05	16	13	11	10	08	06	05	03	03	01
2.6	43	39	34	32	29	26	24	22	20	15	36	32	28	25	23	20	18	16	13	11	29	26	23	20	18	15	14	11	09	08	22	19	17	15	13	11	09	07	06	04	17	14	12	10	08	06	05	03	03	02
2.8	43	39	35	32	28	25	22	21	19	14	37	33	29	25	23	20	17	15	13	11	30	27	23	20	17	15	13	11	09	07	23	20	18	16	13	11	09	07	05	04	17	15	13	10	09	07	05	03	03	02
3.0	43	39	35	31	27	24	21	21	18	13	37	33	29	25	22	20	17	15	12	10	30	27	23	20	17	15	13	11	09	07	24	21	18	16	13	11	09	07	05	03	18	16	13	11	09	07	05	04	03	02
3.2	43	39	35	31	27	23	20	17	17	13	37	33	29	25	22	19	16	14	12	10	31	27	23	20	17	15	12	11	09	06	25	21	18	16	13	11	09	07	05	03	19	16	14	11	09	07	05	04	02	02
3.4	43	39	34	30	26	23	20	17	15	12	37	33	29	25	22	19	16	14	11	09	31	27	23	20	17	14	12	10	08	06	26	22	18	16	14	11	09	07	05	03	20	17	14	12	09	07	05	04	02	02
3.6	44	39	34	30	26	22	19	17	14	11	37	33	28	24	21	18	15	13	10	08	32	27	23	20	17	14	12	10	08	05	26	22	19	16	14	11	09	06	04	03	20	17	15	12	10	08	05	04	02	02
3.8	44	38	33	29	25	22	18	16	14	10	38	33	28	24	21	18	15	13	10	08	32	28	23	20	17	14	12	10	08	05	27	23	19	17	14	11	08	06	04	02	21	18	15	12	10	08	05	04	02	02
4.0	44	38	33	29	25	21	18	16	13	10	38	33	28	24	21	18	14	12	10	07	33	28	23	20	17	14	11	09	07	05	27	23	20	17	14	11	08	06	04	02	22	18	15	13	10	08	05	04	02	02
4.2	44	38	33	29	24	21	17	17	15	10	38	33	28	24	20	17	14	12	09	07	33	28	23	20	17	14	11	09	07	04	28	24	20	17	14	11	09	06	04	02	22	19	16	13	10	08	06	04	02	02
4.4	44	38	33	28	24	20	17	14	14	09	39	33	28	24	20	17	14	11	09	06	34	28	24	20	17	14	11	09	07	04	28	24	20	17	14	11	08	06	03	02	23	19	16	13	11	08	06	04	02	02
4.6	44	38	32	28	23	19	17	14	13	08	39	33	28	24	20	17	13	11	08	05	34	29	24	20	17	14	11	08	06	03	29	25	20	17	14	11	08	06	03	01	23	20	17	13	11	08	06	04	02	02
4.8	44	38	32	27	22	19	16	14	13	08	39	33	28	24	20	16	13	10	08	05	35	29	24	20	16	13	10	08	06	03	29	25	20	17	13	10	08	05	03	01	24	20	17	14	11	08	06	04	02	02
5.0	45	38	31	27	22	19	15	13	13	07	39	33	28	24	19	16	13	10	08	05	35	29	24	20	16	13	10	08	05	02	30	25	20	17	12	10	07	05	02	01	25	21	17	14	11	09	06	04	02	02
6.0	44	37	30	25	20	17	13	11	10	05	39	33	27	23	18	15	11	09	06	04	36	30	24	20	16	13	10	08	05	02	31	26	21	18	14	08	06	05	02	01	27	23	18	15	12	09	06	04	02	02
7.0	44	36	29	24	19	16	12	10	09	04	40	33	26	21	17	14	10	07	05	03	36	30	24	19	15	12	09	07	04	02	32	27	21	17	13	10	07	04	02	01	28	24	19	15	12	10	06	04	02	02
8.0	44	35	28	23	18	15	11	09	08	03	40	33	25	20	16	13	09	07	04	02	37	30	23	19	15	11	08	06	03	01	33	27	21	17	13	10	07	04	01	01	30	25	20	15	12	10	06	04	02	02
9.0	44	35	26	21	16	13	10	08	07	02	40	32	25	20	15	12	09	06	04	02	37	29	23	19	14	11	07	05	03	01	34	28	21	17	13	10	07	04	01	01	31	25	20	15	12	10	06	04	02	02
10.0	43	34	25	20	15	12	10	08	07	02	40	32	24	19	14	11	08	06	03	01	37	29	22	18	13	10	07	05	03	01	34	28	21	17	12	10	07	05	02	01	31	25	20	15	12	10	06	04	02	02

* Ceiling, floor or floor of cavity.

Figure 6-7.

Solution

By referring to Figure 6-7 we find:

$$A_o = \pi r^2 = 100\pi \text{ ft}^2$$

$$A_S = 2\pi r^2 = 200\pi \text{ ft}^2$$

$$\rho_c = 0.80$$

and by applying the formula we obtain

$$\rho_{cc} = \frac{\rho_c A_o}{A_S - \rho_c A_S + \rho_c A_o}$$

$$= \frac{0.80 \times 100\pi}{200\pi - (0.80 \times 200\pi) + (0.80 \times 100\pi)}$$

$$= 0.67\%$$

6-6 Determine the effective ceiling cavity reflectance of a barrel-vault ceiling with the dimensions in Figure 6-8. Given $\rho_c = 0.80$.

Solution

$$A_o = 40 \times 20 = 800 \text{ ft}^2$$

$$A_S = \frac{2\pi r}{2} \times 40 + \frac{\pi r^2}{2} + \frac{\pi r^2}{2}$$

$$= 1570$$

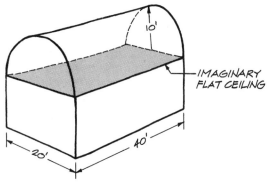

Figure 6-8.

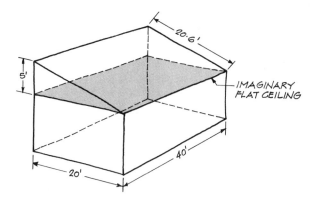

Therefore

$$\rho_{cc} = \frac{800 \times 0.8}{1570 - (0.80 \times 1570) + (0.80 \times 800)} \times 100$$

$$= 67\%$$

6-7 Determine the effective ceiling cavity reflectance of a sloped ceiling with the dimensions in Figure 6-9. Given $\rho_c = 80\%$.

Solution

$$A_o = 40 \times 20 = 800 \text{ ft}^2$$
$$A_S = 2(\frac{1}{2} \times 20 \times 5) + (20.6 \times 40) + (5 \times 40)$$
$$= 1124 \text{ ft}^2$$

Therefore

$$\rho_{cc} = \frac{800 \times 0.80}{1124 - (0.80 \times 1124) + (0.80 \times 800)}$$

$$= \frac{640}{1124 - 899.2 + 640}$$

$$= 0.74 \text{ or } 74\%$$

EFFECTIVE CEILING CAVITY REFLECTANCE OF ROOMS WITH CEILING OBSTRUCTIONS

If the ceiling has beams, joists, twin-tees, mechanical ducts or other obstructions, the following method can be adopted:

(a) Determine the effective cavity reflectance for each cavity formed by the obstruction (beam, duct, etc.).

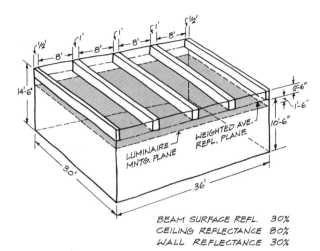

BEAM SURFACE REFL. 30%
CEILING REFLECTANCE 80%
WALL REFLECTANCE 30%

Figure 6-10.

(b) Determine the weighted average reflectance of the plane at the bottom of the obstruction.

(c) Proceed in the conventional manner to determine ρ_{cc} by using ρ_c as found in (b).

6-8 Given the dimensions and surface reflectances of the room with ceiling obstructions shown in Figure 6-10, find the effective ceiling cavity reflectance, assuming that the luminaire mounting height is 10½ ft above the floor.

Solution

By referring to Figure 6-10 we obtain the following:

(a) Each cavity between the beams is 8 × 30 × 2.5 ft. Therefore CCR = 2.0 (obtained from Table 6-1). With $\rho_c = 80\%$, beam wall reflectance = 30%, and CCR = 2.0 the effective cavity reflectance from Table 6-3 is 0.48.

(b) With this figure and the given dimensions and reflectance of beams a weighted average reflectance of the plane at the bottom of the beam can be determined by using the formula

$$\rho_c = \frac{\rho_1 A_1 + \rho_2 A_2}{A_1 + A_2}$$

where A_1 = total surface of beam bottom
A_2 = total cavity opening area
ρ_1 = beam reflectance
ρ_2 = effective cavity reflectance
ρ_c = weighted average reflectance

Therefore

$$\rho_c = \frac{\begin{array}{l}[(0.5 + 1 + 1 + 1 + 0.5) \times 30 \times 0.30]\\ + [(4 \times 8 \times 30) \times 0.48]\end{array}}{\begin{array}{l}[(0.5 + 1 + 1 + 1 + 0.5) \times 30]\\ + (4 \times 8 \times 30)\end{array}}$$

$$= 0.46$$

This is the weighted average reflectance of the plane 1½ ft above the luminaire mounting plane.

(c) With $h_{cc} = 1.5$ ft the ceiling cavity ratio is

$$CCR = \frac{5 \times h_{cc}(L + W)}{L \times W}$$

$$= \frac{5 \times 1.5 \times (30 + 36)}{30 \times 36}$$

$$= 0.458$$

With $\rho_c = 0.46$, $\rho_w = 30\%$ or 0.30 (given), and CCR = 0.458 the effective ceiling cavity reflectance (Table 6-3) is 0.40 (interpolated).

6-9 Given the dimensions and surface reflectances (ceiling = 80%, beam = 30%, wall = 50%) of the room in Figure 6-11a, find the effective ceiling cavity reflectance with a luminaire mounting plane at 20 ft above the floor.

Solution

Assuming that each beam cavity is exactly rectangular with dimensions $L = 15.8$, $W = 8.0$, and $h_{cc} = 2.5$,

$$RCR = \frac{5 \times 2.5(15.8 + 8)}{15.8 \times 8} = 2.35$$

With RCR = 2.35, $\rho_C = 80\%$, $\rho_B = 30\%$, and using Table 6-3 ρ_{cc} is 44%. Therefore this is the effective beam cavity reflectance. With 30% as the given reflectance of the wooden beam bottom the weighted average reflectance of the plane at the bottom of the beam is

$$\frac{(8 \times 0.44) + (1 \times 0.30)}{8 + 1} = 0.42$$

This, however, is the reflectance of the inverted "V" plane touching the bottom of the beams (see Figure 6-11b). The effective cavity reflectance can be deter-

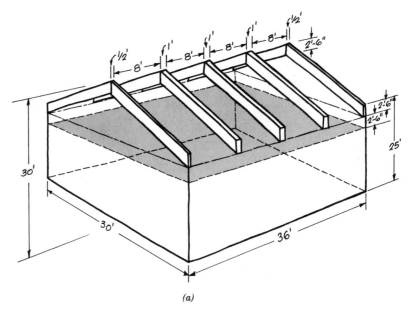

(a)

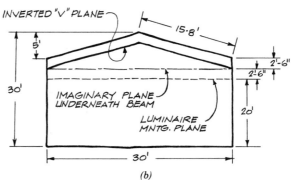

Figure 6-11.

(b)

mined by using the formula for nonhorizontal ceilings; hence

$$\rho_{cc} = \frac{0.42(30 \times 36)}{(2 \times 15.8 \times 36) - 0.42(2 \times 15.8 \times 36)} $$
$$+ 0.42(30 \times 36)$$

$$= \frac{554.4}{1390.4 - 583.96 + 554.4}$$

$$= 0.40$$

which is the reflectance of an imaginary horizontal plane parallel to the floor and just underneath the beam (see Figure 6-11*b*). We are to find the effective ceiling cavity reflectance at the luminaire mounting plane, which is 2.5 ft below this imaginary ceiling. With $h_{cc} = 2.5$

$$RCR = \frac{5 \times 2.5(30 + 36)}{30 \times 36}$$

$$= 0.53$$

With RCR = 0.53, given wall reflectance $\rho_W = 0.50$, and the determined reflectance of the imaginary plane = 0.40 the required ceiling cavity reflectance (Table 6-3) is 37.5% (interpolated).

6-10　A room 20 × 30 ft with a 10-ft ceiling has two separate areas, *A* and *B* (see Figure 6-12*a*), for two different types of work. The luminaires in each room can be individually controlled and are in a mounting plane at 1.5 ft below the ceiling. Determine the ρ_{cc} and ρ_{fc} for (a) the whole room, (b) for *A* with lights on

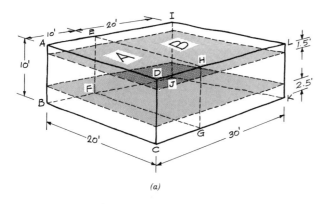

(a)

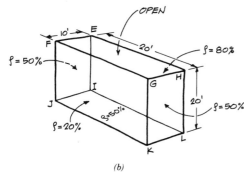

(b)

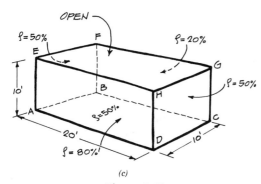

(c)

Figure 6-12.

in that room only, and (c) for *B* with lights on in that room only. Assume a work plane at 2.5 ft above the floor and $\rho_c = 80\%$, $\rho_W = 50\%$, and $\rho_f = 20\%$.

Solution

By referring to Figure 6-12*a* we obtain the following:
(a) Given $h_{cc} = 1.5$, $h_{rc} = 6$, $h_{fc} = 2.5$

$$RCR = \frac{5 \times 6(30 + 20)}{30 \times 20} = 2.5$$

$$CCR = \frac{5 \times 1.5(30 + 20)}{30 \times 20} = 0.625$$

$$FCR = \frac{5 \times 2.5(30 + 20)}{30 \times 20} = 1.0$$

Using these values and the surface reflectances in Table 6-3, we have

$$\rho_{cc} = 70\% \quad \text{and} \quad \rho_{fc} = 19\%$$

(b) In determining the ρ_{cc} and ρ_{fc} of *A*, it is necessary to know the effective reflectance of the opening *EFGH* (see Figure 6-12*a*). For this we tip *B* over, as shown in Figure 6-12*b*, with the open surface *EFGH* at the top. Assuming that this is a new room with *EFGH* as the ceiling, *IJKL* as the floor, and the remaining areas as the new wall surface, the weighted average wall reflectance is

$$W = \frac{\begin{array}{c}(FGKJ \times 0.20) + (GHLK \times 0.50) \\ + (EHLI \times 0.80) + (EFJI \times 0.50)\end{array}}{20 + 10 + 20 + 10}$$

$$= \frac{\begin{array}{c}(20 \times 0.20) + (10 \times 0.50) \\ + (20 \times 0.80) + (10 \times 0.50)\end{array}}{60}$$

$$= 50\%$$

Therefore for *B*, with surface *JIKL* as the floor, the weighted average wall reflectance = 50% and the floor reflectance = 50%. Now with $h = 20$ ft (height of the ceiling of this room),

$$RCR = \frac{5 \times 20(10 + 20)}{10 \times 20} = 15$$

Using Table 6-3, with RCR = 15, $\rho_W = 50\%$, and $\rho_f = 50\%$, we find that the effective reflectance of the cavity at *EFGH* is 13%. Note that because the maximum RCR in the table is shown only up to 10 this value is extrapolated.

When the section is tipped back to its original position, the open side becomes the imaginary wall with 13% reflectance; *A* now has, in effect, three walls with a reflectance of 50% and one with 13%. For *A* the weighted average wall reflectance is

$$\rho_W = \frac{\begin{array}{c}(20 \times 0.5) + (10 \times 0.5) \\ + (20 \times 0.13) + (10 \times 0.5)\end{array}}{20 + 10 + 20 + 10}$$

$$= 0.38$$

Also for A

$$CCR = \frac{5 \times 1.5(10 + 20)}{10 \times 20} = 1.125$$

$$FCR = \frac{5 \times 2.5(10 + 20)}{10 \times 20} = 1.87$$

and, referring to Table 6-3

$$\rho_{cc} = 0.67 \quad and \quad \rho_{fc} = 0.15$$

(c) To determine ρ_{cc} and ρ_{fc} in B we find the effective cavity reflectance of the opening $EFGH$ in a similar manner but with A as the cavity. By redrafting Figure 6-12c we find that the sides or walls of this cavity have reflectances of 50, 20, 50, and 80%. The weighted average reflectance of the walls is

$$\rho_W = \frac{\begin{aligned}(0.50 \times 10) + (0.20 \times 20) \\ + (0.50 \times 10) + (0.80 \times 20)\end{aligned}}{10 + 20 + 10 + 20}$$
$$= 0.50$$

$$RCR = \frac{5 \times 10(20 + 10)}{20 \times 10} = 7.5$$

According to Table 6-3, the effective reflectance of this cavity at EFGH is 0.20. By tipping this cavity back to its original position we find that the weighted reflectance average of the walls of B is

$$\rho_W = \frac{\begin{aligned}(0.20 \times 20) + (0.50 \times 20) \\ + (0.50 \times 20) + (0.50 \times 20)\end{aligned}}{20 + 20 + 20 + 20}$$
$$= 0.43$$

For B

$$CCR = \frac{5 \times 1.5(20 + 20)}{20 \times 20} = 0.75$$

and

$$FCR = \frac{5 \times 2.5(20 + 20)}{20 \times 20} = 1.25$$

By using these values and interpolating (Table 6-3) we have

$$\rho_{cc} = 68\% \quad and \quad \rho_{fc} = 17\%$$

COEFFICIENT OF UTILIZATION (CU)

Once the effective ceiling- and floor-cavity reflectances have been determined finding the CU of a luminaire is made easy. Manufacturers provide tables of CU values for each type of luminaire, typical of which is section J of Figure 5-1. The CU value can be found easily by knowing the values of ρ_{cc}, ρ_{fc}, ρ_W, and RCR. The effective floor cavity reflectance ρ_{cc} in these tables is normally 20%. If this value varies from 20%, a correction factor is used to modify the CU. Table 6-4 contains multiplying factors that will convert a ρ_{cc} of 20% to 0, 10, and 30%. The intermediate values are interpolated. The following example illustrates all steps in the determination of CU values for two situations: (a) when the luminaires are suspended and (b) when they are recessed in the ceiling.

6-11 An office room with dimensions $L = 50$ ft, $W = 30$ ft, and $H = 8.5$ ft has a work plane 2.5 ft above the floor. Ceiling, wall, and floor reflectances are 80, 50, and 20%, respectively. Luminaires are 2×4 ft with four lamps and acrylic prismatic lenses. Determine the CU values if the luminaires are (a) suspended 1.5 ft below the ceiling and (b) recessed in the ceiling. Use the CU table in Figure 5-1.

Solution

(a) Suspended Luminaire

Step 1. Determine the CCR, RCR, and FCR.

$$h_{cc} = 1.5 \text{ ft}, \quad h_{fc} = 2.5 \text{ ft},$$

$$h_{rc} = (8.5 - 1.5 - 2.5) = 4.5 \text{ ft}$$

$$CCR = \frac{5 \times 1.5(50 + 30)}{50 \times 30} = 0.40$$

$$RCR = \frac{5 \times 4.5(50 + 30)}{50 \times 30} = 1.2$$

$$FCR = \frac{5 \times 2.5(50 + 30)}{50 \times 30} = 0.67$$

(These values can also be obtained from Table 6-1.)

Step 2. Determine Ceiling and Floor Effective Reflectances.

Corresponding to $\rho_c = 80\%$, $\rho_W = 50\%$, and CCR = 0.4, ρ_{cc} in Table 6-3 is 74%. Similarly, when $\rho_W =$

TABLE 6-4. MULTIPLYING FACTORS FOR OTHER THAN 20% EFFECTIVE FLOOR CAVITY REFLECTANCE[a]

% Effective Ceiling Cavity Reflectance, ρ_{cc}	80				70				50			30			10		
% Wall Reflectance, ρ_w	70	50	30	10	70	50	30	10	50	30	10	50	30	10	50	30	10
For 30 Per Cent Effective Floor Cavity Reflectance (20 Per Cent = 1.00)																	
Room Cavity Ratio																	
1	1.092	1.082	1.075	1.068	1.077	1.070	1.064	1.059	1.049	1.044	1.040	1.028	1.026	1.023	1.012	1.010	1.008
2	1.079	1.066	1.055	1.047	1.068	1.057	1.048	1.039	1.041	1.033	1.027	1.026	1.021	1.017	1.013	1.010	1.006
3	1.070	1.054	1.042	1.033	1.061	1.048	1.037	1.028	1.034	1.027	1.020	1.024	1.017	1.012	1.014	1.009	1.005
4	1.062	1.045	1.033	1.024	1.055	1.040	1.029	1.021	1.030	1.022	1.015	1.022	1.015	1.010	1.014	1.009	1.004
5	1.056	1.038	1.026	1.018	1.050	1.034	1.024	1.015	1.027	1.018	1.012	1.020	1.013	1.008	1.014	1.009	1.004
6	1.052	1.033	1.021	1.014	1.047	1.030	1.020	1.012	1.024	1.015	1.009	1.019	1.012	1.006	1.014	1.008	1.003
7	1.047	1.029	1.018	1.011	1.043	1.026	1.017	1.009	1.022	1.013	1.007	1.018	1.010	1.005	1.014	1.008	1.003
8	1.044	1.026	1.015	1.009	1.040	1.024	1.015	1.007	1.020	1.012	1.006	1.017	1.009	1.004	1.013	1.007	1.003
9	1.040	1.024	1.014	1.007	1.037	1.022	1.014	1.006	1.019	1.011	1.005	1.016	1.009	1.004	1.013	1.007	1.002
10	1.037	1.022	1.012	1.006	1.034	1.020	1.012	1.005	1.017	1.010	1.004	1.015	1.009	1.003	1.013	1.007	1.002
For 10 Per Cent Effective Floor Cavity Reflectance (20 Per Cent = 1.00)																	
Room Cavity Ratio																	
1	.923	.929	.935	.940	.933	.939	.943	.948	.956	.960	.963	.973	.976	.979	.989	.991	.993
2	.931	.942	.950	.958	.940	.949	.957	.963	.962	.968	.974	.976	.980	.985	.988	.991	.995
3	.939	.951	.961	.969	.945	.957	.966	.973	.967	.975	.981	.978	.983	.988	.988	.992	.996
4	.944	.958	.969	.978	.950	.963	.973	.980	.972	.980	.986	.980	.986	.991	.987	.992	.996
5	.949	.964	.976	.983	.954	.968	.978	.985	.975	.983	.989	.981	.988	.993	.987	.992	.997
6	.953	.969	.980	.986	.958	.972	.982	.989	.977	.985	.992	.982	.989	.995	.987	.993	.997
7	.957	.973	.983	.991	.961	.975	.985	.991	.979	.987	.994	.983	.990	.996	.987	.993	.998
8	.960	.976	.986	.993	.963	.977	.987	.993	.981	.988	.995	.984	.991	.997	.987	.994	.998
9	.963	.978	.987	.994	.965	.979	.989	.994	.983	.990	.996	.985	.992	.998	.988	.994	.999
10	.965	.980	.989	.995	.967	.981	.990	.995	.984	.991	.997	.986	.993	.998	.988	.994	.999
For 0 Per Cent Effective Floor Cavity Reflectance (20 Per Cent = 1.00)																	
Room Cavity Ratio																	
1	.859	.870	.879	.886	.873	.884	.893	.901	.916	.923	.929	.948	.954	.960	.979	.983	.987
2	.871	.887	.903	.919	.886	.902	.916	.928	.926	.938	.949	.954	.963	.971	.978	.983	.991
3	.882	.904	.915	.942	.898	.918	.934	.947	.936	.950	.964	.958	.969	.979	.976	.984	.993
4	.893	.919	.941	.958	.908	.930	.948	.961	.945	.961	.974	.961	.974	.984	.975	.985	.994
5	.903	.931	.953	.969	.914	.939	.958	.970	.951	.967	.980	.964	.977	.988	.975	.985	.995
6	.911	.940	.961	.976	.920	.945	.965	.977	.955	.972	.985	.966	.979	.991	.975	.986	.996
7	.917	.947	.967	.981	.924	.950	.970	.982	.959	.975	.988	.968	.981	.993	.975	.987	.997
8	.922	.953	.971	.985	.929	.955	.975	.986	.963	.978	.991	.970	.983	.995	.976	.988	.998
9	.928	.958	.975	.988	.933	.959	.980	.989	.966	.980	.993	.971	.985	.996	.976	.988	.998
10	.933	.962	.979	.991	.937	.963	.983	.992	.969	.982	.995	.973	.987	.997	.977	.989	.999

[a] Reprinted with permission from the *IES Lighting Handbook,* 1981, Reference Volume.

50%, ρ_f = 20%, and FCR = 0.67, the ρ_{fc} is 19%, rounded off to 20%.

Step 3. Determine the CU.

Corresponding to ρ_{cc} = 74%, ρ_{fc} = 20%, ρ_W = 50%, and RCR = 1.2, the CU value is 0.66 (interpolated).

(b) Recessed luminaire

Step 1. h_{cc} = 0 ft, h_{fc} = 2.5 ft, and h_{rc} = 8.5 − 2.5 = 6 ft.

$$CCR = \frac{5 \times 0(50 + 30)}{50 \times 30} = 0$$

$$RCR = \frac{5 \times 6(50 + 30)}{50 \times 30} = 1.6$$

$$FCR = \frac{5 \times 2.5(50 + 30)}{50 \times 30} = 0.67$$

Step 2. Reference to Table 6-3 yields, corresponding to ρ_c = 80%, ρ_W = 50%, and CCR = 0, ρ_{cc} = 80%; and corresponding to ρ_f = 20%, ρ_W = 50%, and FCR = 0.67, ρ_{fc} = 19% rounded off to 20%.

Step 3. Corresponding to ρ_{cc} = 80%, ρ_{fc} = 20%, and ρ_W = 50%, the CU value for RCR = 1.6 is 0.65 (interpolated).

LIGHT LOSS FACTOR (LLF)

The light loss factor takes into account that light output diminishes with time and must be considered in the lighting calculations to make up for the expected loss in the lighting system.

The factors that constitute the net LLF are divided into two groups: the nonrecoverable and the recoverable. In explaining these factors, we show how an LLF can be constructed for the common situation discussed in Problem 6-11.

Nonrecoverable Factors

The nonrecoverable factors represent the conditions of a lighting system that may reduce light output when nothing in terms of periodic maintenance can be done to recover the loss.

Luminaire Ambient Temperature (LAT)
In essence, luminaire ambient temperature represents the light loss caused by luminaire temperature variation. About the only sources directly affected by ambient temperature are the fluorescents (see Figure 4-21). As a rule of thumb there will be 1% loss in light for every 2°F that the ambient temperature around the lamp (inside the luminaire if it is enclosed) exceeds 77°F.

Voltage Variation (VV)
Light output from almost all sources changes with voltage variation. For incandescents a small deviation from the rated lamp voltage would produce a change in lumens of about 3% for each 1% variation on voltage. In gaseous discharge sources the variation depends on the type of ballast used (see Chapter 4). Variation in incoming voltage is usually unpredictable. If it is stable and of known quantity, an appropriate VV factor can be used in calculations. Otherwise it is assumed to be unity.

Luminaire Surface Depreciation (LSD)
A gradual reduction in light output takes place with the natural changes in the components of a luminaire; for example, enamels suffer constant depreciation because of their porous characteristics, polystyrene and polycarbonate plastic turn yellow with constant exposure to the UV rays, polished metals scratch, and painted surfaces discolor. Glass, porcelain, and processed aluminum, on the other hand, show insignificant depreciation. Most luminaires contain several materials with different depreciating characteristics that make it difficult to predict an LSD factor.

Ballast Factor (BF)
The ballast factor is given by the ratio of light output by a commercial ballast to that by a reference ballast. Each commercial ballast has a BF. If the BF of the ballast used in a luminaire is different from that of the ballast used in the photometry of the luminaire, the light output will vary by the same proportion. This, too, is another unpredictable factor.

The nonrecoverable factors will reduce light output and little can be done to renew them, once installed. The best solution is to select the lamp-ballast-luminaire combination with care. Because these factors are unpredictable, for calculation purposes 1.0 is used for all nonrecoverable factors.

Recoverable Factors

These are the factors that can be predicted and must be used in lighting calculations.

Luminaire Dirt Depreciation (LDD)
LDD constitutes the greatest loss in light output and it is mainly due to the accumulation of atmospheric dirt on lamp, lens, louvers and reflecting surfaces. Three factors must be considered in its determination: the type of luminaire, atmospheric conditions, and maintenance interval. The steps are as follows:

Step 1. According to the luminaire used, select the proper maintenance category from the six given in Table 6-5. The luminaire used in the example fits category V, because it produces 100% down-light and has an unapertured opaque top and an unapertured translucent bottom (prismatic lens).

Step 2. Determine the type of atmosphere most appropriate from the following: (a) very clean, VC, (b) clean, C, (c) medium, M, (d) dirty, D, (e) very dirty, VD. Let us assume that the office in our example has a clean atmosphere (b).

Step 3. Having completed Steps 1 and 2 and derived the interval of maintenance, refer to the appropriate curve in Figure 6-13 and read the recommended LDD factor. In this example the maintenance interval is unknown and must be decided.

TABLE 6-5. LUMINAIRE CLASSIFICATION BASED ON SIX MAINTENANCE CATEGORIES[a]

Maintenance Category	Top Enclosure	Bottom Enclosure
I	1. None	1. None
II	1. None	1. None
	2. Transparent, with 15% or more up-light through apertures.	2. Louvers or baffles
	3. Translucent, with 15% or more up-light through apertures.	
	4. Opaque, with 15% or more up-light through apertures.	
III	1. Transparent, with less than 15% upward light through apertures.	1. None
	2. Translucent, with less than 15% upward light through apertures.	2. Louvers or baffles
	3. Opaque, with less than 15% up-light through apertures.	
IV	1. Transparent, unapertured.	1. None
	2. Translucent, unapertured.	2. Louvers
	3. Opaque, unapertured.	
V	1. Transparent, unapertured.	1. Transparent, unapertured
	2. Translucent, unapertured.	2. Translucent, unapertured
	3. Opaque, unapertured.	
VI	1. None	1. Transparent, unapertured
	2. Transparent, unapertured.	2. Translucent, unapertured
	3. Translucent, unapertured.	3. Opaque, unapertured
	4. Opaque, unapertured.	

[a] Reprinted with permission from the *IES Lighting Handbook*, 1981, Reference Volume.

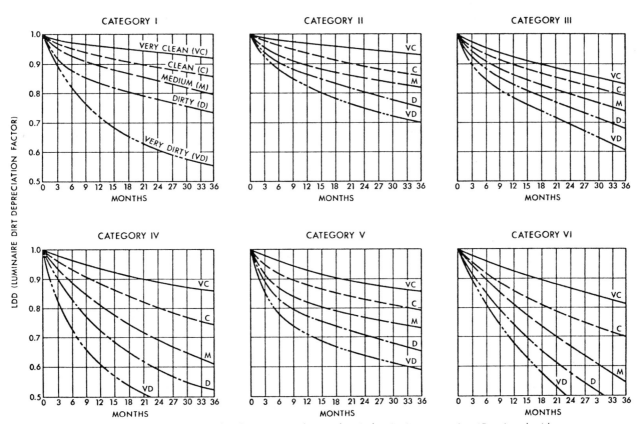

Figure 6-13. *Luminaire dirt depreciation factors for six luminaire categories. (Reprinted with permission from the* IES Lighting Handbook, *1981, Reference Volume.)*

Selection of a maintenance interval depends on how clean the area really is. For air-conditioned offices once a year or once in two years may be sufficient. Nonairconditioned offices or schools may require cleaning at least once a year. In industrial areas, such as foundries or smoke-producing factories, the maintenance interval may be as short as once a month. For food-preparation areas it should be increased to once a week because of the special cleanliness requirement.

Let us assume that the office in this example is air conditioned and clean and that a thorough cleaning is done every two years. According to curve C in category V, the LDD factor for this interval is 0.835.

LDD values recommended by luminaire manufacturers are usually too optimistic because they are based on the assumption that properly scheduled maintenance is done by all owners. In reality this is seldom the case. A more suitable factor can be found from experience with similar luminaires and applications or by consulting a luminaire maintenance company.

Room Surface Dirt Depreciation (RSDD)

RSDD takes into account that dirt accumulates on room surfaces and reduces surface reflectance. A schedule must be maintained for cleaning and possibly repainting. The steps to be taken are the following:

Step 1. Having determined the cleaning interval and the atmospheric conditions, calculate the expected dirt depreciation in Figure 6-14. In this example, which corresponds to a cleaning interval of two years

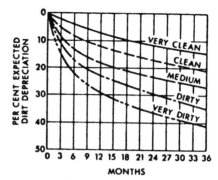

Figure 6-14. *Per cent expected dirt depreciation because of cleaning interval and atmospheric conditions. (Reprinted with permission from the* IES Lighting Handbook, *1981, Reference Volume.)*

and an atmospheric condition C, the expected dirt depreciation factor is 18%.

Step 2. Taking the expected dirt depreciation from Step 1, the luminaire distribution from Figure 5-4, and RCR from Table 6-1, find the RSDD in Table 6-6. In this example the luminaire is a direct type and the RCR is 1.6; therefore the RSDD factor is 0.97.

Lamp Lumen Depreciation (LLD)

The lamp lumen depreciation factor takes into account that lamp lumens decrease with age. Its value can be determined in two ways: (1) by consulting a lamp manufacturer's most recent catalog for a lumen depreciation chart and (2) by dividing the maintained lumens by the initial lamps. Typically, 70% of the average rated life of a fluorescent lamp is the minimum reached when burnouts are promptly replaced.

TABLE 6-6. ROOM SURFACE DIRT DEPRECIATION FACTORS[a]

									Luminaire Distribution Type											
		Direct				Semi-Direct				Direct-Indirect				Semi-Indirect				Indirect		
Per Cent Expected Dirt Depreciation		10	20	30	40	10	20	30	40	10	20	30	40	10	20	30	40	10	20	30	40
Room Cavity Ratio	1	.98	.96	.94	.92	.97	.92	.89	.84	.94	.87	.80	.76	.94	.87	.80	.73	.90	.80	.70	.60
	2	.98	.96	.94	.92	.96	.92	.88	.83	.94	.87	.80	.75	.94	.87	.79	.72	.90	.80	.69	.59
	3	.98	.95	.93	.90	.96	.91	.87	.82	.94	.86	.79	.74	.94	.86	.78	.71	.90	.79	.68	.58
	4	.97	.95	.92	.90	.95	.90	.85	.80	.94	.86	.79	.73	.94	.86	.78	.70	.89	.78	.67	.56
	5	.97	.94	.91	.89	.94	.90	.84	.79	.93	.86	.78	.72	.93	.86	.77	.69	.89	.78	.66	.55
	6	.97	.94	.91	.88	.94	.89	.83	.78	.93	.85	.78	.71	.93	.85	.76	.68	.89	.77	.66	.54
	7	.97	.94	.90	.87	.93	.88	.82	.77	.93	.84	.77	.70	.93	.84	.76	.68	.89	.76	.65	.53
	8	.96	.93	.89	.86	.93	.87	.81	.75	.93	.84	.76	.69	.93	.84	.76	.68	.88	.76	.64	.52
	9	.96	.92	.88	.85	.93	.87	.80	.74	.93	.84	.76	.68	.93	.81	.75	.67	.88	.75	.63	.51
	10	.96	.92	.87	.83	.93	.86	.79	.72	.93	.84	.75	.67	.92	.83	.75	.67	.88	.75	.62	.50

[a] Reprinted from the *IES Lighting Handbook*, 1981, Reference Volume.

In the example given let us assume that the lamps will be replaced as soon as they burn out. According to Figure 4-22, LLD is 0.88 for this interval.

Lamp Burnout (LBO)

This factor predicts the number of lamps that will burn out before the time of scheduled replacement; it is determined by the ratio of the lamps remaining on to the total lamps used:

$$LBO = \frac{\text{lamps remaining on}}{\text{total lamps used}}$$

In the example LBO is 1.0 because it is known that burned out lamps will be replaced promptly.

Therefore the total light loss factor

$$
\begin{aligned}
LLF &= (\text{nonrecoverable factor}) \\
&\quad \times (LDD \times RSDD \times LLD \times LBO) \\
&= 1.0 \times (0.835 \times 0.97 \times 0.88 \times 1) \\
&= 0.71
\end{aligned}
$$

To illustrate the use of the lumen formula let us modify Problem 6-11.

6-12 Find the number of luminaires required in Problem 6-11 to produce 70 fc (maintained) at the task level if the lamps are rated at 3200 lm and the luminaires are recessed in the ceiling.

Solution

We know that,

$$
\begin{aligned}
N &= \frac{E \times A}{L \times CU \times LLF} \\
&= \frac{70 \times (50 \times 30)}{(4 \times 3200) \times 0.65 \times 0.71} \\
&= 17.7 \text{ or } 18 \text{ luminaires}
\end{aligned}
$$

Note that "maintained" footcandles represent the illuminance level at the time of lamp replacement and cleaning. After each cleaning cycle the illuminance level jumps back to the initial value which can be determined by dividing the maintained footcandle by the LLF. Therefore the initial illuminance = 70 ÷ 0.71 = 99 fc.

REFERENCES

Helm, Ronald N. "Energy and Lighting Design—Part One." *Electrical Construction and Maintenance,* 62–70 (November 1979).

Helm, Ronald N. "Energy and Lighting Design—Part Two." *Electrical Construction and Maintenance,* 61–67 (December 1979).

IES, Lighting Design Practice Committee. "General Procedure for Calculating Maintained Illumination." *Illuminating Engineering,* **65,** 602 (1970).

Kaufman, John E., Editor. "Lighting Calculations," *IES Lighting Handbook, 1981,* Reference Volume, pp. 9-1–9-12 and 9-60–9-74.

Levin, Robert E. "On the non-rectangular cavity approximation." *Journal of the IES,* **13,** No. 1, 107 (October 1983).

Sorcar, Prafulla C. "A Study in Energy Savings with Heat-Removal Luminaires." *Electrical Construction and Maintenance,* pp. 66–69 (November 1981).

Sorcar, Prafulla C. *Energy-Saving Lighting Systems.* New York: Van Nostrand-Reinhold, 1982.

7

Short-Cut Methods of Calculation

Short-cut methods allow a lighting designer to avoid conventional lighting calculations and to produce a quick answer with reasonable accuracy. Although many are generic techniques applicable to all luminaires of the same kind, others are furnished by the manufacturers to promote their own products. The main thing to remember is that the results obtained by these methods are only preliminary and must be verified by long-hand calculations whenever accuracy is critical.

LIGHT LEVEL ON A WORK PLANE FROM A SINGLE LUMINAIRE

Figure 7-1 shows curves that represent a quick method of calculating the initial footcandles on a work plane placed directly below a single luminaire. To apply this method two pieces of information are needed: the luminaire mounting height above the point of interest and the nadir candlepower (the candlepower reading at 0°; also known as centerline candlepower).

Let us illustrate this with an example. Let us say that we need the illuminance level on a work plane located 20 ft below a luminaire whose centerline

candlepower is 40,000 cd. Find 40,000 cd on the candlepower reading on the vertical axis and proceed horizontally until it touches the slanted line assigned for a 20-ft mounting height. From this point move straight down to read 100 fc on the horizontal axis. Note that this graphic table can be used for the reversed process as well; for example, if the initial footcandle level and the mounting height are known, a luminaire can be selected by finding the centerline candlepower.

It is important to note that this method provides an accurate answer for luminaires that are like point sources (incandescents, mercury vapor, metal halide, or high-pressure sodium sources). Area sources like fluorescent troffers can be used only if they are mounted at a minimum distance of five times the maximum dimension of the luminaire. For a 2 × 4 ft fluorescent troffer the mounting height should be no less than 4 × 5 = 20 ft above the work plane.

VERTICAL ILLUMINATIONS WITH WALL WASHERS

Figure 7-2 is the quick chart of one manufacturer's recessed wall washers equipped with 150W R-40

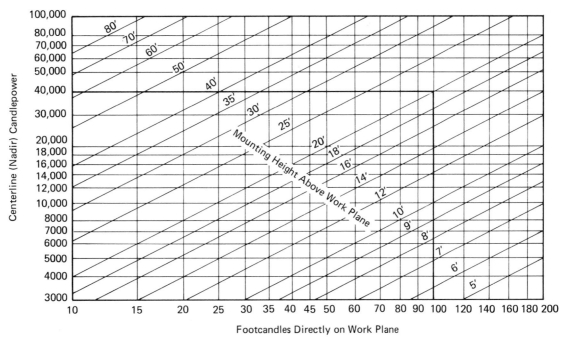

Centerline (Nadir) Candlepower

Footcandles Directly on Work Plane

Figure 7-1. *These curves represent a quick method of determining the initial footcandles directly on the work plane when centerline (nadir) candlepower and luminaire mounting height above the work plane are known.*

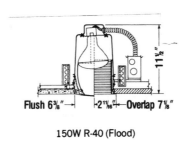

Flush 6⅜″ — 2¹¹⁄₁₆″ — Overlap 7⅛″

11½″

150W R-40 (Flood)

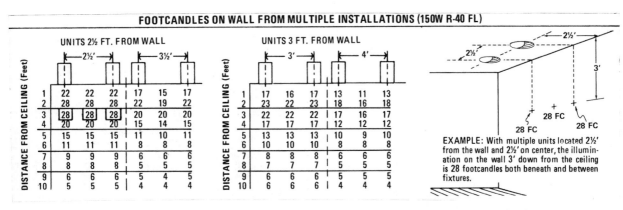

FOOTCANDLES ON WALL FROM MULTIPLE INSTALLATIONS (150W R-40 FL)

UNITS 2½ FT. FROM WALL

DISTANCE FROM CEILING (Feet)	22	22	22	17	15	17
1	22	22	22	17	15	17
2	28	28	28	22	19	22
3	28	28	28	20	20	20
4	20	20	20	15	14	15
5	15	15	15	11	10	11
6	11	11	11	8	8	8
7	9	9	9	6	6	6
8	8	8	8	5	5	5
9	6	6	6	5	4	5
10	5	5	5	4	4	4

UNITS 3 FT. FROM WALL

DISTANCE FROM CEILING (Feet)	17	16	17	13	11	13
1	17	16	17	13	11	13
2	23	22	23	18	16	18
3	22	22	22	17	16	17
4	17	17	17	12	12	12
5	13	13	13	10	9	10
6	10	10	10	8	8	8
7	8	8	8	6	6	6
8	7	7	7	5	5	5
9	6	6	6	5	5	5
10	6	6	6	4	4	4

EXAMPLE: With multiple units located 2½′ from the wall and 2½′ on center, the illumination on the wall 3′ down from the ceiling is 28 footcandles both beneath and between fixtures.

28 FC

Figure 7-2. *A quick chart for wall washing by multiple installations. (Courtesy of Lightolier.)*

flood incandescent lamps. The units are 2-½ or 3 ft from the wall. The spacings between the units are shown on the top of the chart (they vary from 2-½ to 4 ft) and the footcandle readings on the wall are shown for various distances from the ceiling; for example, when the luminaires are spaced 2½ ft apart and 2½ ft back from the wall, at 3 ft below the ceiling the illuminance level is an even 28 fc.

HORIZONTAL ILLUMINATION WITH WALL-COVES

Figure 7-3 shows the quick chart of another manufacturer's wall-cove luminaire which is equipped with an extended aluminum louver and one-or two fluorescent lamps. The louver can be gold specular, ½ in. cube acrylic, or pattern 12 acrylic. The luminaire is mounted 8 ft above the floor and the readings are on a horizontal plane 30 in. above the floor, ranging

from 1 to 10 ft from the wall; for example, with pattern 12 acrylic the luminaire with two lamps produces 50 fc at a distance of 4 ft from the wall. Note that the footcandle readings at the same location for the other two charts (with louvers) are substantially lower (approximately 35 fc). This is expected because a louver is fundamentally a physical barrier to lighting.

AVERAGE HORIZONTAL ILLUMINATION INCORPORATING ROOM SURFACE REFLECTANCES #1

None of the quick methods we have discussed incorporates the room surface reflectances which are a major contributor to the room's illuminance level. Figure 7-4 shows the quick charts of one manufacturer's products which may be used to determine an illuminance level (or the total number of luminaires)

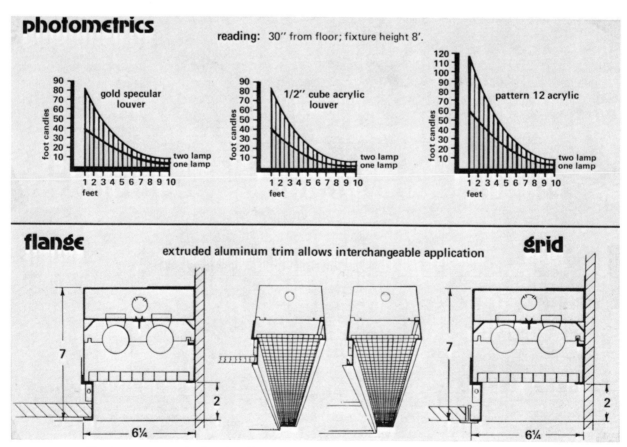

Figure 7-3. A quick chart for illumination on a horizontal plane by a fluorescent cove. (Courtesy of Northern Light.)

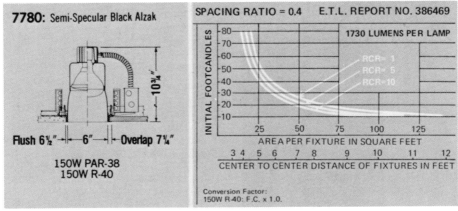

Figure 7-4. *A quick chart for downlights on a horizontal plane. (Courtesy of Lightolier.)*

for a given room whose RCR is 1, 5, or 10. The room surface reflectances are 80% for ceiling, 50% for walls, and 20% for floor.

Let us take an example. Let us say we are to determine how many of these luminaires (equipped with 150-W PAR-38 lamps, 1730 lumens) will be required for 20 fc (initial) of light on the work plane in a room, the width of which is equal to luminaire mounting height above the work plane. According to the guidelines provided, the RCR is equal to 10.

Now we locate 20 fc on the vertical axis and proceed horizontally to hit the curve at RCR = 10. From this point of intersection we go downward vertically to read approximately 45 ft² on the horizontal axis. In other words, for a small room of this size approximately one fixture every 45 ft² is required for an initial illuminance of 20 fc at the work plane.

AVERAGE HORIZONTAL ILLUMINATION INCORPORATING ROOM-SURFACE REFLECTANCE #2

The main disadvantage of the preceding chart is that the results obtained will be fairly accurate only if the RCR is 1, 5, or 10. If the RCR values differ, the result will be inaccurate. This is minimized by charts (Figure 7-5) in which a separate curve is shown for each of the RCR values that range from 1 to 10. If the RCR value is not a whole number, an imaginary curve is easily used for calculation. The chart shown is that for

a typical 2 × 4 ft fluorescent troffer equipped with four F40T12 lamps and a standard acrylic prismatic lens. To illustrate its use let us consider Problem 6-12.

Here, room length = 50 ft, width = 30 ft, luminaire mounting height = 8.5 ft above the floor, work plane = 2.5 ft above the floor, illumination level required = 70 fc, and RCR is 1.6.

First locate the required 70 fc (maintained) on the horizontal axis at the top of the chart. Draw a vertical line straight down onto an imaginary point 1.6, which lies between the lines that represent RCR = 1 and 2. Now draw a horizontal line and read 85 on the vertical axis. This means one luminaire/85 ft² is required for the required illuminance level. Hence the total number of luminaires required is

$$\frac{50 \times 30}{85} = 17.6 \text{ or } 18 \text{ luminaires}$$

Note that the answer received by this method is almost identical to that obtained earlier by the analytical method, primarily because the room-surface reflectances, CU and LLF, are identical in both cases.

An adjusting factor will reflect any change in these parameters. For more details on the use of similar charts of various types of luminaires the reader is referred to *Rapid Lighting Design and Cost Estimating*, another of my books (New York: McGraw-Hill, 1979).

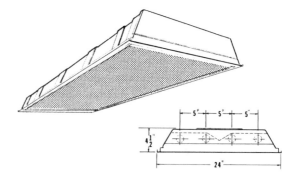

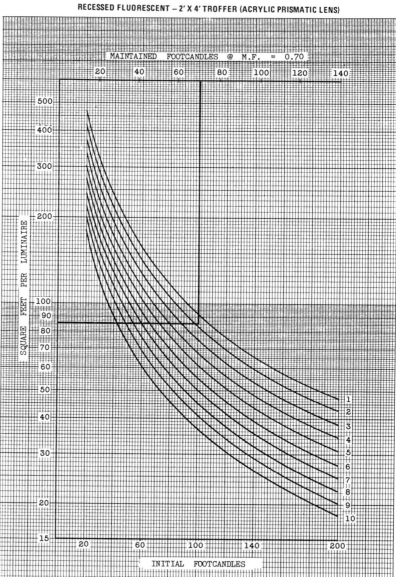

Figure 7-5. A quick chart for a 2 × 4 ft troffer with (4) F40T12 lamps. (Reprinted from Prafulla C. Sorcar, Rapid Lighting Design and Cost Estimating. New York: McGraw-Hill, 1979.)

LIGHT OUTPUT OF LAMPS AND SYSTEM POWER CONSUMPTION

Figure 7-6 can be used for a comparison of the gaseous discharge sources of different wattages with their initial lumens. The numbers on the curves are the rated nominal lamp wattages and the reading directly below on the horizontal axis indicate the total power consumed by the lamp and ballast. The initial lumens are to be read on the vertical axis; for example, to find the total system power consumption and the initial lumens produced by a 250-W HPS lamp draw a vertical and horizontal line from the number 250 on the HPS curve and read 310 W and 30,000 lm, respectively. This lumen value divided by the system wattage will give the initial system efficacy, in this case 30,000/310 = 97 lm/W. The wattage and lumen values found from these curves are approximate and are to be used for comparison purposes only. The actual values will differ from manufacturer to manufacturer and from one type of ballast to an-

other. Note that the relative locations of the curves automatically reveal their overall efficacy differences; low-pressure sodium shows the maximum and mercury vapor, the minimum. Note, also, that basically metal halide continues the ended curve of the fluorescents, which indicates that its efficacy at lower wattages is almost equal to that of fluorescents at upper wattages and gradually improves but is always less than that of high- or low-pressure sodium.

SELECTING FLUORESCENT VERSUS HID

When an even amount of light is required throughout a room and energy saving is a major factor, the dilemma is often in the selection of the source. Fluorescent luminaires are typically more suitable for low-ceiling applications because their brightness is evenly distributed over their entire surface. HID luminaires, on the other hand, are more suitable for high-ceiling applications because a tremendous amount of energy

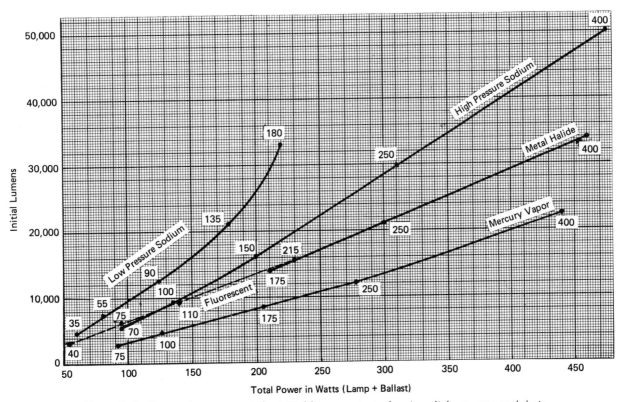

Figure 7-6. Curves that represent the initial lumen output of various light sources and their total input in watts. (Reprinted from Prafulla C. Sorcar, Energy Saving Lighting Systems. New York: Van Nostrand-Reinhold, 1982.)

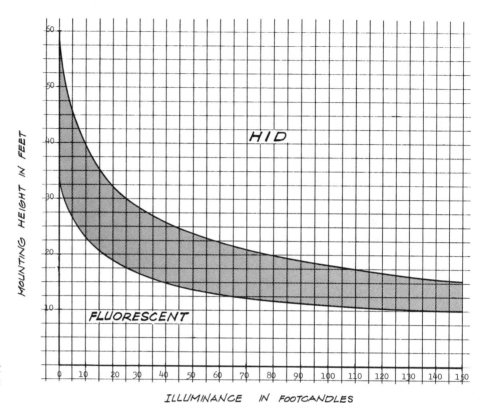

Figure 7-7. A quick chart for determining fluorescents versus HIDs.

emerges from a compact source. Figure 7-7 shows a preliminary idea on the cutoff ranges of each type, the use of which requires two pieces of information: the luminaire mounting height above the work plane and the level of lighting required. First locate the lighting level on the horizontal axis and draw a vertical line through that point. Then locate the mounting height on the vertical axis and draw a horizontal line through that point. Now examine the intersection of these two lines. If it falls below the shaded portion,

fluorescent light is probably the solution; if it is above the shaded area, the solution may be the HID: if it falls inside the shaded area, the solution may be either and needs further investigation.

REFERENCES

Sorcar, Prafulla C. *Rapid Lighting Design and Cost Estimating.* New York: McGraw-Hill, 1979, Chapter B.

Sorcar, Prafulla C. *Energy Saving Lighting Systems.* New York: Van Nostrand-Reinhold, 1982, Chapter 5.

8

Lighting Layout: Perspective Drawings and Drafting

Lighting design is a balanced mixture of science and art. For satisfactory results it is often desirable that the designer become a scientist as well as an artist. In many applications for which a creative lighting design is the only answer it is necessary to exercise artistic skill before planning the layout and specifications. A perspective of a room with various lighting effects will give the client a clearer picture of the designer's concept and result in better communication between the two. It will also help to "preview" the lighting effect.

Most lighting practitioners with technical backgrounds are more than a little frightened by the artistic approach, although they need not be. Some basic skill in sketching will often suffice. The main challenge is to have the proper imagination for which, unfortunately, there are no set rules. Many factors must be considered and each application has its own needs. Each chapter of this book, particularly those under Architectural Tools, makes its own contribution. Some questions that may stimulate the imagination follow:

What is the purpose of the room?

What is the center of attraction? Should it be high-lighted with more light than the rest or perhaps with color?

What are the other attractions? Will there be murals, paintings, or sculptures on the walls or shelves? Should they be given individual or collective attention?

What is the general mood of the room? Should it have perceptual clarity with an abundance of light? What about excitement, drama, and gaiety or perhaps just a pleasant, relaxed atmosphere? What about privacy?

Should the room appear to be more spacious than it really is or just the opposite?

Does it relate to any architectural period?

Should the lighting be uniform or nonuniform, direct or indirect or perhaps in combination?

Is the activity inside for a short time enjoyment or long?

What should the color rendering of the sources be?

Do they complement the mood?

Is there traffic flow to be controlled?

Are special lighting patterns and forms necessary?

Any wall wash, scalloping, highlighting, back-lighting?

What about task and ambient lighting? Should they be combined or separate? Veiling reflections?

Once the design has been formalized it must be expressed by suitable sketches, for which there are four main steps:

1. *Perspective.* Perspective is used to show space in three dimensions in which walls, ceiling, and floor are visible simultaneously. It should represent the focal point or center of attraction as seen by the occupant. If there are several focal points, they can be shown separately or collectively. Including the occupants in the perspective sometimes helps to achieve a better understanding of the space in relation to their size.

2. *Placing Luminaires.* At some point it must be decided what type of luminaires is to be used and where they will be placed. They may be concealed or exposed. In any case, care should be taken that no distracting glare obscures the view.

3. *Color.* Use appropriate colors to represent walls, ceiling, floor, furniture, or other objects in the room. This can be done with colored pencils, chalk, markers, or watercolors by applying a light overlay.

4. *Shade and Fade.* A critical and perhaps the most interesting part of the drawing is the application of light and shadow to the surfaces of the room. Fading is used to show a gradual diminishing of light. A sharp cutoff of light, often necessary in a scalloped effect, represents a drastic change in intensity from one area to another. Accent lighting, which incorporates diffuse, highlight, and backlight effects, is a large part of the total system (explained in detail in Chapter 14) and must be applied with care. In a black and white drawing a ray of light can be shown by shading its surrounding with a pencil and leaving the ray the color of the paper. The same technique is used to show a spot of light on a wall. If the wall is colored, however, it is often necessary that its unlighted areas be treated with a matching color of a darker hue. Here are some tips to be used in the selection of materials for shading and fading:

Colored pencils	Excellent for shading, fading, and color transitions. They are the easiest to use because they are easily available, economical, and erasable.
Colored chalk	Has the same properties as pencils but smears easily and is limited in choice of color.

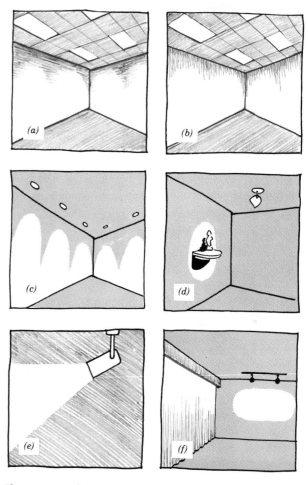

Figure 8-1. These simple sketches show various techniques of shading for lighting effect. (a) Shading can be most easily done with a pencil by varying the intensity. (b) The same effect can be obtained by line-shading with pencil or pen. An increase in the density of lines emphasizes deeper shadow. (c) Shading films are best suited to sharp cutoff light patterns (e.g., scalloping). (d) Use of shading film for the whole room, except for the accent light, dramatizes the effect. (e) A ray of light can be produced by holding down a piece of paper in the shape of the ray and shading around it. (f) A combination of shading film and pencil. The effect of drapery lighting is done best by a line-shading technique, although shading films can also be used (see Figure 22-2). To dramatize the effect of the track light shading film is used in the rest of the room.

Charcoal	Excellent for black and white sketches for shading, fading, and sharp cutoff. Smears easily.
Markers and felt-tip pens	Excellent for sharp cutoff and for filling in brightly colored areas. Erasing is almost impossible.
Shading films	Excellent for sharp cutoff, a homogeneous or diffused environment, and lighting patterns (scalloping or other designs). Needs a special knife to work with. Time consuming.
Watercolors	Can be used for almost any effect but takes skill to use. Time consuming.

Figures 8-1 and 8-2 show some sketches to illustrate many of the factors discussed.

COMPUTER-AIDED DESIGN (CAD)

Computer-aided design, or the CAD system, is used, in general, for drawing floor plans and circuiting; but with special programming it can also be used to de-velop perspectives for lighting-design study. The main advantage of this system is that it saves time and produces professional quality drawings. Although the cost of a CAD system today is considerably less than it was a decade ago, its suitability requires careful economic analysis, which includes anticipated volume of business, training costs, and lease arrangements.

COMPUTER-AIDED RENDERING (SYNTHETIC PHOTOGRAPHY)

Perhaps the most revolutionary achievement in computer-aided design is synthetic photography, which produces architectural renderings in the lighting calculation stage (see Figures 8-3a, b). These photographs, or renderings, provide images created from the calculated surface luminances which are transformed to brightnesses. Shade and intensity in black and white or multicolor, formed with the help of high-resolution, computer-controlled graphic output, imitates real environment and predicts the appearance of the lighted room. These photographs can be used effectively to compare lighting systems, analyze

Figure 8-2. (a) *The owner of the building wanted an inexpensive, but dramatic, lighting effect in the elevator lobby. Indirect fluorescent was used to give a sunrise effect on the metal-strip vaulted ceiling and downlights near the elevators. This perspective was drawn to explain the effect. (b) A photograph of the elevator lobby after installation.*

space, and make presentations to clients. The system has some limitations at present; it works only with certain types of luminaire and cannot incorporate the effects of shadow or brightness from the furniture, paintings, or accessories normally found in a room. In addition, the plotting time is somewhat time consuming but is expected to improve with better computational techniques and availability of resources.

DRAFTING

Once the luminaires and their locations have been decided the next step is to draft the lighting layout, using appropriate symbols. Many lighting practitioners use the symbols specified by USASI (USA Standards Institute) and others modify them to suit their own requirements. In either case, because there are

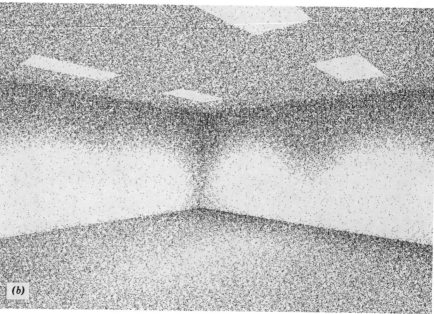

Figure 8-3. Synthetic photography. (a) A photograph of a room with a direct lighting system. (b) A synthetic photograph of the same room from the same viewing angle. (Courtesy of Lighting Technologies, Boulder, Colorado).

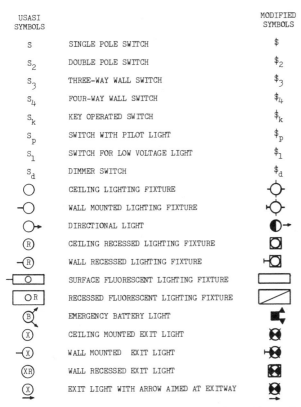

USASI SYMBOLS		MODIFIED SYMBOLS
S	SINGLE POLE SWITCH	$
S₂	DOUBLE POLE SWITCH	$₂
S₃	THREE-WAY WALL SWITCH	$₃
S₄	FOUR-WAY WALL SWITCH	$₄
Sₖ	KEY OPERATED SWITCH	$ₖ
Sₚ	SWITCH WITH PILOT LIGHT	$ₚ
S₁	SWITCH FOR LOW VOLTAGE LIGHT	$₁
S_d	DIMMER SWITCH	$_d
○	CEILING LIGHTING FIXTURE	
–○	WALL MOUNTED LIGHTING FIXTURE	
○→	DIRECTIONAL LIGHT	
Ⓡ	CEILING RECESSED LIGHTING FIXTURE	
–Ⓡ	WALL RECESSED LIGHTING FIXTURE	
▭ O ▭	SURFACE FLUORESCENT LIGHTING FIXTURE	
▭ O R ▭	RECESSED FLUORESCENT LIGHTING FIXTURE	
Ⓑ	EMERGENCY BATTERY LIGHT	
Ⓧ	CEILING MOUNTED EXIT LIGHT	
–Ⓧ	WALL MOUNTED EXIT LIGHT	
ⓍR	WALL RECESSED EXIT LIGHT	
Ⓧ→	EXIT LIGHT WITH ARROW AIMED AT EXITWAY	

Figure 8-4. *Symbol legend frequently used for lighting design.*

no universally mandatory standards, the symbol legend must appear on the drawing to clarify their meanings. Figure 8-4 lists some standard symbols of USASI and their versions modified by consulting engineers.

Luminaires are identified by two general methods: (a) they are specified directly on the drawing; (b) each luminaire is labeled with a key letter that is explained in a separately located lighting fixture schedule. The first system is adequate if the floor plan calls for only a few luminaires, whereas the second system is suitable for any application in which the luminaires exceed four. In either case they are identified by manufacturer's name, catalog number, type of lamp and ballast, power consumed, and a brief description.

In specifying a luminaire for special applications, the designer must always watch for modifications that are necessary to be added to the catalog number; for example, some manufacturers may consider that a luminaire normally used indoors may need a suffix such as "DL" to indicate its suitability in damp locations. If a certain color rendition is desired, it is im-

portant that the lamp carry the correct color code. Specification of voltage is another important item, although easily overlooked. If the luminaire is to operate on a voltage other than 120-V, ac (this is standard in US industry), it is necessary that the lamps and ballasts be properly designated to operate on the desired voltage. Although incandescents predominantly operate on 120-V, fluorescents and high-intensity discharge luminaires may be selected to operate on 120, 208, 240, 277, or 480 V as well. In gaseous discharge sources lamps have no designated operating voltage; ballasts have, however.

DRAWING A LIGHTING LAYOUT

Luminaires and wiring should be designated by darker and heavier lines on the building's floor plan. This contrast makes the lighting layout and its wiring easily readable and minimizes mistakes. The lighting layout may be designed for uniform or nonuniform lighting or their combination.

NONUNIFORM OR UNEVEN LIGHTING

The concept of uneven lighting—or light only where required—breaks out of the traditional practice of providing a uniform blanket of light and has become the state-of-the-art. There are no set rules to follow. Luminaires are provided for ambient, task, or high lighting, as needed. The inverse square law is used to calculate the level of lighting and luminaires are drawn on the plan with their proper symbols. If directional luminaires are used, an arrow will indicate the direction of light. (See Figure 8-5 for a typical example of a nonuniform lighting layout.)

UNIFORM LIGHTING

Although nonuniform lighting is the state-of-the-art, the conventional practice of uniform lighting distribution still remains popular because of the optimum flexibility it offers. In applications such as commercial buildings where tenants move in and out frequently and have a wide range of activity, a uniform blanket of light is often the best solution.

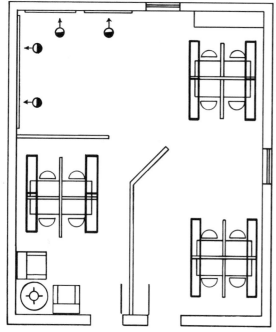

Figure 8-5. *Example of a nonuniform lighting plan.*

Layout of uniform lighting is often a trial-and-error method that coordinates between HVAC, ceiling, spacing criterion (SC), and the levels of lighting requirements. Once their number has been determined the luminaires should be distributed in the ceiling evenly, with the set-back distance from the wall exactly half the size of the spacings between them. This arrangement, however, may not work all the time, especially for troffers, whose spacings are dictated by a grid pattern.

Let us take some examples to illustrate the com-

mon phenomena involved in creating an even, horizontal level of lighting.

PROBLEMS

8-1 Let us suppose we are to do the lighting layout of a room with a length of 60 ft, width, 30 ft, and height, 10 ft, with the following luminaire and data: 175-W metal halide, CU = 0.60, LLF = 0.7, and SC = 1.8. The luminaires are to be recessed in the ceiling and a level of 50 fc is required on the task plane, 2'-6" above the floor.

Solution

Using the lumen method of calculations, the total number of luminaires required is

$$N = \frac{A \times E}{L \times CU \times LLF} = \frac{(30 \times 60) \times 50}{14000 \times 0.60 \times 0.7}$$
$$= 15.3 \text{ rounded to } 15$$

In the next step we determine a suitable layout for an even light distribution. The designer should start with the ratio of the dimensions of the room, which in this example is 60 : 30 or 2 : 1; this means that for uniform distribution the number of luminaires lengthwise should be about twice that widthwise. In this case 5 : 3 appears to be good enough for the purpose because it is the closest to the required ratio and its product is 5 × 3 = 15, which is the total number of required luminaires. Therefore lengthwise there should be 5 luminaires, and widthwise, 3.

The spacing between the luminaires should be twice

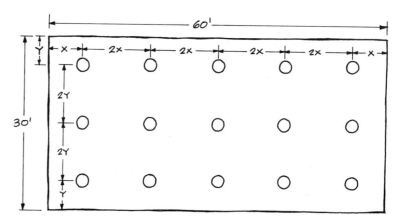

Figure 8-6. *Lighting layout.*

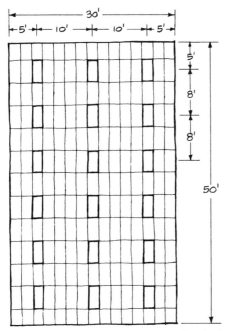

Figure 8-7. *Lighting layout with 18 luminaires.*

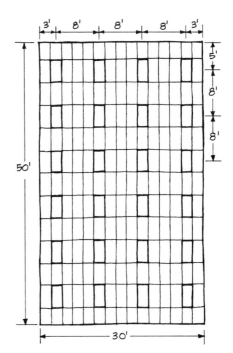

Figure 8-8. *Lighting layout with 24 luminaires.*

that of the setback distance from the walls. With reference to Figure 8-6, the spacing between the luminaires should be 2X if the setback distance is X. Hence lengthwise

$$X + 2X + 2X + 2X + 2X + X = 60 \quad \text{or} \quad X = 6 \text{ ft}$$

Lengthwise the setback distance is 6 ft and the spacing between luminaires, $6 \times 2 = 12$ ft. Similarly, widthwise

$$Y + 2Y + 2Y + Y = 30 \quad \text{or} \quad Y = 5$$

Hence the setback distance is 5 ft and the luminaire spacing, $5 \times 2 = 10$ ft.

The next item is to check the light-level uniformity. To obtain a uniform level of lighting the spacings between luminaires should not exceed the product of the luminaire-mounting height above the work plane times the spacing criterion. In this case the factor is $(10-2.5) \times 1.8 = 13.5$ ft, which is larger than the calculated spacings (12 and 10 ft.). Hence the layout is good and no changes are required. Note that if the spacings of the luminaires had been larger than 13.5

ft a new luminaire with higher SC or an increased number of luminaires with fewer lamps might have to be used.

The ultimate spacings of the lay-in troffers are controlled by the ceiling grid pattern; this is demonstrated by the following example:

8-2 Draw a lighting layout for Problem 6-12; the ceiling is a suspended, 2×4 ft grid.

Solution

It has already been determined that the total number of luminaires needed is 18 (each has four lamps) and the room dimensions are $L = 50$ ft, $W = 30$ ft, $H = 8.5$ ft, and task height, 2.5 ft above floor. Figure 8-7 is the lighting layout. Note that, although crosswise, the setback distance (5 ft) measures half the luminaire spacing (10 ft), lengthwise it does not because of the ceiling pattern.

For uniformity we know that the lengthwise spacing should not exceed 1.35 (SC) $\times$ (8.5 − 2.5) = 8.1 ft and, crosswise, 1.4 (SC) $\times$ (8.5 − 2.5) = 8.4 ft. Here the spacing is satisfactory lengthwise (8 ft center to center); crosswise it is not because the spacing is 10 ft (center to center), which exceeds the calculated limit.

At this point we have three choices. The first is, of course, to review the existing layout closely for the application's suitability and possibly to accept it as it is. Often this insignificant loss of uniformity has little or no adverse effect on the function of the room. As a second choice we replace the luminaires with others of a higher SC. In this case, crosswise, the SC should be a minimum of 10 ÷ 6 = 1.66. Our third choice is to increase the number of luminaires with a reduced number of lamps per luminaire and make a new layout; for example, if luminaires with three lamps are used for the same lighting level, the total number of luminaires increases to

$$(18 \times 4) \div 3 = 24$$

The layout can now be modified as shown in Figure 8-8, in which the uniformity requirements are properly met.

Although increasing the number of luminaires with fewer lamps per unit may provide better uniformity, we must consider the extra expense of this method; for example, the price of a three-lamp troffer luminaire is often almost the same as a four-lamp unit because it uses the same hardware and the same number of ballasts.

9

Electrical Circuiting

Circuiting of lighting layout and their load calculations are based on the fundamentals of electrical engineering, from which it is derived that for an alternating current system, power (watts) = volt − ampere − power factor for single phase, and $\sqrt{3} \times$ line volt $\times$ ampere $\times$ power factor for three phase. The power factor of incandescents is unity and that for fluorescents and high intensity discharge sources can vary from 0.9 and up, if they have a high power factor. In the following examples, for simplification, the power factor of all sources is assumed to be unity. (Light sources with low power factor may significantly affect breaker size and the quantity of luminaires per circuit; this is discussed in Chapter 4).

In the United States three types of voltage systems are common:

1. 120/240 V, single-phase, three-wire
2. 120/208 V, three-phase, four-wire
3. 277/480 V, three-phase, four-wire

The 120/240 V, single-phase, three-wire system is most often adapted to single-family homes and small commercial buildings (see Figure 9-1). It consists of three wires, two phases and a neutral. The phase wires are considered "hot" wires because they provide the current; the neutral carries the unbalanced current. When the currents in both phases are equal, the neutral current is zero. The voltage between any

of the two phases and the neutral is 120 V and that between the two phases, 240 V. The amount of current depends on the wattage of the load and is determined by dividing the wattage of the load by its voltage; for example, if a 200-W lamp is connected between phase A and neutral, the current in phase A is 200 W ÷ 120 V = 1.66 A. Similarly, if another load, say a 500-W lamp is connected between phase B and neutral, the current in the phase B circuit is 500 W ÷ 120 V = 4.16 A. If a lamp is rated for 240 V, it is connected between the two phases and the current is determined by dividing its wattage by 240 V.

The other two systems have four wires that consist of three phase wires (phases A, B, and C and a neutral). In the 120/208-V system the voltage between any of the phases and the neutral is 120 and that between any two phases, 208 (see Figure 9-2). Similarly, in the 277/480-V system the phase-to-neutral voltage is 277 and phase-to-phase, 480 (Figure 9-3). Current is determined in the same manner, as explained earlier, by dividing the wattage by the respective circuit voltage. Here, too, the neutral carries the unbalanced current and is equal to zero when loads at all phases are balanced.

To provide better control and safety in use luminaires are connected through panel boards that consist of a number of circuit breakers to control each lighting circuit (see Figure 9-4). The primary reason for a circuit breaker is to protect the conductors that

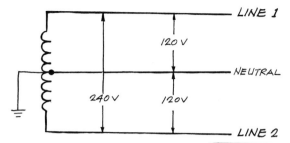

Figure 9-1. *A wiring diagram of a 120/240-V, 1-phase, 3-wire system.*

lead to the lighting loads. In many instances the circuit breaker is also used as a switch.

Circuit breakers in common use are 15 or 20 A and are allowed to carry a maximum of 80% of their amperage, as specified in the National Electrical Code. This restricts the maximum wattage, hence the maximum number of luminaires to be used in a circuit; for example, in a 120-V, 20-A circuit the maximum allowable load is (20 A × 0.8) × 120 V = 1920 W. If each luminaire in use is, say, 200 W, a maximum of 1920 ÷ 200 ≈ 9 luminaires can be installed in this circuit. Similarly, in a 277-V, 20-A circuit this load is (20 × 0.8) × 277 = 4432 W or a maximum of 4432 ÷ 200; 22 luminaires can be installed.

Because the neutral carries only the unbalanced current of the phase loads and its amount is never larger than the maximum carried by any of the

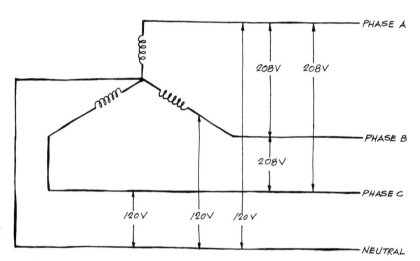

Figure 9-2. *A wiring diagram of a 120/208-V, 3-phase, 4-wire system.*

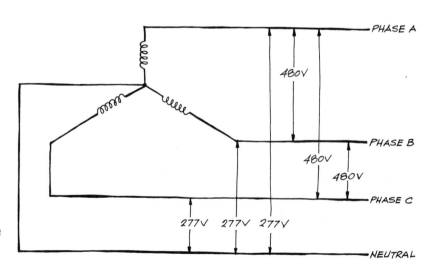

Figure 9-3. *A wiring diagram of a 277/480-V, 3-phase, 4-wire system.*

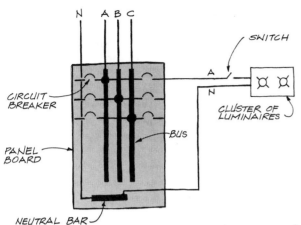

Figure 9-4. *A typical connection diagram between panel-board and luminaires.*

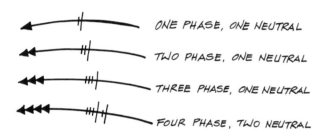

Figure 9-5. *Typical "home runs." The arrowheads indicate phase or hot wires. The short lines across the arrow indicate the number of phase or hot wires. The long lines indicate the number of neutrals.*

phases, a single neutral conductor can be used for as many as three phase conductors (A,B,C) in a three-phase system; for example, if there are 25 luminaires of 200 W each, then in a 120/208-V, three-phase, four-wire system they could be distributed at eight units in each of A and B (1600 W each) and nine in phase C (1800 W). The total number of wires required to feed these luminaires from the panel board is four (A,B,C, and N).

CIRCUITING LIGHTING LAYOUTS

Fundamentally, circuiting lighting layouts means assigning groups of luminaires to circuits and then routing them to the panel board with proper circuit numbers. At some point in the design development the designer must determine the voltage and the panel board location before circuiting. Then, based on the guidelines mentioned earlier, luminaires can be connected, and as many as three circuits can be grouped to be connected to a panel board. The luminaire closest to the panel board shows the "homerun" with arrowheads, one for each of the phases in use, all pointed toward the panel board. The lines that represent the wiring between luminaires may be straight or curved but should be dark and heavy to distinguish them from the background building lines. A curved line is preferred to avoid any confusion with other straight lines on the drawing. Short slash-lines can be drawn across the circuits and the homeruns to indicate the number of conductors. The neutral conduc-

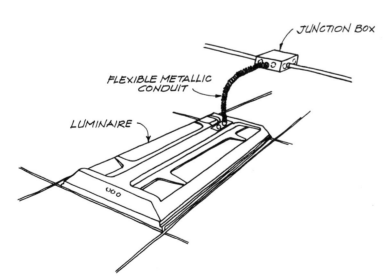

Figure 9-6. *A typical lighting fixture connection above the ceiling.*

tor is usually shown with a longer slash-line than the phase conductors (see Figure 9-5). For economy it is often desirable to connect a group of luminaires to one junction box. This is particularly true for fluorescent troffers which are equipped with flexible metallic conduit leads 6 ft long, (Figure 9-6). Typically, four luminaires can be connected to one junction box and circuiting can proceed as described earlier (see Figure 9-7 for an example).

PANEL SCHEDULE

The panel schedule shows the branch circuit description, loads in watts, circuit-breaker size and number of poles, circuit number, and the phase to which each circuit is connected. Figure 9-8 is a typical schedule. The designer should try to distribute the loads evenly in all phases to give the neutral conductor of the panel board the least amount of current. Total wattage is the sum of individual watts of each luminaire in a circuit. It must be remembered that except for incandescents all other sources (e.g., fluorescents and metal halides) have ballasts that consume power in addition to that required by the lamp.

LOAD CALCULATIONS

After the panel schedule is completed the loads can be added together for each of the phases and for a grand total. To get an average current per phase in a 120/240-V, single-phase, three-wire system, the total load (watts) is divided by 240; for a 120/208-V, three-phase, four-wire system, by $\sqrt{3} \times 208 = 360$, and for a 277/480-V, three-phase, four-W system, by $\sqrt{3} \times 480 = 831$.

Figure 9-8 shows a typical example of load calculations. If lighting is used as a continuous load, NEC requires that this load be calculated at 125% to size the feeder and the overcurrent devices.

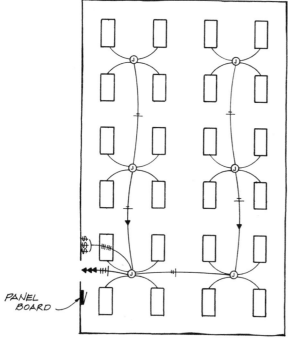

Figure 9-7. A typical lighting layout with a home run, panelboard, and switches.

PANEL LP									
120/208 **VOLTS,**	3	**PH,**		4	**WIRES,**		225	**AMP.BUS**	

load	watts	p	cb	ckt	ph	ckt	cb	p	watts	load
No. office lights	1300	1	20	1	A	2	20	1	1600	West office lights
No. office lights	1200	1	20	3	B	4	20	1	1600	" " "
Conf. room lights	1200	1	20	5	C	6	20	1	1600	" " "
Cafeteria lights	1500	1	20	7	A	8	20	1	1200	Displ. area lights
Lobby lights	1200	1	20	9	B	10	20	1	1400	Library lights
Corridor lights	1200	1	20	11	C	12	20	1	1500	Library lights
Corridor lights	1200	1	20	13	A	14	20	1	1500	Sec. pool lights
So.office lights	1500	1	20	15	B	16	20	1	1200	Sec. pool lights
So. office lights	1300	1	20	17	C	18	20	1	1400	Bookkeeping lights
E. office lights	1400	1	20	19	A	20	20	1	1000	Restroom lights
" " "	1400	1	20	21	B	22	20	1	1000	Gen. office lights
" " "	1400	1	20	23	C	24	20	1	1000	Gen. office lights
Spare		1	20	25	A	26	20	1		Spare
"		1	20	27	B	28	20	1		"
"		1	20	29	C	30		1		Space
Space		1		31	A	32		1		"
"		1		33	B	34		1		"
"		1		35	C	36		1		"
"		1		37	A	38		1		"
"		1		39	B	40		1		"
"		1		41	C	42		1		"

PHASE A _10700_ **W, PHASE B** _10500_ **W, PHASE C** _10600_ **W, TOTAL** _31800_ **W**

DEMAND CALCULATIONS:

LIGHTING _____ 31800 Watts X 1.25 = 39750 Watts

RECEPT _____ 0

MOTORS _____ 0

OTHERS _____ Estimated future load = 10000 Watts

TOTAL DEMAND _49750_ **watts** _138_ **ampere**

FEEDER _____ (4 # 1/0 THW CU)2" C

Figure 9-8. A typical panel schedule and load calculations.

10

Principles of Lighting Control

Unless there is interference, light travels in a straight line. With designed interference light can be precisely controlled. The material used for interference can be opaque, transparent, or translucent. Transparent materials allow almost all light to pass through them, except for a small amount that varies with type and thickness. Objects can be seen through them. Some typical examples are plain glass, plastic, and teflon. Translucent materials transmit light but diffuse it in such a way that objects cannot be seen through it. Some typical examples are opal, configurated glass, and plastic. Opaque materials block light transmission totally but may absorb or reflect it. Their surfaces may be shiny or diffused. Some typical surfaces are painted, polished, or mirrored metal.

When light is interfered with by any of these materials, it is reflected, transmitted, or absorbed.

REFLECTION OF LIGHT

Reflected light can assume various shapes. If the reflecting material is flat and of specular finish, the angle of incident ray is the same as the reflected ray (see Figure 10-1). Typical examples of these reflections

are the polished and electroplated metals, such as gold, silver, copper, and mirrors with their silvered surfaces at the very top. Mirrors with silvered surfaces at the back react differently. Some light is reflected by the top surface as expected, but the remaining passes through the glass at a different angle and is then reflected off the silvered surface at the back, parallel to the reflected ray at the upper surface.

A variety of controlled light output obtained by this method is put into practice:

1. *Concave Reflector.* When parallel rays of light strike a specular reflector of concave shape, the reflected rays merge through its focal point. Conversely, if a point source is placed at the focal point, the reflected rays will emerge parallel to one another (see Figure 10-2).

2. *Convex Reflector.* If parallel rays of light strike a reflecting surface of convex shape, the reflected light will disperse in multidirections, as shown in Figure 10-3.

3. *Spherical Reflector.* When a point source is placed at the focal point of a spherical reflector (focal point is at the center), the reflected light rays pass through the focal point and emerge

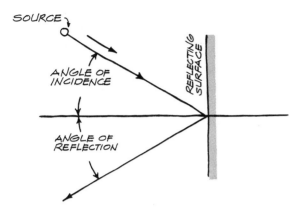

Figure 10-1. *A specular reflection. The angle of incidence is equal to the angle of reflection.*

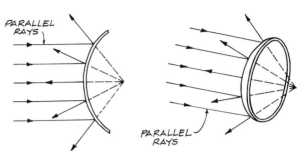

Figure 10-3. *A convex reflecting surface.*

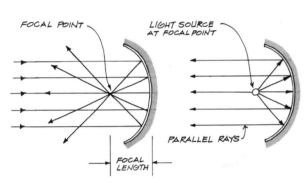

Figure 10-2. *A concave reflecting surface.*

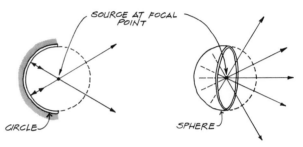

Figure 10-4. *A spherical reflecting surface.*

through the opening as shown in Figure 10-4. Almost all of the energy is reflected back on the source, which may affect its performance.

4. *Cylindrical Reflector.* This operates on the same basic principle of reflection as the spherical reflector except that the source is placed parallel to it through the focal length. Here, too, the reflected light emerges through the focal length which may affect the source's performance (see Figure 10-5).

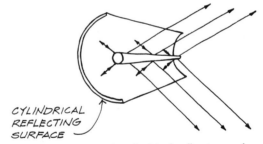

Figure 10-5. *A cylindrical reflecting surface.*

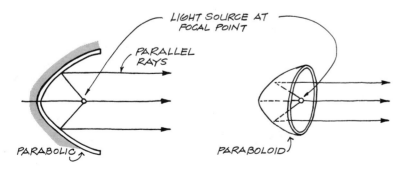

Figure 10-6. *A parabolic reflecting surface.*

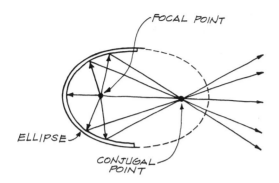

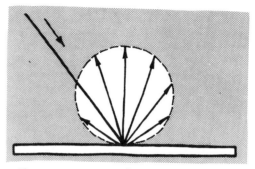

Figure 10-9. *A complete diffuse reflection.*

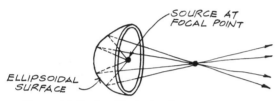

Figure 10-7. *An elliptical reflecting surface.*

OTHER REFLECTION SHAPES

Spread reflection occurs when the reflected light is dispersed in only one general direction (see Figure 10-8). It is used when a smooth beam of light with moderate control is required. Typical examples are corrugated, brushed, dimpled, etched, or pebbled surfaces on metal.

5. *Parabolic Reflector.* When a source is placed at the focal point of a parabolic reflector (or paraboloid reflector), the reflected light emerges parallel to the axis of the parabola (or paraboloid) (see Figure 10-6).

6. *Elliptical Reflector.* An ellipse has two focal points. If a point source is placed at the first focal point, the reflected light emerges through the second (also known as the conjugate point; see Figure 10-7). The main advantage is that a pool of light can be obtained through a very small opening.

Diffuse reflection occurs when the reflected light is dispersed in all directions evenly, independent of the angle of incident ray (see Figure 10-9). Typical examples are reflectors with flat paint or any other matte finish with a rough surface that contains minute crystals or pigment particles. Each ray of light that falls on these tiny particles obeys the laws of reflection and disperses in multidirections to create a total diffusion.

Mixed or compound reflections are a combination of the spread and complete diffusion shown in Figure 10-10. Typical examples are porcelain enamel and the high-gloss painted metals that are used for the reflections of industrial luminaires.

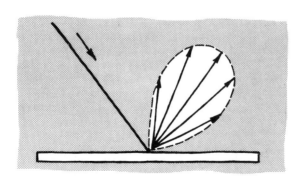

Figure 10-8. *A spread reflection.*

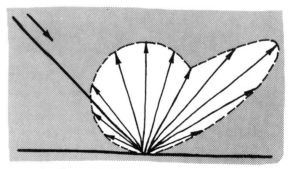

Figure 10-10. *A mixed reflection.*

TRANSMISSION OF LIGHT

Transmission of light may be refracted, spread, or diffused. Refraction refers to the bending or displacement of light as it passes through one medium to another. A variety of refracted light can be obtained by transmitting material of various shapes. Typical examples are prisms, convex or concave lenses, and stepped (Fresnel) lenses (Figure 10-11).

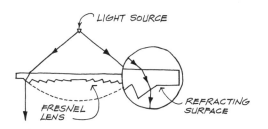

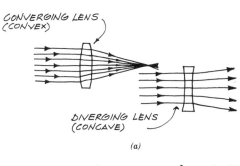

(a)

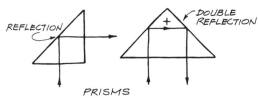

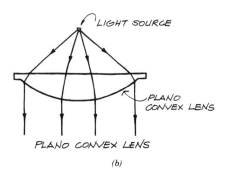

(b)

Figure 10-11. *A refracted light from various transmitting materials (lenses and prisms).*

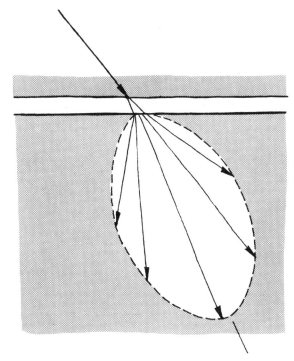

Figure 10-12. *A spread transmission.*

Spread transmission refracts the light but is dispersed in one general direction (Figure 10-12). Typical examples are the frosted or ribbed surfaces of plastic or glass that are used to conceal the source or

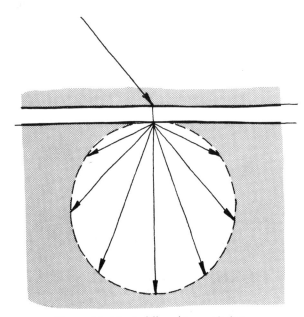

Figure 10-13. *A diffused transmission.*

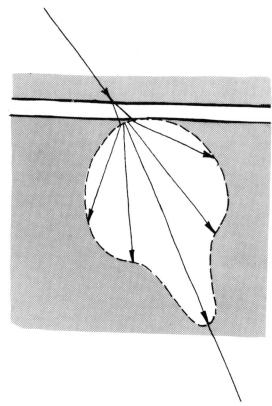

Figure 10-14. A mixed transmission.

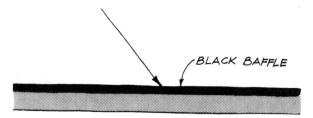

Figure 10-15. An absorption.

increase the beam spread for better candlepower distribution.

Diffused transmission occurs when the refracted light is dispersed in all directions, regardless of the angle of incident ray (Figure 10-13). A typical example is the opal glass, which is used for some interior luminaires. Mixed transmission is a combination of diffused and spread (see Figure 10-14).

ABSORPTION OF LIGHT

Absorption occurs when a material does not reflect or transmit the light it receives. Any material with a matte black finish is absorbing; for example the black baffles as used inside cylindrical downlights (see Figure 10-15).

ARCHITECTURAL TOOLS

11

Incandescent Luminaires

Hundreds of different incandescent luminaires are manufactured today to meet the needs of the many applications. Type of construction, aesthetics, finish, lighting distribution, glare, heat control, size, and cost are only a few of the reasons for their variation, not to mention the type of lamp used, which may vary from a fraction of a watt to thousands. Obviously it is impossible to describe it all.

In this limited space we have covered the frequently used utilitarian incandescent luminaires and others that are new in the market but are suitable for commercial interiors. For convenience they are categorized by their mounting methodology. An in-depth discussion of recessed luminaires whose construction and light distribution are similar to many of the modern surface, pendant, and track-mounted luminaires is presented. In many cases the same luminaire is used for different applications when the only difference is in the decor or in the mounting methodology. For this reason the other utilitarian luminaires are discussed only to the extent that they differ substantially in operating principles from the recessed types.

Regardless of the type, all incandescent luminaires have the following advantages:

1. Because of the small size of the filament (approaching a point source), light distribution is easily controlled.
2. Their low initial cost.
3. The light level is easily and economically controlled (dimming).
4. They are virtually unaffected by ambient temperature and humidity.
5. Their color rendering is excellent.
6. There is more heat per lumen, which may be used for comfort heating during winter.

Their common disadvantages are the following:

1. The lumens per watt are the lowest.
2. Their high operating cost is due to short lamp life.
3. The heat they produce may necessitate additional air conditioning.
4. They are suitable for only low level lighting.

107

RECESSED INCANDESCENT LUMINAIRES

Recessed luminaires are mounted above the ceiling line. The bottom is flush with the ceiling, with or without trim. The purpose of the trim is to cover any disorder at the surface of contact between luminaire and ceiling.

Application

Recessed luminaires are the most popular members of the family of incandescent luminaires with virtually unlimited lighting possibilities that range from general illumination to accent and wall washing. These luminaires are available in 25 to 500 W but are sometimes specially designed to accept three different watt sizes. They are selected largely for their light-distributing patterns, which may be wide, medium, or narrow, depending on their spacing criteria (SC). If the SC is 1.0 or more, it is classified as wide; 0.7 to 0.9 is medium and 0.6 or less is narrow. Spacing criteria are used to determine maximum spacing for even lighting. They are applicable to general and accent lighting and wall washing.

General Lighting

For general lighting there are four major types of downlight: (a) "can", (b) open reflector, (c) ellipsoidal reflector, and (d) lensed. In general can downlights have narrow light distribution and open reflector and ellipsoidal/reflector downlights have narrow-to-wide distribution, depending on the lamps used; lensed downlights have wide light distribution.

As a general rule, wide distributing downlights should be selected for rooms with low ceilings (8 to 10 ft) in which an even general lighting is required and in which "spilling" on the walls is welcome. Medium distributing downlights should illuminate a confined area in a large room with a medium (10 to 16 ft) ceiling. Medium downlights can also be used for even illumination in a room with a high ceiling (16 ft and higher). Narrow distributing downlights provide concentrated illumination in rooms with medium to high ceilings but should not be used for general lighting in rooms of any height. (See Figure 11-1 for applications of all three types of light distribution.)

Accent Lighting and Wall Washing

This class of lighting is comprised of three basic forms: (a) fixed location in the ceiling, with the beam aiming mechanism concealed inside the luminaire, (b) beam-aiming mechanism partly exposed, and (c) retractable beam-aiming mechanism. All are available in narrow-to-wide distribution lighting patterns. Selection should depend on the requirements. As a general rule, however, only narrow or medium spreads are suited to accent lighting and flood lamps are designed for wall washing. A wide variety of accent and wall-washing luminaires is also discussed in the section on track lighting.

Tips on Design Approach and Luminaire Selection

A versatile number of lighting possibilities exists for recessed luminaires. As a first step in planning the space must be analyzed in terms of its application. The designer must identify the areas that need general lighting, those that need downlighting, and the objects that may need highlighting. Should the fixtures be projected from the ceiling or concealed behind a beam? Is there a sloped ceiling? Should a slope adapter be used on regular downlights, or an eyeball? Furniture, plants, pictures, draperies, and textures all have an effect on the selection of an overall lighting system. All items must be checked individually and collectively.

As a general rule, however, downlights will emphasize a horizontal surface, wall washers illuminate a vertical surface, and accent lighting accentuates objects on the floor and walls. A complete interior lighting design can be accomplished with these three basics and by making a wise selection of the luminaires to satisfy the objective.

CODE COMPLIANCE

Since the 1981 edition of the National Electrical Code was published it has been required that all recessed incandescent luminaires have thermal protection, except for those that are installed in poured concrete or designed to be installed in cavities in which the thermal insulation is in direct contact. The thermal protectors consist of a thermostatic switch that will disconnect the power if the temperature of the luminaire rises beyond a preset degree of safety.

Figure 11-1. (a) *Downlights with wide distribution should be used in low-ceilinged rooms for general, even lighting that spills over the walls. The lumen method of calculation is excellent for this purpose. (b) Downlights with medium distribution should be used in medium-to-high-ceilinged rooms for general lighting in confined areas. The point-by-point method of calculation is applicable. These downlights also adapt well to general, even lighting throughout rooms with high ceilings for which the lumen method of calculations should be used. (c) Downlights with narrow distribution should be installed in medium-to-high ceilinged rooms for concentrated lighting in specific areas. The point-by-point method of calculation should be used.*

Application

This downlight is ideally suited to certain applications when the budget is tight and aesthetics are not an important consideration. Use them for general downlighting in medium (75 W, 150 W) to-high (150 W, 300 W)-ceiling areas or to provide a confined amount of light in an area with a medium high ceiling.

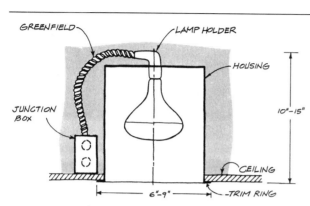

Figure 11-2. Can downlight.

This downlight is designed for applications when widespread general lighting is required and there is no objection to glare.

Use for general, even lighting in a room with low (75 W)-to-medium (150 W) ceilings and for supplementary light above desks and conference tables.

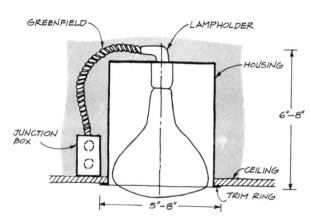

Figure 11-3. Can downlight (partly exposed).

The annular rings cut glare and make these lights suitable for use in medium (50 W-ER, 75 W, 150 W)-to-high-ceiling (150 W, 300 W) areas in which a concealed light source provides soft, narrow, downlighting.

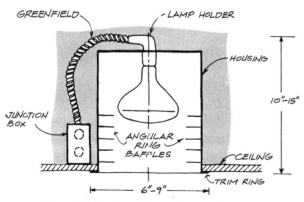

Figure 11-4. Downlight with annular rings.

General Description	*Remarks*
These luminaires utilize R, PAR, or ER reflector-type incandescent lamps. Because of their simple form, they are often called "can" luminaires or "can" downlights. The cylinder is made of steel, painted matte black or white as a baffle. There is no external reflector inside the housing and the light distribution is dependent primarily on the lamp's built-in reflector. The lamp is positioned to provide a 45° shielding angle. To obtain good paint adhesion and a protective finish of superior quality and durability premium grade luminaires are processed and phosphate-conditioned for corrosion resistance before spraying and baking are done.	Simple form, low initial cost. The lamp can be replaced easily from the bottom. Each replacement automatically provides a new built-in reflector, which ensures a good light-loss factor. One disadvantage is that, lacking an external reflector, spill light is trapped inside the luminaire.
Suitable for use with R-type flood lamps, these are can downlights in their simplest form in which the light output is solely dependent on the lamp's reflector. A steel cylinder houses the lamp for safety. Part of the lamp emerges from the luminaire to allow full exposure to the light distribution. Typically, the inside portion of the luminaire is matte black and the exposed part (trim ring) is white enamel.	This luminaire has high efficiency (85 to 95%) because almost all of the lamp lumens emerge without obstruction. The initial cost is low because of the simple form. Perhaps the greatest disadvantage is the discomforting glare caused by the lamp's partial exposure.
This modified version of can downlighting has three to five annular baffle rings of sheet metal attached to the inside surface of the cylinder to intercept spill light and shield the housing. With no visible light at the bottom of the rings and with the lamp regressed to a 45° shielding angle, these luminaires provide a narrow downlight with a low level of internal glow and direct glare. Energy effectiveness can be increased by using ER lamps (in lieu of R or PAR lamps) that allow very little spill light to be trapped in the rings. Typically, the exposed part (trim) is durable white enamel and the inside, including the rings, is matte black.	Glare-free downlight, especially when used with ER lamps. The rings are physical barriers to light output; they cut luminaire efficiency by 25 to 30%, depending on their size. Bands of light are visible at the edges of the annular rings, which become more conspicuous with size. The annular rings also collect dirt and insects.

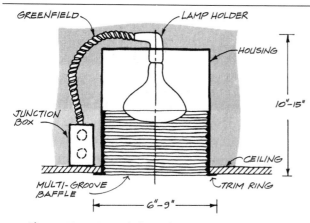

Dark multigrooves cut glare thus making them suitable for use in medium (50 W-ER, 75 W, 150 W)-to-high-ceiling (150 W, 300 W) areas in which a concealed light source is desired for soft, yet concentrated downlighting.

Figure 11-5. *Downlight with multigroove baffle.*

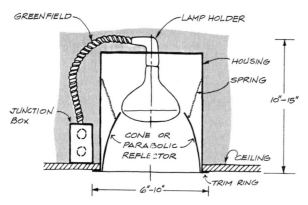

This luminaire should be considered for rooms with medium (75 W, 150 W) to high (150 W, 300 W) ceiling areas when strong downlight with sharp cutoff and low glare is required. It can also be used effectively for scallops on a vertical surface.

Figure 11-6. *Downlight with cone or parabolic reflectors.*

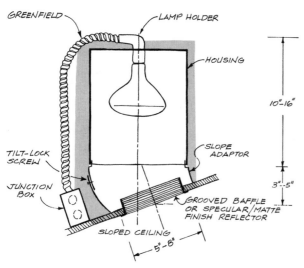

This downlight is suitable for a concentrated amount of virtually glare-free illumination under sloped ceilings. A spot lamp, opposed to a flood lamp, should be adapted to this luminaire.

Figure 11-7. *Downlight for sloped ceilings.*

General Description	Remarks

A multigroove, one-piece aluminum or phenolic rigid baffle is attached to the housing to trap spill light and reduce aperture brightness. Deeply grooved sharp ridges break up peripheral light and are seen as a soft sidewall glow. Like other can luminaires, here, too, the lamp is placed at a 45° shield angle. Reflector lamps with narrow-to-medium beam spread should be used. Typically, the trim is durable white enamel and the baffle is matte black.

Concentrated downlight is achieved with low brightness and a maximum light is attained if ER lamps are used. With R or PAR lamps the black-grooved baffle reduces luminaire light output as much as 25% (slightly better than annual ring downlights). Circular rings are visible if the grooves are widely spaced and their edges are thick.

The one-piece, specular aluminum reflector, normally known as cone or parabolic, is designed precisely to gather spill light from the lamp and reflect it to useful zones. This increases the luminaire's efficiency and light distribution over those already discussed. The reflector is held in position by springs and is designed to accept R and PAR lamps (but not ER). The exterior housing is steel and the reflector has a specular aluminum finish (also known as "clear"), which is standard at most manufacturers. Other optional finishes are gold, black, bronze, and gray. Typically, the housing is matte black and the trim, durable white enamel.

This luminaire achieves its maximum efficiency with a clear reflector (75 to 85%). With others, the efficiency is reduced by the following factors: gold = 0.90, bronze and gray = 0.80, and black = 0.70. Because of the special reflector, the unit cost is approximately three times that of can downlights.

An accessory called slope adaptor is fitted to the bottom of the regular downlight and its built-in, field-adjustable, tilt-lock screw is tightened after matching the ceiling slope. For most luminaires of this type the angle can be varied 5 to 30°. Made of steel, this slope adaptor is sometimes equipped with a baffle. The system produces narrow downlight with little glare. The exposed parts are durable white enamel and the interior is black. The baffle may be matte, specular black, or multigrooved.

The main advantages of this system are the flexibility of the field adjustment to the sloped angle, the slope adaptor can be affixed to any conventional downlight of matching dimensions, and there is virtually no glare because the lamp is concealed deep inside the luminaire.

Luminaire efficiency and distribution in light output however, worsen as the slope angle increases. The light output is never symmetrical to its nadir because the center of the opening does not coincide with the axis of the lamp. The other disadvantage is the inconvenience of changing the lamp.

Application

Downlight with A-lamp is suitable mainly for applications when the budget is tight but a lot of light is required from aesthetically pleasing luminaires. It is ideally suitable for even, general lighting in large or small rooms with low (100 W, 150 W)-to-medium (150 W, 200 W) ceilings in which spilling of light on vertical surfaces is welcome to expand the space visually.

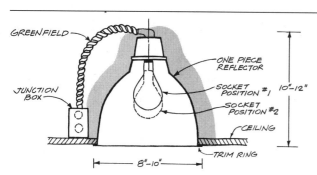

Figure 11-8. *Downlight with A-lamp (vertical).*

Shallow recess depth and a wide distribution pattern make these luminaires ideal for use in rooms with low ceilings (100 W, 150 W) and limited plenum space. They can be combined with their vertical lamp counterparts in the same room for pleasing appearance and equal light distribution.

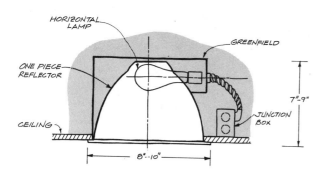

Figure 11-9. *Downlight with A-lamp (horizontal).*

These downlights are designed to produce medium distributing, soft light with precise control of brightness to be used in rooms with low ceilings (100 W, 150 W).

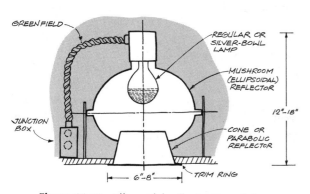

Figure 11-10. *Ellipsoidal reflector downlights.*

General Description	*Remarks*
This is the simplest form of recessed luminaire adapted to general service lamps. It has a one-piece reflector that surrounds the lamp to capture all of its light and to redirect it to useful zones. Because light from A-lamps emerges in all directions (except at the socket), the luminaire's light distribution is totally dependent on the external reflector. Some manufacturers provide a socket-position-changing mechanism that moves the lamp up or down for a change in light output distribution. The closer the lamp to the opening, the wider the light spread. In its higher position the luminaire provides a 45° shielding angle. The one-piece aluminum reflector has a specular, clear, standard finish. The optional colors are gold, black, and bronze.	The main advantages are their use of low-cost general service lamps; and their high efficiency (70 to 80%) and controllable light distribution. In addition, the multisocket position offers flexibility of beam spread. The disadvantage is that the initial cost is slightly higher than that of can downlights. Also, general service lamps, although cheaper and available in a wide range of wattages, have less efficacy (lumens/watts) and life when compared with R and PAR lamps. Because of a larger opening, these luminaires produce more glare.
The precisely designed one-piece aluminum reflector captures the light from horizontally mounted, general service lamps and redirects them to useful areas. The result is a wide distributing light output that has high efficiency yet low brightness from normal viewing angles. The lamp is placed to provide a 45° shielding angle and wide light distribution. The reflector is with a specular clear finish; optional colors are gold, black, and bronze.	The greatest advantage is the shallower recess depth; other advantages and disadvantages are similar to those of the vertical lamp counterparts.
Three reflectors serve three separate purposes. The "mushroom" or ellipsoidal-shaped bowl contains two reflectors. The lower reflector directs the light upward, which is then turned downward by the upper reflector to cover useful areas. The third reflector is a cone or parabolic that redirects the spill light to improve distribution and glare control. With silver-bowl lamps the glare is so precisely controlled that it is hard to tell when the luminaire is on. All three reflectors are made of aluminum in a clear, specular, standard finish. The cone/parabolic reflector comes in optional finishes such as gold, black, and bronze.	A soft amount of light is available from a concealed luminaire with virtually no glare from normal viewing angles. The disadvantages are (a) the reflector system is costly, (b) it requires a deep recessing area, (c) it has low efficiency (45 to 55%) because of the losses in reflecting mechanism, which is reduced to an even greater extent in silver-bowl lamps.

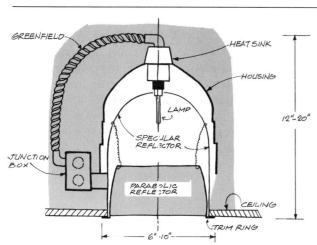

Figure 11-11. *Ellipsoidal reflector, tungsten-halogen downlight.*

Application

These luminaires are designed for medium (250 W, T4) to high (500 W, T4) ceiling areas in which a medium-to-wide light distribution with high quality color is required.

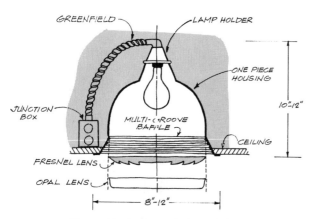

Figure 11-12. *Downlight with lens.*

This downlight is ideally suited to areas with low ceiling heights (100 W, 150 W) in which humidity, corrosion, and environmental dirt are destructive and a wide distribution of soft light is required. The fresnel lens should be considered when a wide, uniform light is needed but a view of the lamp is objectionable. The fresnel lens is "colouvred," a process in which the stepped risers are coated gray to form lens-louvers that filter out the glare of the lamp at high angles. The drop opal lens should be considered for applications in which a general diffuse light is wanted and glare is not objectionable. Polycarbonate opal lens are appropriate for rough service or in vandalprone areas.

General Description	*Remarks*
This luminaire is designed for tungsten-halogen lamps that produce a great amount of light and a high concentration of heat. A cast aluminum radiator and heat sink disperse heat to maintain the lamp's full natural life. The system contains two reflectors: the upper captures the light and directs it downward and the cone or parabolic reflector redirects the spill light to improve lighting spread and glare control. Some manufacturers offer an adjustable socket position that may be used in the field for beam-spread adjustments. The lower the lamp location, the wider the beam spread. In both positions there is wide light distribution. The upper reflector is clear specular aluminum. The parabolic reflector is specular black, a standard for brightness control. Other options are gold, clear, bronze, or multigroove baffle. The trim ring is painted white enamel on metal or matte white polycarbonate.	A compact quartz halogen lamp offers better light control with greater longevity. If 130-V lamps are used, its life is extended to 6000 h, with a 25% drop in light output. At 120 V its rated life is 2000 hr. The disadvantages are that the arrangement requires a deep recessing area and the life of the lamp may be seriously shortened if the heat dissipation system is not adequate. This downlight also has high initial and maintenance costs.

The reflector is a specular anodized aluminum. The fresnel lens refracts the light and provides a widely distributed soft light in useful zones. The multigrooved black baffle cuts glare at wide angles.

The dropped opal lens is a diffuser; basically it scatters light without any precise directional control.

The stepped fresnel lens is made of glass, whereas the opal lens is generally made of acrylic or polycarbonate plastic. The multigroove baffle is matte black.

The main advantages are (a) its ideal suitability to rooms with low ceilings, humidity, corrosion, or dirt; (b) the lens also acts as protection from lamp heat; (c) it is easy to clean; and (d) it has a wide light distribution.

The disadvantages are (a) imperfections in manufacturing allow insects and dirt to collect on the lens; (b) it has a lower efficiency when compared with open-bottom luminaires (lowest with an opal lens).

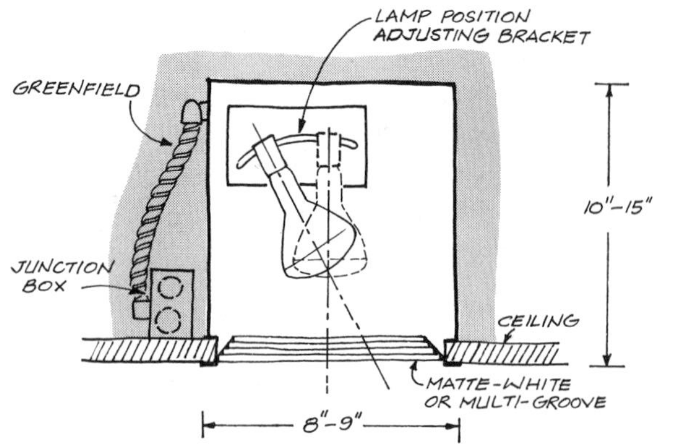

Application

This luminaire throws accent light on displayed objects at a desired direction on a horizontal or vertical plane. It can also be effective for mounting on sloped ceilings at any angle up to 45°.

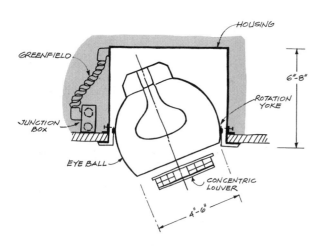

Figure 11-13. Directional recessed round.

This luminaire is used to accent light on objects in a desired direction on a horizontal or vertical plane and can be effective on sloped ceilings at any angle up to 45°.

Figure 11-14. Recessed eyeball.

General Description	*Remarks*
This luminaire basically accommodates a lamp inside the cylindrical housing, which can be moved as a friction lock. The beam tilts up to 45° on the vertical and rotates up to 350° on the horizontal. The remaining 10° are taken up by the swivel-stopping hardware. During installation care should be taken to prevent the object to be lighted from falling into the 10° restricted zone from which it cannot be aimed at. Some luminaires are provided with splay trim, which raises aperture brightness at the ceiling. These units should be used with spot lamps (lamps with narrow beam) only. The housing is made of steel painted matte black like a can-downlight in its simplest form. The trim ring is durable white enamel on metal or matte white polycarbonate.	Its greatest advantage is that light can be aimed precisely at an object without the lamp being visible from the outside. Narrow to wide beams of various intensities are possible with PAR or R lamps. Very narrow beams can be obtained with low voltage lamps (with a built-in transformer). Light distribution is strictly dependent on the lamp's own reflector.
The eyeball can be moved horizontally in a circle (358°) and vertically up to 40° angulation. Some of these luminaires have inconspicuous, regressed construction. The bottom of the eyeball is usually open for maximum light output and has optional concentric louvers mounted on an open face for glare control from normal visible angles. With louvers it should be used with narrow lamps only. The ceiling flange is satin white enamel and the eyeball is satin aluminum or white enamel. The recessed parts are matte black or white.	Because the lamp is enclosed in a ball whose movement is independent of the housing, light output is constant in any direction. Like the preceding luminaire, wide variation in beam is possible with the type of lamp used. Shallow depth allows installation in 8-in. wood-joist construction.

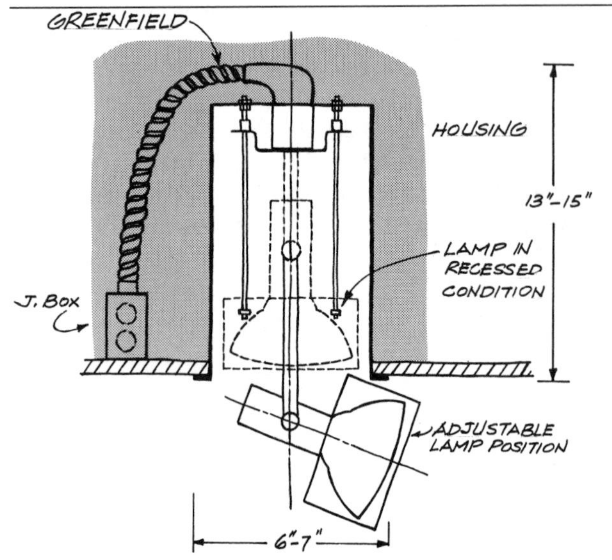

Application

Ideally suitable for situations in which the displayed objects are located very high, especially near the ceiling, or when precise beam aiming is necessary.

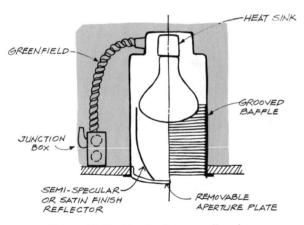

Figure 11-15. Retractable directional recessed.

These wallwashers should be considered for smooth, medium, or high-density wash in rooms with medium-height (150 W, 300 W) ceilings. For an even wall wash they must be placed no closer than 3 to 4 ft from the wall and the spacing between the luminaires must not exceed the distance from the wall.

Figure 11-16. Fixed reflector wallwasher.

General Description

The lamp holder is a separate element that can be totally recessed or projected out of the main housing and is adjustable to a maximum of 358° horizontally and 180° vertically. The remaining 2° in horizontal movement are taken up by the swivel-stopping mechanism, which must be avoided during installation.

The inside of the luminaire is black-matte finished or has a multigroove baffle to reduce glare. The trim ring is painted white enamel on metal or matte white polycarbonate.

Remarks

The main advantage is the beam-aiming flexibility of the retractable lamp holder, which can be (1) totally recessed to give it the appearance of a downlight, (2) partly exposed, to simulate the function and appearance of an eye-ball, and (3) totally exposed, to provide a precise aim of light at difficult angles that cannot be achieved by other directional luminaires.

This luminaire has four main parts for optical control. The first is the built-in reflector of the flood-lamp which provides a wide beam spread downward. The second is the multigrooved black baffle that absorbs and controls the glare at the opening. The third is the semispecular (or satin) aluminum reflector that "scoops" most of the light toward the wall. The fourth, the die-cast aperture plate at the bottom conceals and supports the reflector and allows the light to emerge only through the half-opening. The aperture plate can be removed for relamping. The housing is matte black and the trimming and aperture plate are matte white or black.

Smooth wallwash (fair to good quality) is obtained from floor to ceiling line; the distance to walls and between units determines effect and intensity. Light distribution is preset; leaves are cutoff at the bottom and sides. It integrates visually with round downlights with multigroove baffles.

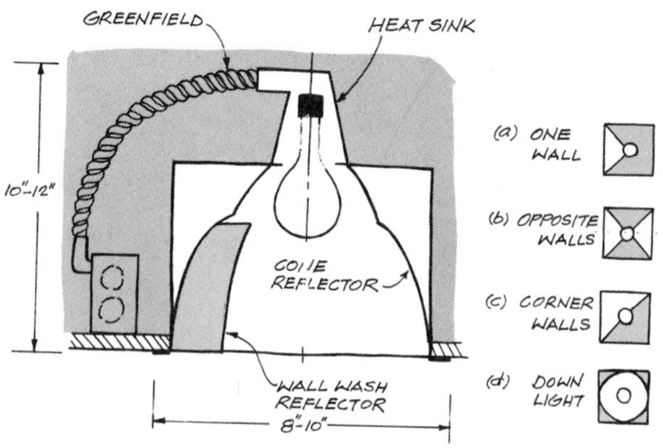

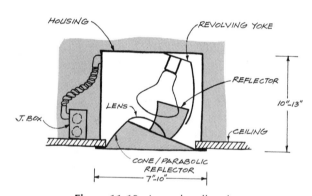

Figure 11-17. Movable reflector wallwasher.

Application

This luminaire uses standard service lamps to light horizontal and vertical surfaces from an inconspicuous recessed source. Suitable for small or large rooms with low (100-W) to medium (150-W) ceilings, this unit can be mounted in the same room with matching open-reflector, downlights. For an even wall wash these units should be placed 3 to 4 ft from the wall and the spacing should be no more than that distance from the wall. Some units have multiple reflectors that can be positioned to light two vertical surfaces at opposite sides or in a corner. Matte wall finishes are recommended to reduce specular reflections and striations.

Figure 11-18. Lensed wallwasher.

This wallwasher should be considered for very smooth, medium, or high-intensity wash in rooms with medium (150 W) to high (300 W) ceilings. For an even wash it must be placed no closer than 3 ft from a wall and the space between luminaires should not exceed that distance.

General Description	*Remarks*
This luminaire has two reflectors: a cone and a wallwasher. The wall-washing reflector is specular and field-adjustable for precise aiming, whereas the specular cone captures the remaining light for downlighting. Factory modification of the reflectors allows incremental wall washing of one wall (Figure a) two opposite walls (Figure b), two corner walls (Figure c), or downlighting only (Figure d). A specular clear finish is standard for the cone. Optional colors are gold, black, and bronze. The housing is matte black and the trimming, durable white enamel.	Wallwash quality is good to very good but it does not reach up to the ceiling line. Whether used exclusively as a wallwasher or for downlighting, it integrates visually with open reflector downlights. When operating as a washer-cum-downlight, it appears to provide more light on the floor than on the walls.
The luminaire's optical system is equipped with an R-type lamp, a "kicker" reflector, and a spread lens to provide even distribution without hot spots or striations. A parabolic cone controls spill light and prevents glare. From outside the appearance of the luminaire matches a downlight with a cone. Both the cone and movable lamp bracket can be adjusted independently to provide a precise light output for a job condition. The cone is finished in black or clear specular as a standard item. Optional colors are gold and bronze. The trim ring is durable enamel paint.	Wallwash quality is excellent. The combination of lens and the reflector provides a very smooth, shadowless, scallopless, gradually fading light over a large surface. Light distribution is preset and integrates visually with downlights by using aperture cones. Matte wall finishes are recommended to reduce specular reflections and striations.

TRACK-LIGHT SYSTEM

A track-light system consists primarily of two main parts: (a) the track and (b) the luminaires.

The anodized, extruded aluminum track is an electrical raceway that supplies power to the luminaires mounted anywhere on its entire length. The luminaires can be moved horizontally and vertically (see Figure 11-19). With this mobility a track-light system offers optimum flexibility in a vast range of lighting effects.

A track can be surface-mounted, pendant, or recessed in the ceiling; the most popular is surface-mounted. Pendant types are used in rooms with high ceilings; recessed types, with low ceilings or where a "clean" appearance is needed.

In its simplest form the track has a service-entrance feed kit, a track section (which houses copper conductors), mounting clips, and endcaps. If the track is to be extended, an electrical connector or "joiner," T, L, X, or I, can be plugged into an end for attachment to a new section. To accommodate large numbers of luminaires, a track may have as many as three circuits, each capable of carrying 1800 W of light. (See Figure 11-20 for a typical surface-mounted track.) The luminaires of a track-light system come in a number of shapes, sizes, and colors but are designed primarily to serve two main functions: (a)

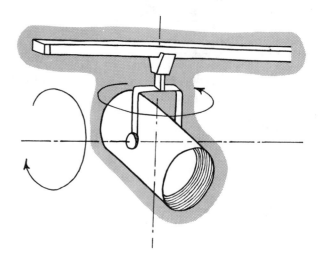

Figure 11-19. A typical track light.

accent lighting and (b) wall washing. Their use in general downlighting is not uncommon, however.

Code Compliance

A track-light system is basically a "flexible power distributing system" that does not qualify as an exclusive interior lighting source when the code specifies "permanent" lighting.

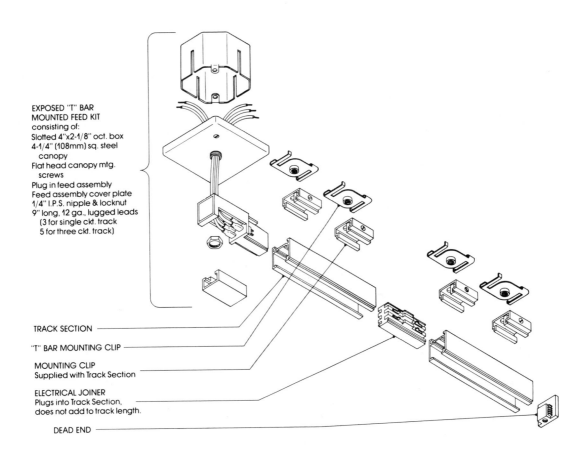

EXPOSED "T" BAR
MOUNTED FEED KIT
consisting of:
Slotted 4"x2-1/8" oct. box
4-1/4" (108mm) sq. steel
  canopy
Flat head canopy mtg.
  screws
Plug in feed assembly
Feed assembly cover plate
1/4" I.P.S. nipple & locknut
9" long, 12 ga., lugged leads
  (3 for single ckt. track
  5 for three ckt. track)

TRACK SECTION

"T" BAR MOUNTING CLIP

MOUNTING CLIP
Supplied with Track Section

ELECTRICAL JOINER
Plugs into Track Section,
does not add to track length.

DEAD END

**SURFACE MOUNTED
FEED KIT**
Matte White & Silver Gray

**SURFACE MOUNTED
"L" JOINER**
Silver Gray

**SURFACE MOUNTED
"T" JOINER**
Silver Gray

**SURFACE MOUNTED
"X" JOINER**
Silver Gray

Figure 11-20. *A typical surface-mounted track and its accessories. (Courtesy of Lightron of Cornwall.)*

Application

This equipment is available in hundreds of shapes, sizes, and colors; Figure 11-21 shows only a few. Track-mounted accent lights should be used for those locations in which mobility of luminaires is important and light is needed to be directed toward one or more objects at various angles.

Figure 11-21. Track mounted accent light (no external reflector).

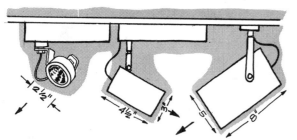

Luminaires designed for MR-16 lamps are usually compact. They should be used on applications for which a precise, customized lighting effect is needed from a conspicuous source. With accessories the beam can be elongated, intensified, or spot-isolated for a tailored appearance.

Figure 11-22. Track-mounted accent light (MR-16 lamp and accessories).

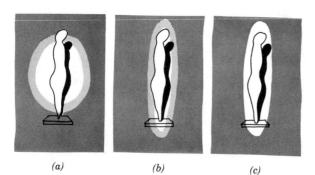

(a)   (b)   (c)

Figure 11-23. Accent light with MR-16 lamp and some accessories. (a) A narrow spot, without any accessory. Circular in shape and spill light is visible. (b) The same spot with a beam elongator. The shape is now stretched vertically; spill light is still visible. (c) The same spot with a beam elongator and an isolation spot. The spill light is captured and an elongated, sharp focus is obtained.

General Description

A majority of the luminaires is made of aluminum and a mechanism holds and allows a reflector type of lamp (R, PAR, ER, MR) to move in the desired direction. Beam distribution (narrow, medium, and wide) is solely dependent on the reflector of the lamp. A very narrow beam can be had with low-voltage lamps for which a built-in transformer is required. Some units include black grooved baffles or concentric ring louvers clipped onto the openings to reduce glare.

Remarks

Only narrow or medium beam-spread lamps should be used with a louver or baffle. Because of the enclosed configuration that leads to high heat build-up, a higher wattage lamp than that is recommended by the luminaire's manufacturer should never be used.

The aluminum housing can be of any shape, size, or color. An MR-16 lamp operates on 12 V, for which a transformer is necessary. When the transformer is mounted on the track, the luminaire can be compact. When it is enclosed inside the housing, the luminaire is the same size as a conventional track light. The light output is strictly dependent on the lamp's reflector and its accessory. There are, in general, three types of accessory: (1) an elongator (lens) that changes the normal, round light beam to an oblong pattern; (2) an intensifier that extends the reflecting surface of the lamp to capture wasted spill light; and (3) an isolation spot baffle that cuts off all illumination beyond the edge of the main beam (Figure 11-23).

With the appearance of MR lamps creative-accent lighting has reached a new dimension. The tiny tungsten-halogen filament, which operates on a low voltage, offers long life and precision in light control that has never before been possible. The accessories produce a tailored match, and the overall compact form of the system is architecturally attractive. The built-in transformer and the lamp produce continuous heat in operation and adequate ventilation in the luminaire is essential.

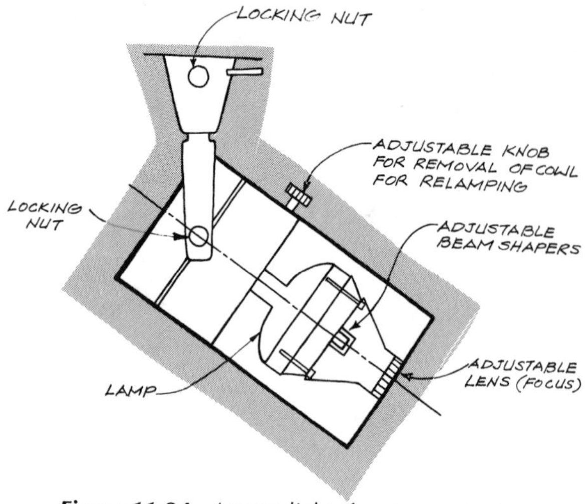

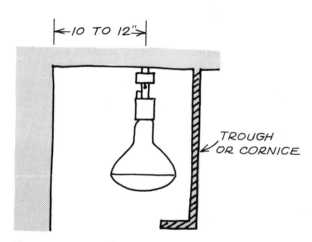

Figure 11-24. Accent light: framing projector.

Application

This luminaire should be used when a uniform, medium intensity beam is needed to meet a precise shape (e.g., round, rectangular, or oval). Some applications are paintings, murals, and art objects mounted on walls.

This wallwasher should be considered for a uniform, high-intensity wash in a room with a low (75 W) to medium (150 W) ceiling. Units can be spaced as desired on a track; for best effect they should be mounted 10 to 12 in. from the wall and spaced 12 in. apart.

Figure 11-25. Track-mounted wallwasher (grazing with R lamps).

General Description

This unit may be described as a precise optical instrument for cutting light beams to the shape and size of the vertical display. It operates a compact 100 or 150 W, T-4, clear tungsten-halogen lamp, which is located behind adjustable stainless-steel beam shapers with insulated finger grips. A tensioned, adjustable lens at the front allows the light to be focused precisely on the framework of the display. Concealed adjustable shutters provide a wide range of quadrilateral shapes. Additional sharp-edged shapes can be obtained by inserting drop-in templates into the system. For replacing the lamp the cowl (front of the housing) can be removed by unscrewing an adjustable knob.

Remarks

This luminaire provides sharp delineation of the lighted area; for the best effect it should be used with wallwashers or other accent lighting to maintain a comfortable luminance ratio between the display and wall. If used alone, it should be focused to overlap the display. Precise framing is sometimes difficult and the color of the light may not complement some paintings. In some models lamps suffer a short life because of inadequate heat dissipation design.

It is primarily a lamp holder with a mechanism at the back to be clamped on a track. It should use R type lamps only.

It is simple in form, economical, and easy to maintain. Wallwash quality is fair to good and improves with distance from the sources. A shallow grazing angle strongly emphasizes texture and also reveals surface imperfections. A trough or cornice should be used to shield the source. Spot lamps should be used for high ceilings.

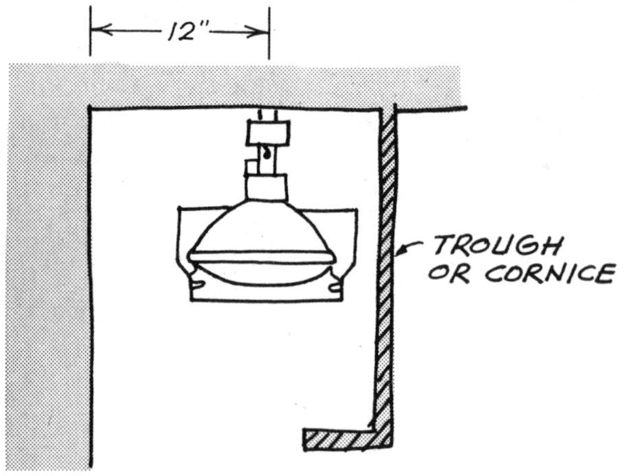

Application

This unit should be used for uniform, high-intensity wallwash for a room with a medium (150 W) to high (200 W) ceiling. For even distribution the units should be mounted as close as 12 in. to the wall and spaced 12 in. apart.

Figure 11-26. *Track-mounted wallwasher (grazing with PAR lamps).*

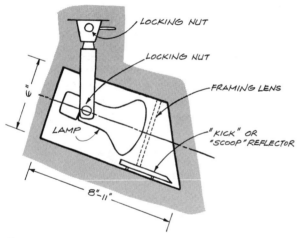

A smooth, medium intensity for low (75 W) to medium ceiling (150 W) areas is provided by this unit. It can be used successfully to erase undesirable scalloping produced by other luminaires or can be combined with a frame projector. For an even wallwash the setback distance from the wall should be a minimum of 3 ft; the spacings between units is the same as the setback distance.

Figure 11-27. *Track-mounted wallwasher (with kick reflector).*

SEMIRECESSED AND SURFACE-MOUNTED INCANDESCENT LUMINAIRES

All downlight luminaires with R, PAR, and ER lamps are in general available for semirecessed or surface-mounted arrangements. For these purposes the luminaires are enclosed inside decorative cylinders or squares (there may be other shapes) that are available in a number of different colors and finishes. Most, however, are white, black, or natural.

General Description	*Remarks*
The housing is a diecast aluminum cylinder with a serrated locking arrangement. Designed for PAR type lamps, it has a mechanism to be clamped onto a track.	Wallwash quality is good to excellent, but the smoothness does not reach up to the ceiling line. A shallow grazing angle strongly emphasizes texture and also reveals surface imperfections. To shield the source a trough or cornice is recommended.
This unit contains an embossed, anodized aluminum "kick" reflector that spreads light to upper angles for a smooth and even wall wash. The locking nuts hold the luminaires in any fixed aiming position. Some versions of this unit are also available with a spread lens in front of the lamp for a smooth light distribution.	The quality of distribution is good to very good; the walls are lighted evenly right up to the ceiling line. A spread lens provides an even smoother distribution. When used for wall wash, a matte finish is recommended to avoid reflection.

Part recessed and surface-mounted luminaires may be selected for aesthetic reasons or when the ceiling space (plenum) is too tight to accommodate a recessed luminaire. When a luminaire is mounted on a vertical plane (wall-mounted), a special bracket, which is basically an arm, connects the luminaire body to the electrical junction box on the wall.

Surface-mounted luminaires (wall or ceiling) are good alternates to recessed luminaires that cannot be used for fire-rated ceilings.

12

Fluorescent Luminaires

Regardless of type, the following is listed in relation to fluorescent luminaires:

Advantages

1. High amount of light per watt used
2. Lamps have long life
3. Wide range of lamp color rendering is possible
4. Long linear lamps cover larger areas and provide uniform and diffused light distribution even in rooms with low ceilings.

Disadvantages

1. Light output is sensitive to ambient temperatures and humidity
2. Dimming requires special ballast and is expensive

Various factors affect the performance of a fluorescent luminaire.

NUMBER OF LAMPS AND THEIR RELATIVE LOCATIONS

A bare lamp produces maximum efficiency because its light output is virtually unobstructed except where the metallic channel holds the lamp. As the number of lamps increases more light is trapped between them and between the lamps and the channel and efficiency decreases. When lamps are placed inside the housing for light-direction control, the efficiency decreases even more because of an additional light trap and heat build-up. As a general rule, regardless of its type, the efficiency of a fluorescent luminaire decreases as the number of lamps is increased and their relative locations become closer (see Figure 12-1).

LUMINAIRE HOUSING

Except for strip luminaires (in which lamps are exposed and attached to the channel through sockets), all fluorescent luminaires contain housings that serve two functions: to protect the lamps and ballast(s) from external abuse and to direct the light to useful areas. Most luminaires used today are made with 22-gauge (0.0229-in.) cold-rolled steel (CRS), although a 20-gauge (0.0359-in.) is not uncommon. The door frame, usually the weaker part of a fluorescent luminaire, is designed to hold a plastic lens. When a nonstandard lens like a glass model or louver grid is specified, it should be made certain that the luminaire is capable of handling the additional weight.

In vibrating environments, in which the lamp may

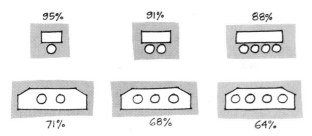

Figure 12-1. *Light output and the luminaire's efficiency decrease with the increase of number of lamps, due to heat build-up and light trap.*

come loose from lampholders, luminaires with spring-loaded lampholders are preferred. A full urethane foam gasket around the luminaire door prevents light leakage and reduces vibration.

REFLECTOR AND FINISHES

Except for the doors, virtually all the remaining features in the interior of a house are reflectors. The most common reflecting material used in fluorescent luminaires is white enamel paint, dried in air or baked for durability. The reflecting surface is the main element that increases the luminaire's efficiency and its value should be as high as possible. On the average, a 1% rise in painted reflectance will result in a 0.9% rise in CU values and efficiency. Premium-grade luminaires are coated with synthetic enamel of high reflectance that is baked at a high temperature (350°F) onto physically and chemically prepared surfaces .The result is a tough finish that protects the reflecting surface from scratches and other damage.

Aluminum reflectors are anodized or painted, and some manufacturers use lacquer or plastic coatings to protect the anodized surface.

APPEARANCE AND COST

The appearance of a luminaire is important because it is also a decorative object. This is especially true with surface-mounted or pendant luminaires whose exterior surfaces (except for the top) are visible from all directions. Most nonrecessed luminaires are usually available in a wide variety of designs and finishes; a selection should be made for reasons of aesthetics as well as for durability and maintainability.

Although most owners are more concerned with the initial cost of luminaires, the net savings, if any, cannot be judged until the related maintenance costs have been evaluated. Popular luminaires are manufactured by a number of companies at prices that are indicative of their quality. Although the exterior appearance may be the same, a cheap luminaire often has a thinner body and lens, inferior quality ballast, lower surface reflectance, exposed or uncovered ballast wiring, and an overall weaker structure—all of which is in addition to unsatisfactory photometrics.

LENS

To control its light a fluorescent luminaire can have an open bottom or be equipped with a lens or louver. The open-bottom luminaire is strictly dependent on its reflector for light distribution. Other units rely on the combined effect of reflector and lens or louver.

The main purpose of the lens is to hide the lamps from direct vision by spreading its intensity uniformly over the bottom area and controlling the light output in a predetermined manner. In general, there are two different types of lens: the diffusers and the refractors. Diffusers can be made of plastic or glass and are used when brightness control is required but there is no need for precise photometric control. Light emits in all directions and the efficiency is low.

Diffusers known as "etched", "frosted", or "sandblasted" usually offer poor diffusion and lamp shielding (high transmission of light). Opal glass diffusers offer excellent diffusion and shield lamps uniformly with high absorbtion. Plastic diffusers, too, offer excellent diffusion and are sometimes more desirable than glass because of their lighter weight and lower cost.

The main purpose of a reflector is to intercept rays that arrive from all directions and to redirect them from the glare zone to more useful areas. A variety of refractor lenses designed to serve specific purposes is discussed elsewhere in this chapter.

LOUVERS

Louvers, which are physical barriers to light output in the glare zone, allow light to move freely downward. This characteristic provides high visual comfort (VCP) but may cut light output substantially, thus reducing overall efficiency. Louvers vary substantially in size, shape, and color. The most common shapes of metal or plastic are circular, rectangular, and square. As a general rule, the smaller the size and the darker the color, the lower the efficiency. Only well engineered louvers are capable of producing high VCP with moderately high efficiency. Louvered luminaires are also discussed later in this chapter.

BALLASTS AND LAMPS

The main purpose of a ballast is to control the flow of current inside the lamp. Heat produced by the ballast has a considerable impact on its own life as well as on the lamp's light output; the designer should investigate the many different options available and devise a combination of the products most suitable for the application. The reader is advised to refer to Chapter 4 in which ballasts and lamps are already discussed.

AIR-HANDLING LUMINAIRES

An improvement in light output added to possible energy savings can be accomplished by air-handling luminaires that generally come in three different types: heat removal, supply, and supply-return. The main idea is to integrate the air-handling system of the space through the luminaires. Heat removal luminaires have air-intake openings around the door frame that allow the return-air of the space to enter the lamp cavity and remove the trapped heat through slots at the top (see Figure 12-2a). The heat-removal

slots may be provided with adjustable dampers to control the amount of air. The supply types provide air in the space with the help of an air-supply boot installed at the top of the luminaire (Figure 12-2b). A flexible duct carries air into the boot, which in turn discharges through the supply slots around the door frame, by-passing the lamp cavity. A supply-return luminaire is a combination of the two systems.

Heat-removal luminaires often offer better efficiency than their static counterparts because a constant removal of heat from the lamp cavity lowers the bulb's operating temperature closer to the desired 100°F.

RECESSED FLUORESCENT LUMINAIRES

Fluorescent luminaires come mainly in rectangular form, although circular or other shapes are also available. The smaller circular luminaires use circular lamps of matching diameter. The larger circular or other nonrectangular luminaires have linear fluorescent lamps all of the same or varying sizes.

More than 90% of the fluorescent luminaires in use today are in rectangular or square form and their popularity is attributed mainly to the fact that the light from linear lamps is best controlled when they are placed in a rectangular (or square) housing (see Figures 12-3 through 12-7).

SELECTION BY LIGHT CONTROLLER

A variety of lenses and louvers is designed to serve a specific purpose (Figures 12-8 through 12-18). Most can be used in all types of housing (described earlier) and some are designed to operate with luminaries in special lamp locations.

In general two processes are used to form plastic lenses: extrusion embossing (extruded) and injection molding. In the extrusion-embossing process plastic is melted in the extruder and emerges in sheet form. It is then passed through rollers that emboss the plastic with the prismatic design. The formed product is then cooled to room temperature and cut to the dimensions of the luminaires.

Formed plastic has a tendency to deform during the process of cooling unless precautions are taken; extrusion embossing process sometimes becomes a victim of this. The prisms of a poorly manufactured lens may "round -off" at the corners and perform unsatisfactorily.

In the injection molding process plastic is melted

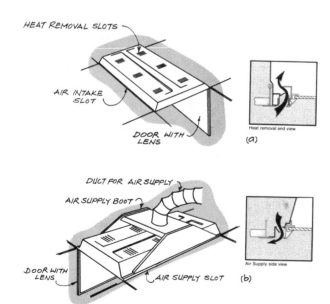

Figure 12-2. Air handling luminaires: (a) a typical heat-removal troffer; (b) a typical air-supply troffer.

in the machine and the molten product is injected into a closed mold of the lens design under extremely high pressure. This forces the molten plastic to reach every fine detail of the mold. The lens is then allowed to cool gradually while still under high pressure. This prevents the prismatic plastic from deforming.

Luminaire	Application	Remarks
2 × 4 ft *Figure 12-3.*	This luminaire can be used for almost all rooms with low-to-high ceilings, including lobbies, offices, and conference rooms.	Available with 2, 3, 4, or 6 lamps; units with four lamps, followed by three lamps, are the most common and are normally equipped with 2 two-lamp ballasts. The efficiency of the luminaire decreases as the number of lamps increases.
1 × 4 ft *Figure 12-4.*	This luminaire is mainly suitable for areas that are long and narrow like corridors, hallways, and aisles.	Available with 2 or 3 lamps; vertically stacked lamps offered by some manufacturers, provide finely defined "batwing" distribution.
2 × 2 ft *Figure 12-5.*	This luminaire is mainly suitable for smaller rooms, corridors, and hallways or in "problem" areas with a 2 × 4 ft grid ceiling in which only half the space is available.	Available with 2, 3, 4, or 6 F20 lamps or 2, 3 F40 U lamps; U-shaped rapid-start lamps outperform the F20 (2 ft long) lamps by providing more light, better longevity, and higher power factor.
3 × 3 ft *Figure 12-6.*	This luminaire is available for nongrid ceilings only and is suitable mainly for medium-to-small rooms and in corridors and hallways.	Available with 4 or 6 lamps (rapid-start, 36 in. long).
4 × 4 ft *Figure 12-7.*	This luminaire should be used only in rooms with medium to high ceilings.	Available with 4, 6, 8, or 12 lamps; the efficiency of the luminaire is drastically reduced with the increment in the number of lamps.

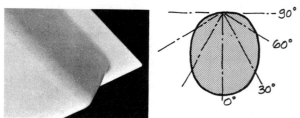

Figure 12-8. *Opalescent diffuser*

Commonly known as the opal lens, the opalescent diffuser is made of plastic or glass. Light is totally diffused and scattered in all directions. It is suitable for areas in which directional control of light is not important; such as, in vestibules, lounges, cafeterias, corridors, hallways, and restrooms. Visual comfort and efficiency are quite low. These diffusers should not be used in offices or drafting rooms in which a high level of glare-free lighting is desirable.

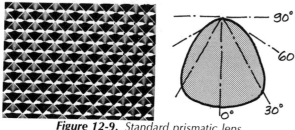

Figure 12-9. *Standard prismatic lens*

Standard prismatic lens represents the most popular lens in the lighting industry. It can be made of polystyrene or acrylic plastic. Acrylic plastic is slightly more expensive than the polystyrene, but its superior performance in terms of light output, longevity, and light stability (polystyrene turns yellow within five years) justifies the cost difference. These lenses are designed to direct the light at lower angles (0 to 30°). Available at 0.09 to 0.125 in., these lenses are suitable for all rooms with medium to low ceilings, from general to offices in which a pool of light is required. A thinner lens provides higher efficiency, but that should not be the only reason for its selection. A thin lens has a tendency to sag at the middle; it also makes the lamps visible from certain angles and reduces VCP.

A high impact acrylic lens has approximately 10 times the impact strength of the standard acrylic prismatic lens and its light stability duration is about the same (10 to 15 years). The cost is almost twice as high.

Extra strength makes it suitable for indoor games like racquet ball, handball, and softball and for applications in schools, gymnasiums, correctional institutions, or any other places in which breakage is highly probable and protection is a necessity.

Polycarbonates are 30 times stronger than standard acrylic lenses, but their light transmission efficiency (hence luminaire efficiency) is substantially lower (85% as opposed to 92%). Light stability duration is approximately three to four years, after which the light output is drastically reduced (turns yellow) and the material becomes brittle.

Polycarbonates should be considered in vandal-prone and other interior areas in which the luminaires may be subject to abuse.

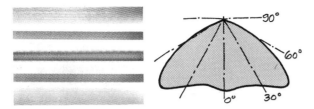

Figure 12-10. *KSH 3E #1*

These lenses are designed primarily for luminaires with three lamps to provide even lighting on horizontal surfaces. They consist of four different types of lens, each of which serves a specific function. For proper operation the lamps must match the lens pattern in which each lamp is directly above the three straited patterns. If the two side lamps are switched separately from the one in the middle, three levels of evenly distributed horizontal lighting ($\frac{1}{3}$, $\frac{2}{3}$, 1) can be created. The best results are obtained if the luminaires are installed in a continuous row or in a checkered pattern. High SC (1.8) place the luminaires farther apart than a standard prismatic lens (SC = 1.3). With a high amount of light in the upper zones (above 45°) these lenses are capable of producing good contrast on task at a sacrifice of visual comfort (VCP). The multiprismatic pattern of the lens lends a distinct straited appearance from some angles that may cause unfavorable aesthetics.

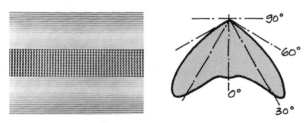

Figure 12-11. *KSH 3E #2*

Designed to work with 1 × 4 ft or narrower luminaires, this one-lamp version of the KSH 3E lens provides a batwing-like candlepower distribution. The greatest amount of light emerges through the 30° to 60° zone, much smaller amount between 0° to 30° and almost none above 60°. This allows good task contrast and little glare at normally viewing angles. Excellent for use in coffer ceilings, which is discussed in a later part of this chapter.

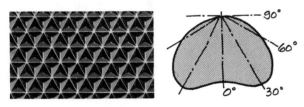

Figure 12-12. *Extruded clear prismatic*

This lens has a smaller prismatic pattern on the top and a flat surface on the bottom. The result is the production of radial batwing distribution with slightly higher upper-angle brightness and a high SC. The VCP in particular is low, because no prisms appear on the bottom. To cut the lens brightness and increase VCP it is sometimes recommended for use with an overlay diffuser. This improves VCP and prevents the lens from collecting dirt but it reduces luminaire efficiency substantially. The main advantage is that, unlike the multiprismatic lens, the extruded prismatic lens is independent of the requirements of the number of lamps or their locations; its appearance is uniform from all angles, with or without the overlay, and good task contrast is produced.

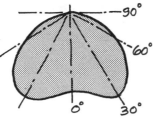

This grid has a recess pattern on the top (female) and a male prism on the bottom. It, too, produces a radial batwing light distribution and offers a high SC. The lens, which is about 0.24-in. thick, possesses strength and good light control but at a loss of efficiency. An overlay (0.04-in.) diffuser is sometimes recommended to improve VCP, but this reduces luminaire efficiency to a substantially low level.

Figure 12-13. Injection molded refractive grid

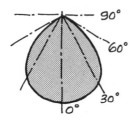

This refractor has a round array of hemispherical refractive prisms, concave at the top and matching convex-shaped at the bottom. The result is a low brightness downlight with lamps that are visible only when observed directly from the bottom. Use of an overlay obscures surface brightness at a loss of approximately 20% of the light output.

Figure 12-14. Hemispherical refractors

A polarized lens consists of multilayers of polarizing materials that absorbs all vibrations of light except those in the vertical plane. This transmits a high degree of polarized light by reflection and refraction and results in improved visibility, truer color rendering of objects, and reduced brightness.

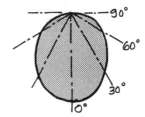

These louvers are made of ½ × ½ × ½ in. translucent polystyrene cubes that provide 45° of lamp shield. Light emits primarily downward; SC is low. The net result is a small amount of downlight (because of poor efficiency), closer spacings, and lower visual comfort. An additional problem is that the small cubes are hard to clean.

Figure 12-15. Egg-crate louvers

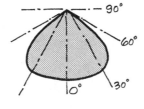

Figure 12-16. *Specular egg-crate louvers*

These louvers are a modified version of the egg-crate in that the vertical fins are parabolic and have a clear or colored specular aluminum finish (film). Light output is still primarily downward, efficiency is low, but because of the finish and shape there is a slight improvement in spacing criteria and significant improvement in glare control.

These louvers, as well, are hard to clean. In addition, the film peels when the unprotected specular cells are soiled and the louvers begin to show light passing through.

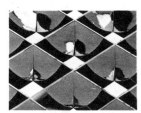
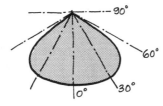

Figure 12-17. *Parabolic louvers (small)*

These louvers are made of $1\frac{1}{2} \times 1\frac{1}{2} \times 1$ in. parabolic reflector cells of injection-molded acrylic with a specular finish of vacuum-deposited aluminum, protected by baked acrylic lacquer of palest gold or silver tint, all of which provide an extremely low surface brightness, much improved spacing criteria, and slightly better efficiency. These louvers must be cleaned after installation, since they show finger prints.

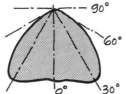

Figure 12-18. *Parabolic louvers (medium to large)*

These large-cell parabolic louvers (typically 8 in. square and 2 to 6 in. deep) have a specular or satin finish. Precisely located to match lamp locations, they produce widely distributing light, low apparent brightness, and moderate efficiency. The metallic cells avoid the electrostatic accumulations of dirt that are typical of plastic louvers and the large sizes are easier to clean. As a general rule, light distribution patterns improve with deep, precisely designed louvers. One disadvantage is that these units tend to produce multishadows.

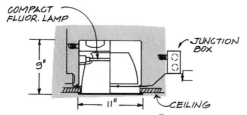

Figure 12-19. Compact fluorescent.

This unit is ideally suited to areas in which a great deal of soft light is required from low-glare luminaires and energy conservation is of special interest. It can be used in corridors, hallways, lobbies, and other spaces in which light is constantly needed and the ambient temperature does not drop below 60°F.

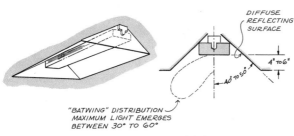

Figure 12-20. Coffered lighting.

Coffered lighting is suitable for all applications in which quality lighting with high visual comfort, and low energy use are required; for example, schools, offices, drafting rooms, libraries etc.

MOUNTING SYSTEMS OF RECESSED LUMINAIRES

Recessed fluorescent luminaires are mounted in a number of ways; the technique depends on the ceiling. In general, there are two types of ceiling; wet and dry construction. Whereas wet construction utilizes only plaster, dry construction is achieved with a variety of materials such as hardboard, Sheetrock, dry plaster, gypsum boards, and the many forms of tile that are suspended mechanically. The National Electrical Manufacturers Association (NEMA) classifies hung ceilings into five categories (see Figure 12-21):

Type F (flange)	Used for wet and dry ceiling construction. A flange luminaire has a projected trim around its perimeter that conceals any irregularity or gap between it and the ceiling. This luminaire makes use of a spline as support and an adjustable screw for proper fitting.
Type G (grid)	This grid ceiling features an exposed inverted T-system to support "lay-in" luminaires.

General Description	*Remarks*
The housing is made of diecast aluminum and the reflector is one-piece Alzak specular aluminum. Two lamps (9 or 13 W each) are critically located to provide a 45° cutoff angle. The trim in the ring is a matte white enamel on metal or polycarbonate. The reflector is available in a clear or gold finish.	Perhaps the greatest advantage displayed by this unit is its compactness. It houses two compact lamps that offer high efficiencies (as high as 69 lm/W) and long life (10,000 h). Color rendition is excellent. In comparison to an incandescent of the same light output, it can reduce energy consumption by as much as 70% and last up to 13 times longer. This compact fluorescent is available in 120 and 277 V. It is suitable mainly for indoor use. The minimum starting temperature is approximately 25°F, and light output is drastically reduced in low temperatures.
The luminaire is a narrow profile, wraparound with a specially designed acrylic lens to produce batwing light distribution. It is available for one or two lamps and is designed to operate in a coffered, or inverted V-shape ceiling. A coffered ceiling is usually custom-made and can be expensive. Some manufacturers offer an economical model that can be installed in a conventional inverted Tee-grid ceiling. Tiles are used for the inclined reflecting surface.	The main advantage of the coffered ceiling is that quality lighting with high visual comfort is available in an aesthetically pleasing lighting system. The luminaires can be installed far apart because the SC is high; but that should not be the only reason for their location. For best results the following should be observed (Figure 12-20): (1) The cove angle should be between 40 and 50°; (2) the luminaire is concealed as deeply as possible (typically 4 to 6 in. from ceiling line to luminaire bottom); (3) a minimum number of lamps per luminaire allowing an increased quantity of coves; and (4) a diffuse, reflecting surface of the cove should preferably match the rest of the ceiling. The disadvantages in a coffer system are (1) there is no flexibility in luminaire relocation; (2) visual comfort lengthwise is not so good as it is widthwise (for lamps 4 ft. long); and (3) a coffered ceiling can be expensive.

	It is hung from the ceiling by wires.	ports the luminaire. Like types M and F, it adopts an adjustable screw mechanism for fine tuning luminaire positioning.
Type H (hook)	In this system the luminaires are suspended directly from the structure which also supports the ceiling.	
Type M (metal pan)	In this system T-bars are used on a metal pan ceiling, which also supports the luminaire. Fine tuning to position the luminaire is done with an adjustable screw.	
Type S (spline)	Z-spline or concealed Z sup-	

SPECIAL WIRING METHODS FOR MOBILITY

To cut installation costs and time and to provide mobility of lighting-fixture relocation industry has pro-

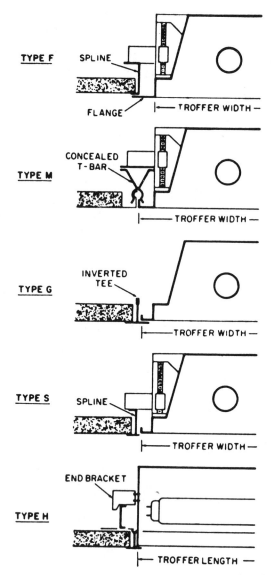

Figure 12-21. *Suspended ceilings. (Courtesy of NEMA, Publication No. LE1-1963.)*

vided two major above-ceiling, flexible power distribution systems. A number of manufacturers offer these products with some modifications, but their basic principles of operation are the same as we describe.

Flexible Power Distribution System With Rigid Metal Raceways

Rigid metal raceways with prewired outlets (see Figure 12-22) are installed in the ceiling space above the suspended ceiling. The outlets are energized by connecting them to a panel board which is similar to

feeding a wall-mounted receptacle (plug mold) strip. The metal raceway can have one or more circuits and two separate voltages (120 or 277 V) for simultaneous operation of lighting and receptacles. They may also have separate chambers for telephone or communication wiring which are usually connected to tele-power poles. Flexible metallic conduits with a plug at one end are used to energize luminaires or receptacles.

This system has some disadvantages: The rigid raceways must be placed within reach of the luminaires that form a grid system in the ceiling space; only one luminaire can be connected to an outlet and the cost tends to be high.

Flexible Power Distribution System With Flexible Metal Raceways

This system offers more flexibility than the preceding system in that the luminaires are connected by flexible metallic conduits and no rigid metal raceways are installed in the ceiling. It has a distribution box located in the ceiling space (see Figure 12-23), which is fed from the panel board by a conventional hard-conduit wiring system. Power is extended from the distribution to the switches and then connected to the luminaires, all with a flexible metallic conduit system with plugs at the end. The luminaires are specially equipped with a plug-in system to receive power (in) and extend (out) to other luminaires. Except for the first, all other luminaires receive power from adjacent luminaires. This system, like the preceding one, can carry more than one circuit in the same raceway.

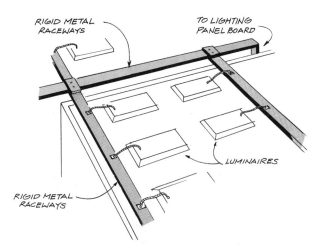

Figure 12-22. *A flexible power distribution system with rigid metal raceways.*

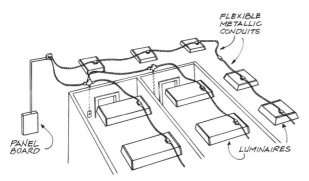

Figure 12-23. *A flexible power distribution system with flexible metal raceways.*

The main disadvantage in this system is the temptation to connect to the nearest luminaire for power to feed the newly added luminaires. This may overload the circuits. Also, unlike the preceding system, each voltage (120 or 277 V) must have its own raceway.

SURFACE-MOUNTED LUMINAIRES

Most surface-mounted fluorescent luminaires are identical to recessed luminaires except that the sides may be modified for decorative purposes. However, no matter what finish is selected, a surface-mounted luminaire functions as a direct lighting source (light emitting only from the bottom) unless it is a wraparound which also emits light from the sides.

Surface-mounted luminaires are used when access is unavailable above the suspended ceiling and when the ceiling is nonpenetrable or fire-rated. The wiring can be exposed or concealed above the ceiling, depending on the type of application. In general, wiring for a surface-mounted luminaire system is much cheaper than for the recessed types. Following is a description of the utilitarian luminaires that are different from those discussed earlier.

Strip or channel

Available for one to four lamps of various lengths, strip or channel luminaires (Figure 12-24) are the most economical in areas in which a high amount of light is required and aesthetics is not important, as in storage rooms, warehouses, and closets.

These luminaires can also produce aesthetic effects like indirect lighting in coves, cornices, and above drap-

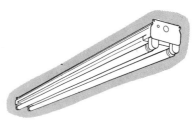

Figure 12-24.

eries, where they are wall-mounted in series behind a decorative, opaque plate. The result is a glare-free, indirect wall light throughout its length except for the areas in which the ends meet (shadow).

Staggered strips

Shadows are minimized with the help of staggered strips (Figure 12-25). Lamps are staggered so that light from at least one lamp is always available at each joint.

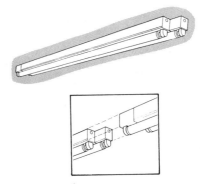

Figure 12-25.

Industrial fluorescent

This strip light (Figure 12-26) with reflectors redirects all high-angle lights toward useful zones. Some reflectors have slots to provide a small amount of uplight. Industrial fluorescents should be considered when abundant downlight and a sharp cutoff at vertical illumination are desirable.

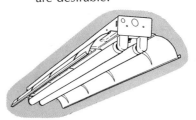

Figure 12-26.

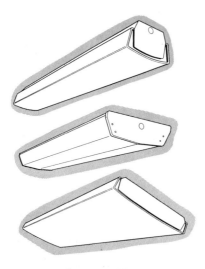

Figure 12-28.

Special wraparound   This wraparound (Figure 12-28) is enclosed and gasketed and is suitable for use in damp and wet locations.

Figure 12-27.

PENDANT-MOUNTED LUMINAIRES

Wraparound   A wraparound luminaire (Figure 12-27) should be considered when horizontal and vertical illumination from aesthetically pleasing, moderately bright, area-type sources is required. The narrow profile is appropriate to long and narrow areas such as corridors, stairwells, hallways, and in between aisles.

These are basically surface-mounted luminaires, suspended from the ceiling by a "stem" or chain and should be considered for rooms in which the ceiling is high and/or slanted and light is required in selected areas. The stem is a narrow decorated pipe that carries the conductors to the luminaire. A pendant-mounted luminaire can be direct, indirect, semidirect, semiindirect, or direct-indirect. The stem is connected through a swivel at the ceiling to hold the luminaire perpendicular to the floor.

13

High-Intensity Discharge Luminaires

Mercury vapor, metal halide and high-pressure sodium are the high-intensity discharge (HID) sources. Regardless of type, all HID luminaires have the following advantages:

1. Substantially more light per watt than the incandescents and fluorescents is produced; mercury vapors whose light output is better than the incandescents are the exception.

2. All have a longer life than incandescents and in many cases even longer than fluorescents.

3. Light distribution control is much easier than that of the fluorescents because of their compact form.

4. Operating costs are lower because of their excellent efficacy.

5. Unlike fluorescents, HID luminaires are not affected by ambient temperature or humidity variation.

The principal disadvantages are the following:

1. The initial cost (luminaire) is much higher

2. The lamps can be more expensive, thus affecting the cost of relamping.

3. Like fluorescents, HIDs need ballasts, which can be noisy and expensive to maintain.

4. The lamps may take 18 min or more to come to full brightness.

5. Some lamps may shatter during operation, radiating ultraviolet rays that may be harmful for body.

6. HIDs are suitable mainly for medium-to-high ceiling areas.

HID luminaires were designed to be used outdoors and in industrial areas, but with the variety of color corrections now possible they can be used effectively indoors as well. Extensive coverage of HID sources is provided in Chapter Four: here we will review the color aspects from the standpoint of the user.

MERCURY VAPOR LAMPS

The clear lamps are deficient in red and preponderant in blue and green, which may result in marked distortion of object and color. Phosphor-coated lamps improve color, but because no standardization has been established among lamp manufacturers, descriptive names such as Deluxe white, Warm deluxe white, and Beauty Lite have been given to identify the color rendition produced by different types of phosphor. For design purposes the following is a general comparison of products:

Deluxe white (Brite White Deluxe): Apparent color temperature, 3700 to 4000K; rendition is similar to cool white fluorescents.

Beauty Lite: Apparent color temperature, 4000K; rendition provides a moderately cool atmosphere and more pleasing skin tones at no light loss over deluxe white. These colors may be used in corridors, lobbies, stores, shopping malls, banks, supermarkets, and terminals.

Warm deluxe white (warm white deluxe): Apparent color temperature, 3300 to 3600K; provides a warmer atmosphere than standard deluxe white

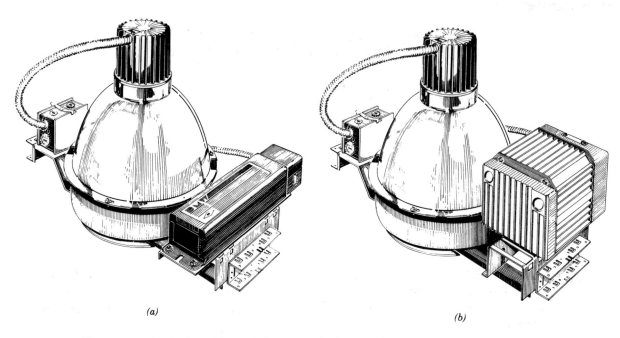

Figure 13-1. *Luminaire with, (a) industry standard encased type (FE) HID ballast, and (b) "Silent-Pak" ballast. (Courtesy of Prescolite.)*

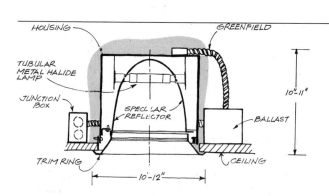

Figure 13-2. *Recessed downlight with compact metal halide.*

Application

This luminaire should be considered for high illumination in a room with a medium (75 W) to high (150 W) ceiling.

with some reduction in light output. It is excellent for the same areas as deluxe white and others when skin tone is important.

Style-Tone: Apparent color temperature 3000 to 3200K; color rendition is warm and closest to the incandescents (2850K). It produces less light than deluxe white and is excellent in areas in which warm tones are preferred.

METAL HALIDE LAMPS

Coated metal halide lamps provides a slightly warmer diffused light than clear lamps at apparent color temperatures that vary from 3400 to 3900K. With 50% more light output than the deluxe white mercury vapors, the halides are suitable in all areas with medium-to-high ceilings. Use of clear lamps in place of coated lamps may produce a shadow ring on the floor for some luminaires.

HIGH-PRESSURE SODIUM LAMPS

Among the three, high-pressure sodium lamps produce maximum light for the same wattage but poorer color rendition. Described as ''golden-white,'' it emits a pinkish orange light and can be used in some special indoor areas in which the background is compatible with the color rendition.

BALLAST NOISE

Ballast noise is generated by the ac magnetic flux collapsing on the core of the transformer. To minimize this sound the industry standard ballast (FE) is encased in a metal housing with core and coil and other circuit components potted together in a class A insulation (105°C) compound. These are offered with a noise rating of A to indicate a low noise level.

Some manufacturers provide exceptionally quiet ballasts by encasing the core, coil, and circuitry in an extruded aluminum housing and potting them in a thermally conductive class F (155°C) emulation material (see Figure 13-1). They, too, carry a sound rating of A and are claimed to have a quiet performance that lasts much longer than the standard FE type of ballasts.

Quiet ballasts are important in areas like libraries or recording studios, but for complete silence they can be mounted separately in an adjacent ventilated room.

General Description	*Remarks*
The exterior of this downlight is a 0.20-gauge steel housing that accommodates a clear, specular aluminum reflector. The lamp is a tubular, compact metal halide source with recessed, press-in, double bases. Some manufacturers provide an automatic power cutoff mechanism in the lens assembly that permits safe lamp changing. The luminaire has a spread distribution and its regressed cone and trim are satin white.	The main advantages of this downlight are high efficiency, excellent color rendering (CRI index 81 to 86), long life, and compact form. It may be used in stores, restaurants, banks, and merchandising areas for general lighting. One disadvantage is its cost; a 175-W compact lamp costs three times as much as an equivalent E or BT lamp.

Application

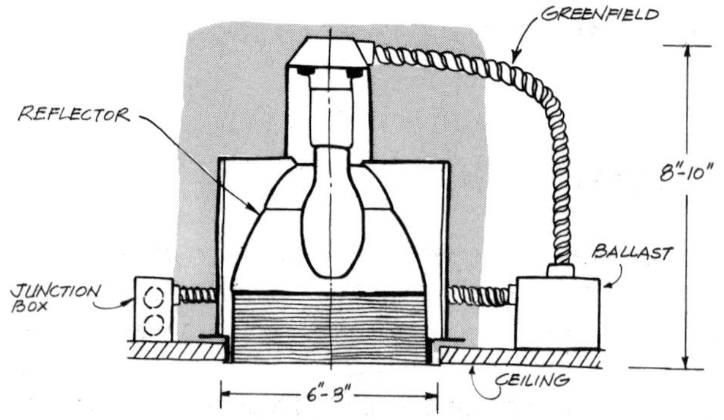

This downlight is designed for mercury-vapor and high-pressure sodium lamps in a room with a medium-height ceiling (70 W, 100 W).

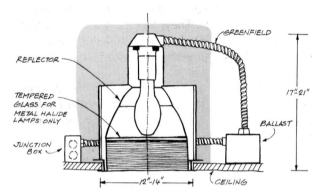

Figure 13-3. Open reflector downlight.

This downlight is a larger version of the preceding type except that it also utilizes metal halide lamps. It should be considered for a room with a medium (175 W) to high (250 W) ceiling.

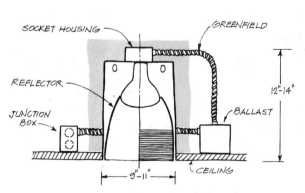

Figure 13-4. Open reflector downlight.

This luminaire uses a reflector-type (R) mercury-vapor lamp and should be used in a low (100 W) to medium (175 W) high ceiling area only. With a specular reflector, light is widespread; with a baffle it is medium to narrow spread.

Figure 13-5. Reflector downlight (R lamp).

General Description	*Remarks*
Light distribution is due to a specular aluminum reflector with a clear standard finish or in other optional colors like gold, bronze, or black. Some manufacturers provide field-removable reflectors. A black milligroove baffle is another option that cuts down the glare in a normal viewing angle. The trim is painted white enamel.	This downlight has high-efficiency and widespread distribution on vertical surfaces; relamping is easily done from below. Peak efficiency occurs with a clear reflector, but a reduction follows with color: gold = 0.90, bronze = 0.80, black = 0.70, and baffle = 0.50.
This larger version is identical to those mentioned earlier except that for metal halide lamps (250 W) a protective tempered glass is placed above the milligroove baffle to comply with the lamp manufacturer's safety precautions.	The light output is further reduced by 10% because of the protective glass.
The light distribution is due to the lamp's built-in reflector and the specular aluminum parabolic reflector that gathers spill light from the side and reflects to useful zones for a wide spread. With a multigroove baffle, light is partly absorbed and the distribution is narrower. A regressed lamp has a 45° shielding.	One advantage is that each time the lamp is replaced its main reflector, which is a part of it, is replaced automatically. A baffle unit should be considered for glare control and may also be used in areas of high dirt accumulation. With the baffle luminaire efficiency is reduced by approximately 20%.

Application

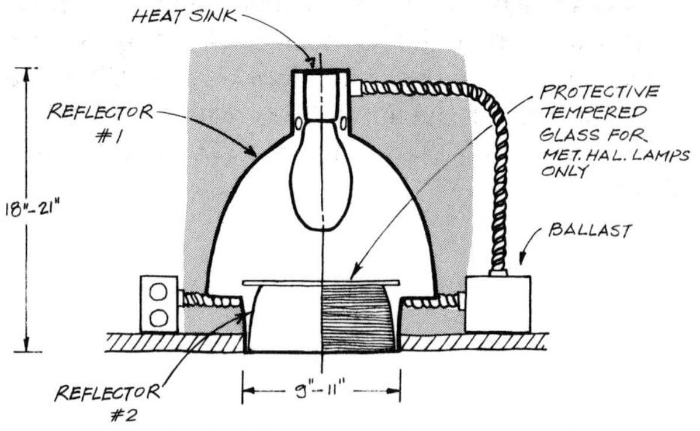

This luminaire is suitable for mercury vapor, metal halide, and high-pressure sodium lamps. It may be considered for a concentrated to medium distribution of light with little glare for a room with a low (70 W, 100 W), medium (150 W, 175 W), or high (250 W) ceiling.

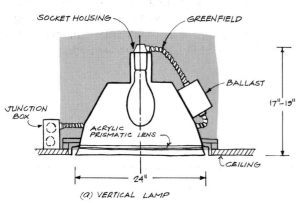

Figure 13-6. Ellipsoidal reflector downlight.

This downlight is suitable for low (70 W, 100 W) to medium (175 W, 250 W) ceiling heights when humidity, corrosion, and environmental dirt are a problem and a wide distribution of light is required. It can use mercury vapor, metal halide, or high-pressure sodium lamps.

The fresnel lens should be considered for cutting glare at high angles and drop opal lens, for general diffuse light (when glare is not a concern). Polycarbonate lens should be used for rough service areas.

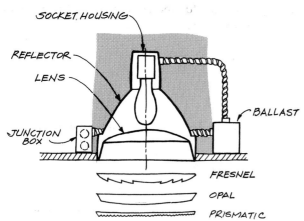

Figure 13-7. Downlight with lens.

This downlight is used primarily with mercury vapors or metal halides to produce medium to widespread light from a suspended grid (2 × 2 ft) or from a flat ceiling; 175 to 250 W lamps are suitable for medium-high (10 to 14 ft) and 400 W for high (14 to 18 ft) ceiling areas.

It can be used in shops, supermarkets, atriums, halls, gymnasiums, and handball and squash courts where abundant general lighting is required. In gym-

Figure 13-8. Regressed lens downlight.

General Description	*Remarks*
There are two reflectors. The upper one, which is clear, specular, and mushroomshaped, reflects light downward. The lower reflector redirects spill lights to useful zones. The lower reflector can be clear, gold, bronze, or gray; it may also be equipped with a multigrooved black baffle. A protective tempered glass must be used for metal halide lamps up to 250 W.	Light is obtained from inconspicuous openings in the ceiling, but because of the multireflections and light traps inside the luminaire their efficiency is low (35 to 50%). Use of a colored reflector, baffle, and tempered glass lowers it even more. It also costs twice as much as open reflector downlights.
The lens is usually a deeply regressed, shielding light source. The reflector is a one-piece specular (or semispecular), anodized aluminum that reflects the light downward to be refracted or diffused by the lens. The regressed steps up to the lens are usually black to give a floating effect. The trim is painted white enamel.	This lens also acts to protect from heat and lamp shatter, but unless manufactured with precision it may give access to insects and dirt. The efficiency of the fresnel lens is moderate (50 to 60%), but it may be substantially lower (25 to 35%) in an opal diffuser.
The housing is aluminum, the inside of which is a baked, white, semigloss enamel reflector of high reflectance. The lens is a acrylic prismatic 0.125 in. thick. The trim frame is matte white, the lens frame, white or black.	This downlight can be installed to blend with a 2 × 2 ft fluorescent troffer in appearance and color rendition. The higher wattage luminaires (400 W) tend to be very bright and should be considered for high-ceiling areas only. For metal halide lamps no separate lamp guard is necessary because the lens serves the purpose.

Application

nasiums or on handball courts the lens should be high-impact acrylic, fastened securely to the frame. In libraries or music rooms, where noise is a concern, ballasts should be the low-noise type, or remote-mounted.

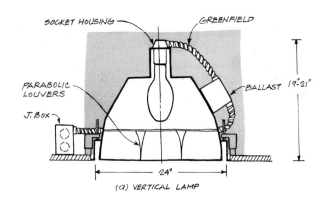

(b) HORIZONTAL LAMP

Figure 13-8. (Continued)

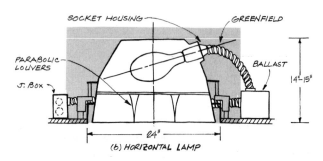

(a) VERTICAL LAMP

This downlight is also designed to work with mercury vapor or metal halide lamps and is suitable for medium-to-high-ceiling areas with lamps that vary from 175 to 400 W. The deep parabolic louvers provide low brightness and excellent glare control.

It is used in shops, supermarkets, atriums, halls, and libraries for 2 × 2 ft grid suspended or gypboard ceilings.

(b) HORIZONTAL LAMP

Figure 13-9. Parabolic, louvered downlight.

General Description	*Remarks*
	The horizontal lamp types are suitable for applications in which ceiling space is tight, but because of the inclined operating position of the lamp the light output is significantly reduced and a change in color, lamp life, and striking time is possible.
This downlight is identical to the unit described for the preceding luminaire except that in lieu of the lens deep, parabolic louver cells of semispecular aluminum are used.	Deep parabolic louvers provide an extra wide light distribution with low apparent brightness. It can be matched in appearance with fluorescent troffers with similar louvers and lamp colors. Because of the principle involved (physical barrier to light output), the efficiency of this luminaire is lower (55 to 60%) than those with lenses (70 to 77%). The horizontal-lamp types need less mounting space, but light output is significantly lower. Horizontal operation of lamps may change lamp color, life, and striking time. To avoid distortion of reflector surface the lateral movement of the cells should be prevented by securing the intersection joints.

Application

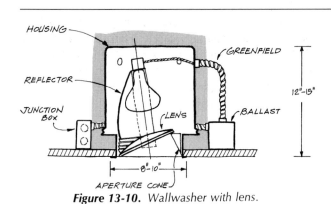

Figure 13-10. *Wallwasher with lens.*

This wallwasher is used with reflector-type (R) mercury vapor lamps and can be utilized for wall washing without "scallops." Designed for 100 to 175 W lamps, it can be effective with low to medium-height ceilings. For an even wall wash the setback distance from the wall should be the same as the luminaire spacings (3 ft minimum).

INDIRECT LIGHTING

The main advantages of indirect lighting are the following:

1. Indirect lighting provides an almost shadow-free homogeneously lighted atmosphere on vertical and horizontal surfaces alike.

2. Absence of bright sources minimizes veiling reflection on horizontal (books) as well as vertical tasks (CRT) alike.

3. The system uses interior surfaces to illuminate and expand a room without the interruption and visual clutterness usually found in direct-lighting patterns.

4. In the absence of harsh shadows and veiling reflections, people may see better even at lower illumination level. From this respect, it may be potential of saving energy under some circumstances.

Some noted disadvantages are the following:

1. Overall uniform brightness in indirect lighting can result in marked monotony, especially if the surroundings are in a uniformly white finish.

2. Patches of distracting hot spots are visible on the ceiling if the ceiling is too close to the luminaires.

3. The luminaires collect environmental dirt.

Some design guides in the use of indirect luminaires are:

1. The finishes of room and furniture should be complemented by the light source selected (or vice versa).

2. The stem length should be a minimum of 24 in. and no more than 36 in. from the ceiling for lamps up to 400 W.

3. The luminaires should be mounted at least 5 to 6 ft from the walls.

4. The ceilings must have a matte finish.

5. For color consistency relamping should be done in groups and lamps of different wattages should not be mixed in the same area.

6. To maintain optimum light output the luminaires should be cleaned often.

Whether they are furniture-mounted, pendant, self-standing, or wall-mounted, all indirect luminaires operate on the same basic principle: a HID lamp is placed above a precisely designed reflector, which directs the light outward to be reflected by the ceiling. Almost all reflectors are made of specular or semispecular aluminum, and, like the housing, can be round, hexagonal, or some other shape. Some examples are given in Figures 13-11 through 13-14.

In general, there are three light distribution patterns in indirect lighting systems: (a) even lighting in a circular pattern, (b) unidirectional or light directed in one direction, and (c) bidirectional or light distributed

General Description	*Remarks*
Inside the housing is an unidirectional semispecular aluminum reflector that pushes spill light toward the heat-resistant spread lens. The main reflector of the luminaire is the built-in reflector inside the lamp, which is automatically renewed each time the lamp is changed. Concealed springs secure the aperture cone-retainer assembly in a trim frame after installation and for relamping. The aperture cone that controls spill light and prevents glare may be specular clear, gold, or black to match other HID downlight finishes. The trim is painted enamel.	The greatest advantage is the striation-free or hot-spot-free wall wash that gradually fades on a large vertical surface. The unit tends to be expensive.

in two directions, 180° apart. Some manufacturers also provide down lighting with indirect lighting (direct-indirect). The luminaires usually have a tempered glass at the top.

Figure 13-11. *Examples of furniture-mounted and self-standing indirect luminaires. (Courtesy of SPI Lighting.)*

Furniture-Mounted

Furniture-mounted indirect luminaires are the simplest kind and are rectangular or cylindrical in shape for placement above furniture or low partitions. They should be considered when clutter on the ceiling or walls is undesirable. The greatest advantage is their mobility; they can be moved easily to exactly where light is required. The other advantage is that they can be matched with the design of the furniture or surroundings.

Self-Standing

These are luminaires-cum-furniture. The luminaire is located at the top, the ballast at the base. Some units have shelves as an optional feature and should be considered if there is little furniture in the room and clutter on the ceiling is undesirable. They, too, can be mobile and can match the decor of the surroundings, although not to the same extent as the furniture-mounted.

Wall-Mounted

Wall-mounted luminaires are suitable for walkways, corridors, or other areas in which clutter is undesirable on ceiling or floor, and light must be directed in certain patterns (uni- or bidirection). They may also be considered for wall washing. Unlike the self-standing and furniture-mounted, they lack mobility, unless they are the modular wall-hanging type that can be moved from one wall to another as required.

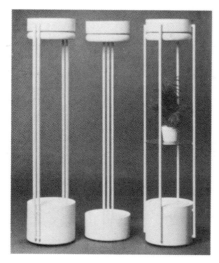

Freestanding styles include one, two and four stem configurations, shelves and under desk models.

(a)

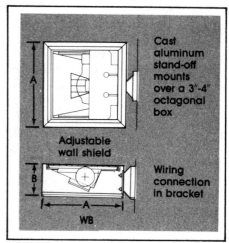

Wall mounted Motif 3 asymmetrical forward distribution patterns for perimeter locations.

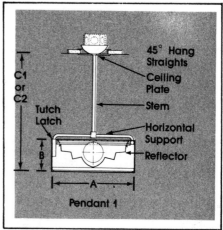

Pendant mounted single stem remote ballasted Motif 3 with symmetrical or asymmetrical distribution patterns.

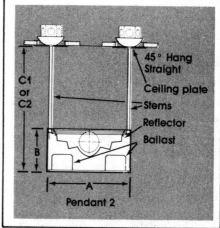

Pendant mounted twin stem integrally ballasted Motif 3 with symmetrical or asymmetrical distribution patterns.

Figure 13-12. *(a) Self-standing luminaires. (b) A cross section of a wall-mounted and pendant luminaires. (Courtesy of Gardco Lighting.)*

(b)

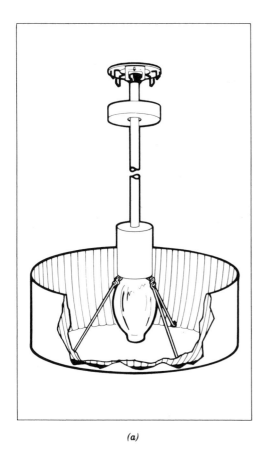

(a)

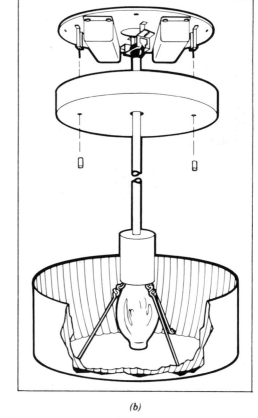

(b)

Figure 13-13. *(a) Pendant luminaires with remote mounted ballast. (b) Pendant luminaires with the ballast at the top. (Courtesy of LAM Lighting Systems.)*

Pendant

A variety of pendant indirect luminaires is available for hanging from the ceiling with the help of one or more stems. The stems can be cylindrical in diameters of ½ to 3 in. (or larger) or in other shapes. The thickness of the luminaire depends on the lamp size and its mounting (vertical or horizontal) and ballast location. Units with horizontal lamps and remote ballasts are the slimmest and can be hung with a single stem for a clean appearance. Units with self-contained ballasts and vertically operated lamps usually require the greatest depth.

To keep the depth of vertical lamps to a minimum, some manufacturers offer units with remote mount ballasts or provide a mechanism with which they can be mounted inside the cover at the top of the stem.

Figure 13-14. *Pendant twin units. (Courtesy of Indalux.)*

14

Lighting Patterns and Forms

Lighting patterns and forms can be used for architectural emphasis. This chapter discusses a general approach and gives design details whenever necessary.

LUMINOUS CEILING

A luminous ceiling is usually a large continuous surface of transmitting material of a diffusing or louverlike character with light sources mounted above it. Hundreds of types of transmitting material are available. Typically the light source is fluorescent strips. This system produces an evenly distributed, diffused, soft light that is of practical value if installed 8 to 10 ft from the floor. Above 10 ft it becomes mostly decorative. Arrangement and design tips follow (see Figure 14-1):

1. The entire space above the luminous ceiling should be painted white.

2. If translucent louvers of a light color are used, the ratio of the spacing (S) to mounting height (H) should not exceed $1 \cdot 5 : 1$.

3. For opaque louvers the S-to-H ratio should not exceed $1 : 1$.

SKYLIGHT

Based on the concept of the luminous ceiling, an artificial skylight can be created. Important features to be considered are:

1. The lens must be an opal-type diffuser at least 0.15-in. thick, preferably in acrylic plastic or glass. Avoid using polystyrene or polycarbonate plastic because over the years they will turn yellow.

2. The color of the lamps should simulate daylight (approximately 6400 K).

3. The ratio of the spacing-to-mounting height (S-to-H; see Figure 14-2) should be kept within $1.25 : 1$. The minimum height H should be 7 in.

4. Paint the entire interior surface white.

A dark trim (e.g., black or brown) around the recessed opal lens produces a floating effect. A regressed lens concept (above the ceiling plane) will avoid the appearance of a conventional troffer luminaire.

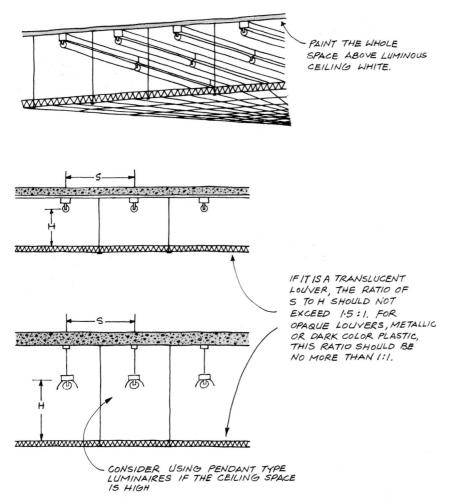

PAINT THE WHOLE SPACE ABOVE LUMINOUS CEILING WHITE.

IF IT IS A TRANSLUCENT LOUVER, THE RATIO OF S TO H SHOULD NOT EXCEED 1.5 : 1. FOR OPAQUE LOUVERS, METALLIC OR DARK COLOR PLASTIC, THIS RATIO SHOULD BE NO MORE THAN 1:1.

CONSIDER USING PENDANT TYPE LUMINAIRES IF THE CEILING SPACE IS HIGH

Figure 14-1.

These points should be considered when the effect of a skylight is desirable but practical or economical reasons preclude the use of natural skylights.

LUMINOUS BEAMS

These light sources in translucent glass or plastic form (lens) simulate beams. Luminous beams can be con-

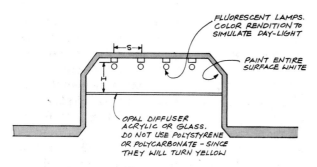

FLUORESCENT LAMPS. COLOR RENDITION TO SIMULATE DAY-LIGHT

PAINT ENTIRE SURFACE WHITE

OPAL DIFFUSER ACRYLIC OR GLASS. DO NOT USE POLYSTYRENE OR POLYCARBONATE - SINCE THEY WILL TURN YELLOW

Figure 14-2.

structed with surface-mounted, wraparound, fluorescent luminaires (Chapter 12). They are excellent for emphasizing length (see Figure 14-3). Parallel, longitudinal lines will expand a room visually; conversely, horizontally arranged lines running across the room will appear to expand the width of a room. For a visual balance these beams should be spaced parallel to the structural beams.

COVE LIGHTING

Cove lighting is indirect light emitted from a continuous wall recess (or projection) and distributed toward the ceiling. It is a decorative or architectural feature that is also used for diffuse illumination. The main points are the following:

1. An efficient lighting system of pleasing brightness is obtained if the light at the ceiling and wall space above the cove is fairly uniform.

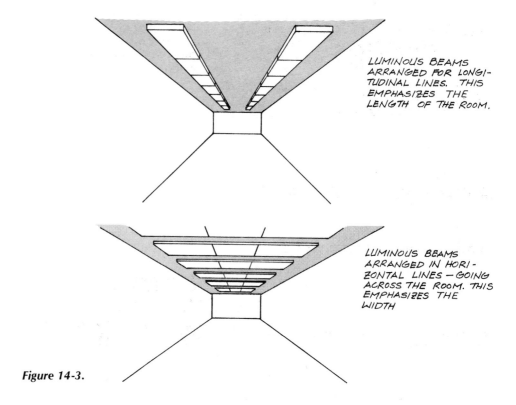

LUMINOUS BEAMS ARRANGED FOR LONGI-TUDINAL LINES. THIS EMPHASIZES THE LENGTH OF THE ROOM.

LUMINOUS BEAMS ARRANGED IN HORI-ZONTAL LINES — GOING ACROSS THE ROOM. THIS EMPHASIZES THE WIDTH

Figure 14-3.

The ratio between the space (S) and distance D (see Figure 14-4) should be 1 : 4 to 1 : 6.

2. To reduce wall brightness (this space is closest to the lamp) the luminaire should be side-mounted with the lamp away from the wall.

3. The lamps should be staggered to avoid shadows.

4. The location of the cove should be above normal eye level but not too close to the ceiling (12-in. minimum). If one cove is used, the distance D should be approximately 25% of the length L. If there are two, one at each end, D should be 15% of the length L on both sides.

Cove lights should be used only on matte, white, or off-white surfaces, preferably in rooms with high ceilings and in areas in which ceiling height changes abruptly. It is also effective in diluting the brightness of ceiling apertures (from recessed incandescent downlights).

LUMINOUS COLUMNS

Luminous columns are used for decorative purposes and graphic display. When tastefully designed, they can be most effective in drawing attention to the display and defining structural elements. The fluorescents are installed inside columns of translucent panels. For best effect brightness should be low, especially at and below eye level (Figure 14-5), and the luminance ratio should not exceed 20 : 1 between the bright surface and the adjacent darker areas.

INDIRECT UP (DOWN) LIGHTING

Wall-mounted indirect, unidirectional or bidirectional (up and down) lighting with a shielding medium can be pleasing aesthetically as well as functionally. Similar to cove lighting, here, too, the light output is soft and uniform but lacks punch or emphasis. It is best used to supplement other lighting. The distribution of light can be down or up and down simultaneously, and light spread can be precisely controlled by the shielding medium. Wooden blocks can be used to project the lamp away from the wall and spread light over draperies or wall displays. The main design features are shown in Figure 14-6.

The inside surface of the shielding should be painted matte white for good light distribution. Note that the illustrations represent typical designs; the dimensions may need to be job-tailored to match.

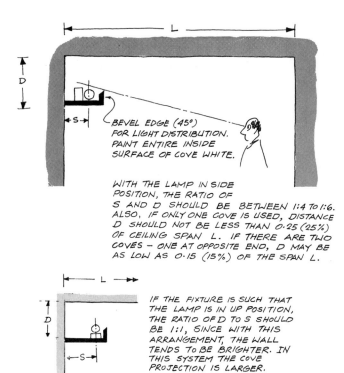

BEVEL EDGE (45°) FOR LIGHT DISTRIBUTION. PAINT ENTIRE INSIDE SURFACE OF COVE WHITE.

WITH THE LAMP IN SIDE POSITION, THE RATIO OF S AND D SHOULD BE BETWEEN 1:4 TO 1:6. ALSO, IF ONLY ONE COVE IS USED, DISTANCE D SHOULD NOT BE LESS THAN 0·25 (25%) OF CEILING SPAN L. IF THERE ARE TWO COVES — ONE AT OPPOSITE END, D MAY BE AS LOW AS 0·15 (15%) OF THE SPAN L.

IF THE FIXTURE IS SUCH THAT THE LAMP IS IN UP POSITION, THE RATIO OF D TO S SHOULD BE 1:1, SINCE WITH THIS ARRANGEMENT, THE WALL TENDS TO BE BRIGHTER. IN THIS SYSTEM THE COVE PROJECTION IS LARGER.

Figure 14-4.

SOFFIT LIGHTING

Soffit lighting is a structural lighting element suitable for a high level of downlighting. It is often used in furred-down areas, over a kitchen sink, or in a niche over a sofa or built-in furniture. The basic concept is based on fluorescent strips inside the soffit equipped with a suitable diffuser or louver at the bottom. The main design features are shown in Figure 14-7 and are described in the following:

1. The entire inside surface should be painted white.
2. Lenses opposed to louvers in areas in which cleaning is a problem should be considered.
3. For restrooms lenses or louvers that emit light at upper angles to illuminate the face should be selected. Warm white or deluxe warm white lamps will enhance skin color.

ACCENT LIGHTING TECHNIQUES

All objects are three-dimensional. The proper application of accent light can make it partly or fully visi-

Figure 14-5.

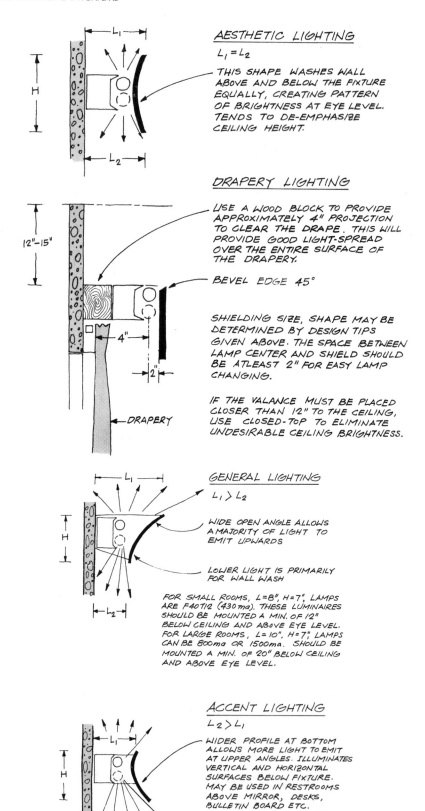

AESTHETIC LIGHTING

$L_1 = L_2$

THIS SHAPE WASHES WALL ABOVE AND BELOW THE FIXTURE EQUALLY, CREATING PATTERN OF BRIGHTNESS AT EYE LEVEL. TENDS TO DE-EMPHASIZE CEILING HEIGHT.

DRAPERY LIGHTING

USE A WOOD BLOCK TO PROVIDE APPROXIMATELY 4" PROJECTION TO CLEAR THE DRAPE. THIS WILL PROVIDE GOOD LIGHT-SPREAD OVER THE ENTIRE SURFACE OF THE DRAPERY.

BEVEL EDGE 45°

SHIELDING SIZE, SHAPE MAY BE DETERMINED BY DESIGN TIPS GIVEN ABOVE. THE SPACE BETWEEN LAMP CENTER AND SHIELD SHOULD BE AT LEAST 2" FOR EASY LAMP CHANGING.

IF THE VALANCE MUST BE PLACED CLOSER THAN 12" TO THE CEILING, USE CLOSED-TOP TO ELIMINATE UNDESIRABLE CEILING BRIGHTNESS.

DRAPERY

GENERAL LIGHTING

$L_1 > L_2$

WIDE OPEN ANGLE ALLOWS A MAJORITY OF LIGHT TO EMIT UPWARDS

LOWER LIGHT IS PRIMARILY FOR WALL WASH

FOR SMALL ROOMS, L=8", H=7", LAMPS ARE F40T12 (430 ma). THESE LUMINAIRES SHOULD BE MOUNTED A MIN. OF 12" BELOW CEILING AND ABOVE EYE LEVEL. FOR LARGE ROOMS, L=10", H=7", LAMPS CAN BE 800ma OR 1500ma. SHOULD BE MOUNTED A MIN. OF 20" BELOW CEILING AND ABOVE EYE LEVEL.

ACCENT LIGHTING

$L_2 > L_1$

WIDER PROFILE AT BOTTOM ALLOWS MORE LIGHT TO EMIT AT UPPER ANGLES. ILLUMINATES VERTICAL AND HORIZONTAL SURFACES BELOW FIXTURE. MAY BE USED IN RESTROOMS ABOVE MIRROR, DESKS, BULLETIN BOARD ETC. AVOID USING OVER DOORS.

Figure 14-6.

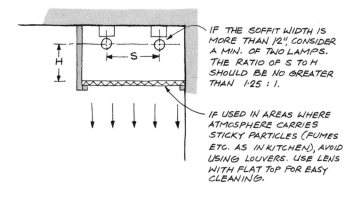

IF THE SOFFIT WIDTH IS
MORE THAN 12", CONSIDER
A MIN. OF TWO LAMPS.
THE RATIO OF S TO H
SHOULD BE NO GREATER
THAN 1.25 : 1.

IF USED IN AREAS WHERE
ATMOSPHERE CARRIES
STICKY PARTICLES (FUMES
ETC. AS IN KITCHEN), AVOID
USING LOUVERS. USE LENS
WITH FLAT TOP FOR EASY
CLEANING.

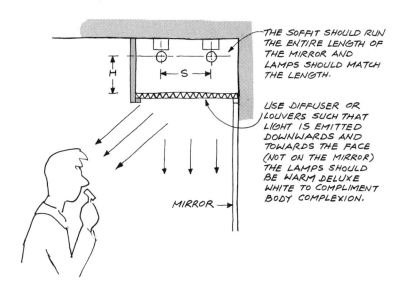

THE SOFFIT SHOULD RUN
THE ENTIRE LENGTH OF
THE MIRROR AND
LAMPS SHOULD MATCH
THE LENGTH.

USE DIFFUSER OR
LOUVERS SUCH THAT
LIGHT IS EMITTED
DOWNWARDS AND
TOWARDS THE FACE
(NOT ON THE MIRROR)
THE LAMPS SHOULD
BE WARM DELUXE
WHITE TO COMPLIMENT
BODY COMPLEXION.

MIRROR

Figure 14-7.

ble, reveal its contour, intensify its character, add solidity, emphasize bulk, and, above all, create a dramatic effect! The techniques of accent lighting can be divided into four parts:

Diffuse Lighting

This technique provides a uniform amount of light on and around the object. But the shadowless diffuse light fails to emphasize the particular features (e.g., relief work, carving, color variation) of the object, and produces a flat appearance (Figure 14-8). It is best achieved with wide beam floodlights.

Highlighting

Highlighting is done with a reflector lamp with narrow to medium beam spread, aiming at the object from an angle or from above. It reveals the object's surface and color detail but may not isolate the object from its background. In addition, when lighted with a single source, the object may seem to be both intensely lit and deeply shadowed (Figure 14-9). For best effect, the intensity ratio between the object and its surroundings should be between 2 : 1 and 6 : 1. Within this range the transparent shadow effect tends to reveal the true color and three-dimensional rendering of the object. Ratios higher than 6 : 1 casts a veil on the object, whereas ratios lower than 2 : 1 would tend to make it look too flat.

Backlighting

In this technique light is placed behind the object to illuminate the background material and to create a silhouette effect (Figure 14-10). The contour of the

Figure 14-8. *Diffuse lighting provides even illumination.*

Figure 14-10. *Backlighting produces a silhouetting effect.*

object is well defined, but the color, finish, and physical characteristics are hidden by darkness. Backlighting can be done successfully with A-lamps or reflector lamps with a wide beam spread (floodlight).

For balanced lighting, it is sometimes desirable that all three techniques be used simultaneously. The de-

signer needs to make a skilled judgment in selecting luminaires that provide the best combination of beam spread, beam angle, intensity, and color to reveal the special character of the object. Accessories such as beam elongators, intensifiers, isolation spot-baffles (Chapter 11), and dimmers may be used for fine tuning.

Shadowing

A shadowing technique is used to enhance with light and shadow the beauty of objects with finely detailed carving and modeling. The number of light sources and their locations are critical. If the object is illuminated by only one source, strong shadow will darken it on one side, which for most application is unsatisfactory. If the source is at a distance, it tends to give the object a flat appearance. The effect is best when a number of sources from multidirections, locations and angles create a certain amount of fill light that softens the sharp contrast between extremely dark and light areas.

In shadowing human figures, the most naturalistic resolution is achieved when the light sources are placed at an angle approximately 45° above the face. If the sources are located directly above, they produce telltale shadows that expose baggy eyes, furrowed brows, and flabby cheeks; if aimed from below, long, upward shadows of nose, eyebrows,

Figure 14-9. *Highlighting brings out surface detail and color. It also provides undesirable harsh shadows.*

cheeks, and lips produce an unnatural, ghostly expression (Figure 14-11). From a theatrical standpoint large, dark shadows imply dejection, power, distress, or suspense, whereas soft shadows indicate friendliness, liveliness, safety, joy, and beauty.

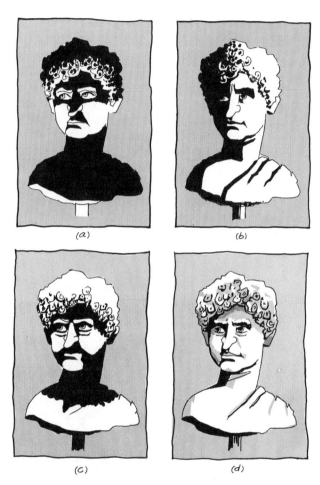

(a)

(b)

(c)

(d)

Figure 14-11. *Shadows on human figure.* (a) *Lighting from the bottom casts shadows upwards (opposite to what is seen normally) and results in an unnatural appearance. It emphasizes horizontal lines and shows fullness of cheeks. It also simulates the appearance of someone standing near a fireplace in darkness.* (b) *Lighting from the side shows vertical lines; it emphasizes a long face and thoughtful appearance. The contrast of light and shadow on two sides of the face is sometimes used as a symbol of the happiness and sadness of life, or a split personality.* (c) *Lighting from the top shows horizontal lines; it emphasizes flabby (or flat) cheeks, baggy eyes, furrowed brows, and age. Harsh shadows indicate dejection, distress, or suspense.* (d) *Lighting from multidirections (particularly at 45° above the face, from both sides), produces soft shadows revealing all characteristics. Soft shadows indicate friendliness, happiness, and safety.*

Wall Washing

When a vertical surface is washed with light, the visual impression is of a large space; it emphasizes textures, dramatizes entrances or exits, and accentuates murals and graphics. A variety of wall washers is discussed in Chapters 11 and 13.

Smooth Wall Wash

For a smooth wall wash on a vertical surface it is necessary to use nonscalloping wallwashers and to place them at a distance away from the wall without creating a hot spot. As a rule of thumb, the setback distance from the wall should be one-half the SC of the luminaire times the mounting height above the floor. In an average room (8-to-10-ft ceiling) this distance is 3 to 4 ft. The spacing between the luminaires may vary from a half to full setback distance from the wall, depending on their candlepower distribution, and the degree of smoothness required. Luminaires with wide beam, or with spread lens, may be spaced as far as the full setback distance, whereas others may be set at half the setback distance (see Figure 14-12).

A few words of caution. Do not try to wash a vertical surface with specular finish (polished marble, mirror tiles, or glossy paint). A specular surface will

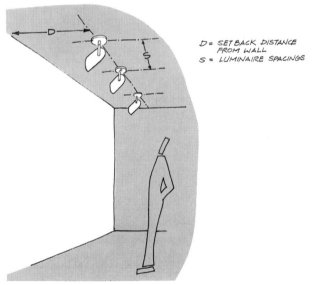

D = SETBACK DISTANCE FROM WALL
S = LUMINAIRE SPACINGS

Figure 14-12. *For an even wall wash the setback distance D should not be any less than 3 ft from the wall. If unscalloping, lensed wallwashers are used, the spacing S can be the same as the setback distance D. For non-lensed type units this may be half of the setback distance, D.*

reflect the light sources. For best results, the vertical surface should be highly reflective matte finish.

Do not wall wash a door or window, or the surfaces above them, unless you are sure that the location of the wallwashers will not "blind" people entering the room or standing outside the window.

Textured Walls

Textured walls (e.g., brick or moss-rock) are best enhanced by a grazing lighting technique in which the luminaires are placed 10 to 12 in. from the wall. Any closer than that would tend to create large shadows on the textured surface and lose the effect of solidity. Conversely, if the luminaires are too far apart, they will produce a flat appearance of the textured surface (Figure 14-13). The grazing effect can be created with a grazing wall-washing system, or conventional downlights (Chapter 11), by using R or PAR lamps with a narrow (for high ceiling) or wide (for low to medium ceiling) beam spread. For an even wash the spacings between the luminaires should not exceed 12 in. Some words of caution: (1) be careful when using a grazing wall-wash technique on a flat surface; it exposes imperfections. (2) For a track or surface mounted grazing system trough or cornices will shield the sources. (3) Be careful when grazing the textured surface from the bottom; undesirable shadows may be reflected on the ceiling.

Scallop Lighting

A scalloping pattern gives new dimensions to a flat or uninteresting vertical surface. It lowers a high ceiling visually and helps to move traffic. Scalloping can be created with downlights (and some wallwashers) that produce distinct cutoffs (Chapter 11, 13). The size of the scallops depends on the cone of the light beam and the luminaire location. For distinctly-shaped scallops the luminaires should be installed 12 to 16 in. from the wall and their spacings varied to suit individual taste (average 4 ft; see Figure 14-14). Re-

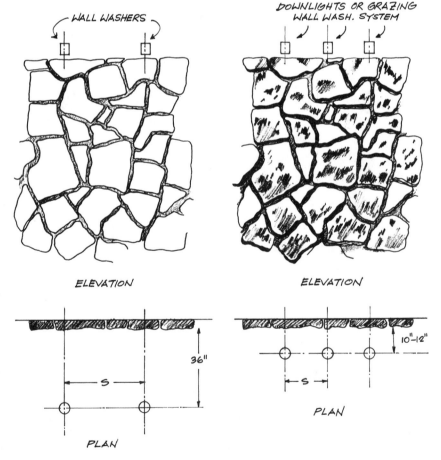

Figure 14-13. *The textures of an interesting vertical surface such as brick walls or moss-rock walls, etc. can be grazed dramatically by "grazing wall washing systems," or with the help of conventional downlights. Textures are more defined as the luminaires are placed closer to the wall. For best effect, these should not be placed any closer than 10 in.–12 in. and the spacing between luminaires should not exceed the same distance as the setback. This is shown in the figure on the right. General illumination on the whole surface (no grazing) can be created by wall-washing technique, with the help of wall-washers placed no closer than 3 ft. from the wall, and spaced no more than the setback distance. This is shown in the figure on the left.*

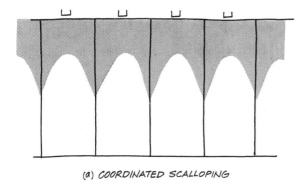

(a) *COORDINATED SCALLOPING*

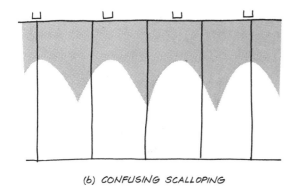

(b) *CONFUSING SCALLOPING*

Figure 14-14. *If the wall contains a regular pattern such as wooden panels, coordination with light is important. Otherwise it may produce confusing scalloping.*

petitive patterns (e.g., wood paneling and columns) can be emphasized by coordinating patterns of scalloped light in between the rows. Irregular application produces a confusing design (Figure 14-14*b*).

Lighting of Paintings

Lighting of paintings (or murals and notice boards) uses accent luminaires and a combination of accent and wallwashers in two general techniques. For best results it is recommended that the luminance ratio between painting and wall be no more than 5 : 1 and no less than 3 : 1. If the wall is already served with a satisfactory amount of illumination from ambient lighting, only accent lights should be used to supplement it. Wallwashers are required if the wall is dark or if the surface is to be set apart from the immediate surroundings.

In both cases the placement and aiming of the accent luminaire is critical. Although there is no hard and fast rule, the following should be observed for satisfactory results:

Locate the accent luminaire in such a position that its source or direct glare is not visible at normal angles.

If the painting has a glossy finish, care must be taken that the reflected glare is never in the field of view.

The luminaire may, however, have to be aimed from an oblique angle that must be field-verified.

If the painting has a matte finish, the accent light can be installed on the ceiling at the centerline of the painting. The setback from the painting should have its center-of-beam at a 30° angle from nadir (see Figure 14-15). This also means that the angle from the horizontal ceiling to the center of the painting (fixture-aiming angle) is 60°. With this arrangement the setback distance can be expressed as follows:

$$D = \text{(luminaire mounting height} - \text{eye height)} \times \tan 30°$$
$$= 0.5774 \text{ (luminaire mounting height} - \text{eye height)}$$

By knowing the dimensions of the painting the cone of the lamp can be determined. The cone represents the solid angle of the beam spread, which should be large enough to cover the painting on the vertical surface. If, in the example given, the length of the painting is, say, 50 in., a reflector lamp of 30° beam spread will suffice.

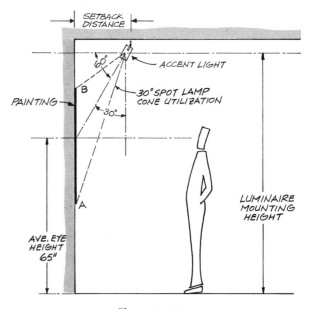

Figure 14-15.

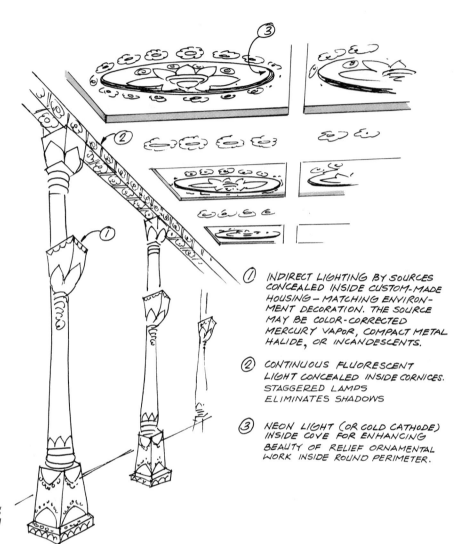

① INDIRECT LIGHTING BY SOURCES CONCEALED INSIDE CUSTOM-MADE HOUSING — MATCHING ENVIRONMENT DECORATION. THE SOURCE MAY BE COLOR-CORRECTED MERCURY VAPOR, COMPACT METAL HALIDE, OR INCANDESCENTS.

② CONTINUOUS FLUORESCENT LIGHT CONCEALED INSIDE CORNICES. STAGGERED LAMPS ELIMINATES SHADOWS

③ NEON LIGHT (OR COLD CATHODE) INSIDE COVE FOR ENHANCING BEAUTY OF RELIEF ORNAMENTAL WORK INSIDE ROUND PERIMETER.

Figure 14-16. *Some lighting considerations for ornamental ceilings.*

If the painting has a heavy frame, its shadow can be minimized by installing the luminaire away from it and by increasing the setback distance. If the painting has a glossy surface, the reflected glare can be avoided by decreasing the setback distance.

Staying within the luminance ratios outlined earlier is important to good lighting of paintings. If the wall is dark, supplementary lighting (e.g., wall washers) must be used with accent lighting. For symmetry it is desirable that these luminaires, as well, be installed on the ceiling, possibly at the same setback distance as others; but it may not always be possible because of the variation in the type of luminaire and lamps used.

If an accent light must be used alone, it should be positioned to make sure that its beam spread on the wall overlaps the painting, frame included. Light falling on the wall reflects and creates a spilled ambient light that tends to decrease the strain on the eyes. This is especially important for the frame-projector accent luminaire which has an optical arrangement for cutting light beams to the exact shape and size of the painting (see Chapter 11 for details). Using a frame projector on the painting alone is like watching television in the dark. Wall washing should always be considered when a painting is lighted with a frame projector.

Lighting an Ornamental Ceiling

When a ceiling is decorated with a lot of ornamental work, a combination of direct and indirect lighting is

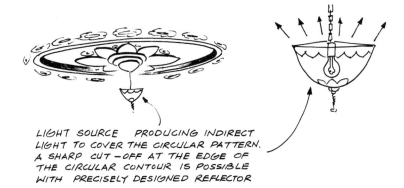

LIGHT SOURCE PRODUCING INDIRECT
LIGHT TO COVER THE CIRCULAR PATTERN.
A SHARP CUT-OFF AT THE EDGE OF
THE CIRCULAR CONTOUR IS POSSIBLE
WITH PRECISELY DESIGNED REFLECTOR

USE OF CHANDELIER MAY
BE CONSIDERED FOR AESTHETICS
AS WELL AS SPARKLES ON
GOLD-FINISHED ORNAMENTAL
WORK

Figure 14-16. (Continued)

often the best solution. Use of fluorescents in cornices and coves, neon or cold cathodes recessed in curved contours and sparkling chandeliers below ornamental work can enhance its beauty. Figure 14-16 provides examples.

The highlights are as follows:

1. The sources must not be visible, yet their glow will increase the beauty of finely-detailed work and provide sufficient indirect ambient lighting.

2. Fewer luminaires cast strong shadows and more luminaires tend to erase them. This concept must be used to determine the total number of luminaires and their spacing.

3. Fluorescent for linear and neon or cold cathodes for curved coves will highlight important areas. Color rendition of the sources should complement the surroundings. If there is a shortage of mounting space or a noise problem, the ballasts can be remote-mounted.

4. If there is a lot of ornamental work, the use of incandescents should be considered for sparkles. Chandeliers with a number of incandescent flames are often a good solution.

REFERENCES

Flynn, J. E. and S. M. Mills. *Architectural Lighting Graphics.* New York: Van Nostrand-Reinhold, 1962.

J. E. Flynn, "A Study of Subjective Responses to Low Energy and Nonuniform Lighting Systems." *Lighting Design and Application,* 8 (February 1977).

J. Panero and M. Zelmik. *Human Dimension and Interior Space.* New York: Watson-Guptill, 1979.

Shemitz, S. R. "Lighting: Tools that Suit Architectural Objectives." *Architectural Record* (March 1968).

Spencer D. E. and V. E. Spencer. "Narrative Luminous Ceilings." *Lighting Design and Application* (April 1977).

G. Zekowski. "The Art of Lighting is a Science/The Science of Lighting is an Art." *Lighting Design and Application* (March 1981).

15

Human Reaction to Light

PHYSIOLOGICAL REACTION

Whether artificial or natural, light has a significant impact on the human body. Experts in the medical field conclude that in addition to making the skin visible the "powerful physical force of light" may penetrate the muscles and tissues of the body "enough to affect the internal compounds and metabolic processes." Only visible and infrared light has this penetrating ability, and according to some experts in photobiology the effect of this penetration of environmental light is healthful for the body and the basis for leading a normal life. The effect of ultraviolet, however, can be serious. It does not penetrate but may have a vital affect on the skin, even to causing cancer. For this reason all light sources that produce ultraviolet rays that may shatter during operation (e.g., metal halide lamps) must have a protective shield.

Not all photobiologists agree on the effects of ultraviolet light on the human body. According to F. Greiter, "while the west in a rather simplistic way blames increased exposure to sunlight for the increasing incidence of malignant melanoma without taking into account any other environmental parameters,

children in Russia are exposed to artificial sunlight during school-breaks in order to make-up for the lack of natural sunlight."

Among these controversial issues there is some good news. Photobiologists today use light and ultraviolet successfully (sometimes with chemicals) to control certain incurable diseases.

There are other physiological responses to light. Prolonged exposure is found to be just as harmful as living in darkness; for example, miners who spend most of their time in darkness or semidarkness may have eye trouble. Prolonged exposure also breaks the light and dark rhythms of the body, so vitally important to the control of body temperature and secretion of hormones into the bloodstream.

Color attained by finishes and/or by light also affects the human body. According to Faber Birren, noted expert in color psychology:

"In human beings, red tends to raise blood pressure, pulse rate, respiration, and skin response (perspiration) and to excite brain waves. There is a noticeable muscular reaction (tension) and greater frequency of eye blinks. Blue tends to have reverse effects, to lower blood pressure and pulse rate, skin response is less, and brain waves tend to decline. The green region of the spectrum is more or less neutral. Reactions to orange and yellow are akin to reactions to red but less pronounced. Reactions to purple and violet are similar in reaction to blue.''

It is important for the lighting designer to remember that all physiological effects of color are only temporary. Faber Birren also states: ''The reaction to color is not unlike the reaction to alcohol, tobacco, coffee—up for a short period and then down.''

VISUAL REACTION

Much of the visual reaction to lighting has already been discussed in Chapter 2. Here we carry on to other forms that are useful to the lighting designer in practical applications.

A visual task requires two important aspects of light: quality and quantity. Although quantity of light is undoubtedly an essential element, the quality of light is also important in many applications. The principal elements that control this quality are glare and color. Glare is classified as direct and indirect, and each has a significant impact on visual response.

Direct glare is the product of two sources. The first is excessively bright, like the headlights of an oncoming car or the television studio lights that cause ''disability glare'' by shining directly into the viewer's eyes. The second is the peripheral stray light from a cluster of luminaires, like the fluorescent troffers in a large office that cause visual discomfort. In an office-like atmosphere discomfort glare is more of a problem than disability glare. Discomfort glare caused by excessive brightness in the normal field of view produces stress in the eye muscle that regulates pupil size and induces fatigue.

Brightness of objects produces fatigue during the transient adaptation of the eyes. Looking up, down, and around requires constant eye adaptation to varying light. In each occurrence the eye focuses its lens and changes the pupil size and over an extended period of time there is fatigue. But this does not necessarily mean that to see properly all objects in the field of view should be of uniform brightness. In fact, the peripheral of uniform lighting and colors of constant brightness may cause sensory deprivation such as monotony and boredom. According to Faber Birren, ''people require varying, cycling stimuli to remain sensitive and alert to their environments. Comfort and agreeableness are normally identified with

moderate if not radical changes, and this change concerns brightness as well as all other elements in the environment. If overstimulation may cause distress, so may severe monotony.'' The important message here is that to satisfy visual and mental response a change in brightness must exist in the objects of the field of view, but never too radically.

SOME BRIGHTNESSES ARE A BLESSING:

Although it is well recognized that ''disability brightness'' and ''discomfort brightness'' impair visual response, there are applications in which the presence of strong brightness in the field of view is a favorable feature. In a large gathering of multiactivity, in which a perceptual clarity with high amounts of lighting is constantly required, visible brightness from direct light fixtures often provides, at least psychologically, a higher amount of light and security. A good example is found when we compare the customers' reaction to the lighting systems of two identical national-chain grocery stores both with the same level of task lighting, but one with exposed fluorescent strips in the conventional manner and the other with metal halide downlights concealed in the pockets of a modified ceiling with no ceiling brightness. It is interesting to note that when customers were asked about the lighting systems the majority preferred the first because ''it provided more light'' and the other was ''too dark and things were hard to find.'' The eye develops under daylight and sun. Grocery stores with high ceilings and bright lights possibly imitate the natural sense of security.

AESTHETICAL AND EMOTIONAL REACTION

When an observer looks at a lighting system (which is a part of the environment), reactions may be loosely divided into two types; aesthetical and emotional. The aesthetical response may be good or bad, bright or dark, too red or too blue, which in general, is an expression of instant reaction. The emotional reaction, on the other hand, can be cheering, boring, pleasing, exciting, tranquil, depressing, cozy, inviting, and so on, which is an expression of deeper feeling, a conclusion possibly gained subconsciously after being in the environment for some time. Needless to say, both aspects are important to the lighting designer, because each may have to be used individually or collectively, depending on the application.

Crudely speaking, although any lighting system may share both, the aesthetic response is important to applications in which it must impress the transient observers in a very short time. A good example is the lighting system in a store front or showwindow in a shopping mall, which must attract the attention of passersby. The aesthetic response must stand out from any adjacent lighting. It may be dramatic, based on items like special light patterns, effects, projections, bright colors, colored lights, glitter, backlit signs, light sculptures, and moving lights.

The emotional response is important when observers spend a long time in the environment. In the preceding example the environment of the shop interior must be such that it makes the customers "comfortable", "happy", and "invited" inside the store. It must encourage them to stay and shop for a longer time.

For most people emotional excitement is largely due to the visual experience of association. It is like the reaction of any of the senses; the fragrance of a particular perfume may bring to mind a special person and make us happy, or the rain may make us sad because of a bitter experience. In the case of lighting it may be a particular color or setting, or their combination, with which we may associate an earlier experience. A lovely shade of blue may remind us of the sky; green, of the ocean, red, of the roses received on St. Valentine's Day, and so on. This superficial association leads from one to another, all subconsciously, possibly awakening deeper, happier, or sadder memories.

Of course, emotional response varies with an individual's personal interpretation and experience. The designer's challenge lies in creating an environment that works for the majority.

Although it is impossible to make claims for specific colors, certain moods can be produced with the help of some lighting patterns of varying levels of illumination, color, or light source:

For gaiety	Use high levels of light, color, and movement. Changing effects in illumination levels and color should be smooth, gradual, and warm.
For solemnity	Use subdued patterns of light with emphasis on the dramatic points. Color should be used sparingly and with atmospheric effect.
For restfulness	Use no visible light sources, low illuminance, subdued color, and low wall brightness that fades into the dark upper ceiling.
For activity	Use high levels of light with warm colors. Perceptual clarity.
For warmth	Use high levels of illumination with red, orange, yellow, amber, gold, pink, or any combination of colors in the red end of the spectrum.
For coolness	Use moderate amounts of illumination with blue, blue-green, and violet mixed with white.

More about light patterns and color association with environmental design is discussed in Chapters 16 and 17.

AGE AND BEHAVIOR RESPONSE

The age of the occupants has a significant impact on environmental design. In lighting, apart from the visual aspects (more light for aging eyes), the preference for light and color will also vary. Again, although it is true that the choice will vary from person to person and it is impossible to make specific claims, some general conclusions will probably hold for the majority.

Infants and the toddlers are attracted by the light source, concentrated light areas, and bright colors, primarily because of the visual (not emotional) attraction. Experts claim that babies stare the longest at luminous colors like yellow, white, pink, and red. Sparkling and flashing lights fascinate them. Movement of light sources and/or bright-colored articles cause an infant's eyes to follow their track. Although the general fascination for bright light and color continues to grow, the order of preference does show some variation as the child matures. Attraction to yellow fades slowly and is replaced by red and then blue. Black, brown, and gray are the least preferred.

In the teen years the choice of light and color probably reaches its most varied and versatile. Sparkle, motion, flash and glitter, and wild colors in bizarre combinations seem to provide emotional and psychic pleasure (mostly applicable to the entertainment areas). As to personal preference, experts claim that with maturity the order becomes blue, red, green, violet, orange, and yellow. Black, brown, and gray still remain the least in favor.

In old age, as eyes become feeble and vision blurs, an appreciation of the environment becomes increasingly dependent for biological reasons on abundant light and bright colors.

Regardless of age, some conclusions due to lighting can be drawn on the behavior patterns of human beings. Activity, including talking, increases with light. A vivid example can be found in the theaters, in which noise increases as the light level in the auditorium increases and subsides as the lights go down. Another example of a change in human activity is in supermarkets, where light level is suddenly reduced to notify the patrons of approaching closing time. The customers hurry to finish their shopping.

Traffic is efficiently controlled by attracting people toward the location of the lights, a phenomenon that can be implemented in museums, and art galleries by providing concentrated light from one display to another, following a predetermined traffic pattern.

La Guisa and Perney, in their experiments with school children, showed that power of lighting directs activity. They noted that students paid more attention and spent more time on a displayed card when it was more brightly lighted than the rest of the room.

People, in general, are attracted to light and like their surroundings to be lighted, at least for safety, if for no other reason. In large gatherings they like the lighting to be slightly less intense than the surroundings or uniform at a level. They usually try to avoid an area in which higher amounts of light fall on them, unless, of course, they are the center of attraction (e.g., on stage or a public speaker). The general inclination to enjoy a more subdued light is evident when we observe their behavior in restaurants. A good example of this characteristic is described by Flynn and the others in their experiment in a coffee bar, which was illuminated in two different ways for two experiments. In the first they had a wall, lighted in a way considered "interesting" and "pleasant." In the second the room was halved and only one wall was lighted. In both cases the participants in the experiment chose to sit in an underlighted bar facing the lighted wall. They preferred to look at the light rather than being in it, thus indicating a preference for privacy and comfort. Unlike the supermarket, a sudden increase in the general light level would probably serve to provide notice of closing.

REFERENCES

Birren, Faber. *Light, Color and Environment.* New York: Van Nostrand-Reinhold, 1969.

Birren, Faber. "Psychological Implications of Color and Illumination." *Illuminating Engineering* (May 1969).

Birren, Faber. *Color and Human Response.* New York: Van Nostrand-Reinhold, 1978.

Boyce, P.R. Human Factors in Lighting. New York: Macmillan, 1981.

Flynn, J. E., T. J. Spencer, O. Martyniuck, and C. Hendrick, "Interim Study of Procedures for Investigating the Effect of Light on Impression and Behaviour." *Journal of the Illuminating Engineering Society,* **3** (1973).

Heerwagen, Judith, H. and R. Dean. "Lighting and Psychological Comfort." *Lighting Design & Application,* 47–51 (April 1986).

Helene, C., M. Charlier, Th. Montenay-Garestier, and G. Laustriat, Editors. *Trends in Photobiology.* New York: Plenum, 1984.

La Guisa, F. and L. R. Perney, "Further Studies on the Effects of Brightness Variations in Attention Span in a Learning Environment." *Journal of the Illuminating Engineering Society,* **3** (1974).

Sorcar, Prafulla C. "Magic of Light and Light of Magic." Research work for All India Magic Circle, India, 1981.

16

Human Reaction to Color and Application

To select a color it is advisable first to know its values. Color is usually associated with physical objects that stand out distinctly from their surroundings, such as the children's toys on the floor, leaves in autumn, paintings on the walls, wallpaper, and flowers. In design it is often considered an integral part of the material; for example, carpets, walls, ceilings, fabrics, and appliances. In addition, color is associated with visual atmospheric impressions that are not directly related to physical objects; a rainbow, a sunrise or sunset, or artificially colored light for mood setting. Although the use of color on physical objects goes back to the walls of caves, lighting to manipulate color is a recent development.

EFFECTS OF COLOR

The many effects of color can be divided loosely into three groups: biological (physiology), visual (style), and psychological (emotion). Each group is strongly dependent on the others; therefore the discussion of one automatically overlaps the others.

Although reaction to color reflects individual pref-

erences, some effects are universal; for example and as mentioned earlier (Chapter 15), the stimulating effects of the warmer and soothing effects of the cooler tones. What might be interesting to know is that for some colors there is a reversal effect before returning to normalcy. For example, with red, after all initial excitement, the biological measurements actually fall below normal readings. The important thing to remember here is that in order to maintain physiological and psychological color-related reactions periodic changes are required.

The emotional effects of color can be significant. Warm colors like red, orange, and yellow can be stimulating, yet may have a negative effect; for example, red represents heat and danger, orange to some can be discomforting and upsetting, and yellow can cause a conflict of moods. Cool colors like blue, green, and violet tend to sooth. Experts claim that cool colors suppress interaction among people in large numbers and are suitable therefore for applications such as in self-service stores and supermarkets.

Another significant effect is visual or aesthetic, for which the selection of color is made primarily for "style." The trend today appears to be moving toward light, neutral colors (mostly earth tones) with bright accents in an overall balanced scheme. Floors and trim are usually a deeper hue.

SELECTING COLOR FOR INTERIORS

All interiors have a ceiling, four walls, a floor, and furnishings. For almost all applications the ceiling is white or off-white with high reflectance. The walls and the floor are the largest visible areas; the dominant colors and patterns depend on their size. Typically the floor is of low reflectance and the walls have a coordinated color of higher reflectance. The furnishings blend or contrast with the dominant hue. Some points that may be helpful in color selection are the following:

1. Association of colors with mood:

Red	Warmth and comfort
	Exciting and stimulating
	Heat and danger
Gold	Royalty and luxury
	Cheering, joyous, glittering
	Ornamental
Orange	Social, cheerful, and luminous
	Warm and exciting
	Discomforting, upsetting
Blue	Tranquility and calmness
	Soothing and peaceful
	Cool, soft, and restful
	Sadness
Green	Tranquility and calmness
	Soothing and peaceful
	Natural
	Cool and restful
White	Purity and cleanliness
	Monotonous and boring
	Glaring
Purple	Devotion and quietness
	Solemnity
	Elegant
Yellow	Cheering and joyful
Brown	Unhappy, dejected
	Earthtone and neutral
Black	Mourning, solemnity
	Death and despair
	Sadness

2. The reflectance of color is proportional to its value (Chapter 3), which in essence measures its lightness or darkness. For a room that requires a high level of light, the dominant color scheme should have high reflectance. Similarly, in areas of low light level requirements the reflectance of the dominant colors should be proportionally lower. A mixture can be uncomfortable; for example, 100 fc of light in a room with dark brown walls (say, 20% reflectance) can result in an uncomfortably large brightness ratio between light colored objects and the room's perimeters.

3. A large pattern with strong contrast (value) makes a room visually smaller, whereas a small pattern with soft contrast makes a room appear larger.

4. Strong contrast in some bright colors (e.g., orange, yellow) can be stimulating and exciting, but they may also be the causes of restlessness, irritation, and making time seem longer. They can be effective for use in areas where it is desirable that patrons spend a short time (e.g., washrooms, corridors, and fast-food stands). Conversely, a gentle contrast is restful and make time seem shorter.

5. Warm, exciting color tones are required in rooms in which higher stimulation is suitable, for example, rooms with northern exposure, cool temperatures, smooth textures, and low noise elements. Conversely, cool, subdued colors create a restful atmosphere in rooms with southern exposure, abundant sun, lots of noise and excitement, and rough textures.

6. In areas in which low contrast is effective without losing the environmental interest, a single hue should be used exclusively with slight but tasteful variations of its value.

7. Contrasting hues (two hues) of high saturation can be safely applied in small rooms or areas. Light colors are effective in dark surroundings, and dark colors are best in light spaces. For most applications contrasting colors must be complementary.

8. Where triads of hues are selected, two of them should be related. The third should complement an average of the pair. For the best effect, related hues of the triad should be equally divided for a complete visual balance.

9. The chroma of a color is particularly important in retail environments (Chapters 22 and 23). Strong chromas (bright colors) are essential for areas in which a sense of excitement must be generated in a relatively short time,

for example, a store front, sign or window displays, and advertisements. Low chromas (grayed colors) are needed in areas in which the time exposure is long, a dignified atmosphere is desirable, and responsibility in high (e.g., a store interior).

10. The apparent size and position of an object is affected by its color. The warm colors appear to advance, whereas cool colors recede. A light color makes an object appear larger, whereas a dark color makes it appear smaller.

COLOR OF LIGHT FOR APPEARANCE AND ENVIRONMENT

When skin tone is a consideration, warm light sources rich in red are preferred to flatter the complexion.

From the standpoint of practical application warm light to enhance the human complexion should be used for lower levels of lighting and a cooler or whiter light at high levels; for example, in powder rooms, rest rooms, or dressing rooms, in which a low level of lighting is the choice, incandescents, followed by deluxe warm white fluorescents, should have the first preference. In offices, drafting rooms, and other work areas that need high levels of light cool white or deluxe cool white fluorescent or deluxe white mercury or metal halide should be the choice.

As far as the appearance of the material is concerned, the main thing to remember is that the light will be effective only with those colors whose energy is present in the spectrum. The absence of an energy band will produce an unreal color. Similarly, a predominance of some energy will flatter that color and may raise questions of credibility (this is particularly applicable in merchandising areas and food stores).

REFERENCES

Birren, Faber. *Color and Human Response*. New York: Van Nostrand-Reinhold, 1978.

Birren, Faber. "Color and Man-Made Environments: Reactions of Mind and Emotion." *Journal of the American Institute of Architects* (October 1972).

Evans, Ralph M. *The Perception of Color*. New York: Wiley, 1974.

17

Environmental Impression

Although the main purpose of light is to make things visible, its scope is much broader than that; for example, it can create an environmental impression. The room can be spacious or cluttered; it can be inviting, exciting, depressing, boring, relaxing, or pleasing, all of which ultimately have an impact on the mood and behavior of the occupant. Environmental lighting, in many ways, is responsible for the occupant's working efficiency. On the other hand, no visual task is necessary to create the character of environmental lighting.

From the very beginning environmental lighting has been a subject of great curiosity in the minds of environmental and illuminating designers. Experts have conducted a variety of experiments with varied results and conclusions limited to experimental parameters. In the general outline we have prepared it is important to note that although these simple guidelines are useful, their application still requires skilled judgment.

IMPRESSION OF SPACE

An impression of spaciousness can be created with a moderate amount of general ambient lighting and a greater amount of perimeter (wall) lighting. The perimeter must be bright and uncluttered, possibly with in light tone. Warm colors appear to advance and cool colors to recede, characteristics that can be adopted to "open up" space.

Use of specular surfaces such as mirrored walls can double the sense of space. Mirrors, as we know, reflect opposite walls to stretch a room's boundaries. To maximize this impression lighting should be directed toward the unmirrored walls. In a large room a separate ambient lighting system may be necessary. Brightness is a reinforcing factor but not a decisive one.

Windows with a view also help to create a feeling of space. In interior windowless rooms, however, small openings in partition walls often provide similar results. Architecture is important here. The room by itself may be small, but the arrangement allows the eyes to focus on distant objects and thus erases possible claustrophobia. It is important to remember that the distant object should be illuminated to catch the attention.

In a group of small rooms one common high ceiling (e.g., cathedral or sloped), visible to all, will increase the sense of space. The partitions between the

Figure 17-1. *Cleverly used, mirrors can expand a room visually. It is important to note that lighting should be directed toward the walls, not the mirrors.*

rooms may be varied heights for privacy. Peripheral or perimeter lighting is important here just as much as task lighting in separate rooms. If the rooms are very small, the furniture should be kept to a minimum.

IMPRESSION OF PERCEPTUAL CLARITY

An impression of perceptual clarity is obtained with a high level of uniform, white light. Emphasis is placed on overhead lighting with large, visible, direct type of luminaires (e.g., fluorescent troffers, luminous ceiling), as opposed to perimeter lighting with cove or indirect light or wall brackets. Painted surfaces (walls and ceiling) in a light color of high reflectance, opposed to patterned wallpapers, are preferred.

If the visual task is uninteresting or if there is none at all, this lighting may contribute to boredom because there are no stimulating elements in the spatial information. In a large gathering this environment tends to be noisy—noise that usually increases with the light level.

In a room with a luminous ceiling the dominating ceiling pattern reduces the focal emphasis.

IMPRESSION OF RELAXATION

Relaxation implies rest for the tired body. All glare is to be avoided, especially if it is on the ceiling. Low

levels of ambient light in the form of a spill from accentuated or wall-wash light in a nonuniform pattern provides this relaxed atmosphere.

Table lamps, accent or wall-wash, rather than large ceiling-mounted luminaires should be used, and dimmer switches can fine-tune the lighting level to individual requirements. In general, invisible light sources, low illuminance, subdued color, low wall brightness, fading to a dark upper ceiling, are most restful.

IMPRESSION OF PRIVACY

A nonuniform lighting pattern, with a center lighting level dimmed but a higher brightness beyond, yields an impression of privacy. Typically, people enjoy a relaxed underlighted area, but need the bright lights nearby for security. This lighting is particularly effective in restaurants or bars, where customers tend to congregate in underlighted areas but prefer a view that is brighter. This is one of the few applications in which visual-task (drinking and eating) light level is much lower than that of other areas. Experiments show that the preferred visual task light is a warm tone (e.g., incandescents or candles), as opposed to the cooler tones produced primarily by fluorescents or mercury vapor. Following the characteristics of black-body radiation, the white color rendition is often indicative of a very high level of illumination,

Figure 17-2. *If there are glass partitions or large windows between two rooms, one can be visually extended to the other by their lighting systems.*

Figure 17-3. *Perceptual clarity is achieved with large, visible area sources with white color rendition and bright surroundings.*

Figure 17-4. Impression of relaxation. In general, no directly visible light sources, subdued color, and low level illumination directed at a dark ceiling are relaxing and restful.

Figure 17-5. The level of light to achieve an impression of privacy goes back to the fundamentals: lower than the surroundings, nonuniform, and warm in color.

which might be one of the reasons for its lack of acceptance in such applications.

IMPRESSION OF PLEASANTNESS

Perhaps this is the most sought after environment in almost all applications, particularly in an officelike atmosphere, in which a sedentary task or steady use of the eyes is involved.

Exactly what kind of lighting makes an atmosphere pleasant is inconclusive. Practical experiments conducted by experts in the field have provided a general answer—a nonuniform lighting with strong emphasis on peripherals (walls in particular).

This was well demonstrated by R. J. Hawks, D. L. Loe, and E. A. Rowland, in 1979, when they collected ratings related to people's impressions of a small office illuminated by 18 different lighting combinations which included conventional uniform lighting, downlighting, wall washing, local desk lighting, and spot lighting; the desk light remained unchanged at a predetermined light level. The most preferred were the installations that had a "bright" look and a nonuniform pattern of interesting wall lighting with incandescent focused sources (spotlights). The least preferred were the recessed fluorescent luminaires that provided a blanket of uniform diffuse light. Earlier experiments conducted by Flynn produced these findings.

Note that nonuniform perimeter lighting is crucial here. It is an important means by which the fatigue caused by uniform task lighting can be diluted and stimulation preserved. Experts in color are in agreement here. According to Faber Birren, "people require varying, cycling stimuli to remain sensitive and alert to their environment. Comfort and agreeableness are normally identified with moderate if not radical changes, and this change concerns brightness as well as all other elements in the environment."

What kind of nonuniform lighting satisfies these conditions is an open question that varies with application; but, in general, it includes special effects like scalloping, wall washing (brick or moss-rock walls), concentrated light on sculpture, flowers, murals, and paintings, primarily with focused incandescent sources. From time to time a change in the lighting arrangements and its highlighted objects continues to stimulate and to renew pleasantness and interest.

Although all of this information is helpful and fairly accurate, it must be remembered that it alone may not be sufficient to serve the purpose. Pleasantness is a comparative term and its judgment varies from person to person.

IMPRESSION OF BOREDOM AND MONOTONY

Boredom and monotony occur when the visual tasks are uninteresting, and no stimulation emanates from the spatial elements, including environmental lighting. Uniform blankets of light throughout the room and a consistent dull-colored perimeter often contribute to boredom, monotony, and other effects at least of partial sensory deprivation.

IMPRESSION OF DEPRESSION

Dim light and dim, dark-colored surroundings in black or dark brown are often the major contributors to depression. A room paneled dark brown, covered

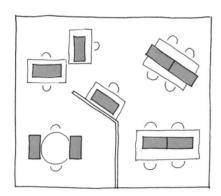

(a) ON DRAWING THE LUMINAIRES MAY APPEAR TO BE IN THE RIGHT LOCATIONS

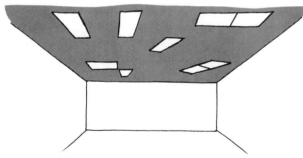

(b) IN REALITY, INCONSISTENCY IN LIGHTING PATTERN MAY GENERATE SPATIAL CONFUSION.

Figure 17-6. Irregular task locations often provide an unsymmetrical pattern of light as shown here, and result in spatial confusion.

WHERE DID I GO WRONG?

Figure 17-7. Impression of clutter and confusion. Selection of luminaires, wallpapers, and floor design, all are contributing factors.

in dark brown or black carpet, and equipped with low-level lighting is an example.

IMPRESSION OF DRAMA, EXCITEMENT, GAIETY

Nonuniform lighting of varying brightness, including such extremes as sparkles and glitter, moving or flashing lights, and peripherals of stimulating color patterns express drama and excitement. This environment also tends to encourage conversation.

IMPRESSION OF CONFUSION AND CLUTTER

An impression of confusion is felt when nonuniform lighting and/or color patterns clash with spatial information.

The ceiling (overhead zone) is usually of subordinate interest in relation to the activity; the lighting used and its mounting arrangements are expected to maintain a consistent pattern. Any major deviation from the orientation creates a state of clutter and con-

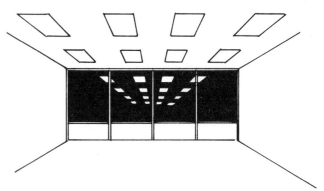

Figure 17-9. *Reflection of the luminaires on window panes creates a black hole. The effect is maximized if there are windows at opposite ends.*

Figure 17-8. *A cave effect takes place when a high level of illumination is directed toward the task area and the surroundings remain in the dark.*

fusion. A similar impression is obtained if wallpaper and carpet designs are both clashing and "busy".

IMPRESSION OF CAVE EFFECT, INSECURITY, SPOOKINESS

A cave effect is achieved when a highly illuminated task area is located inside a large room with dark peripherals. If the visual task is illuminated with table lamps or localized, self-standing forms (not on the ceiling) and no other light sources exist for ambient and perimeter lighting, the effect is at its maximum.

"Spookiness" occurs when a very low level of light in the perimeter, gathered as a spill from the task or ambient light, gives the furniture or other spatial material a deformed appearance.

IMPRESSION OF "BLACK HOLE"

This is a special condition of the cave effect. At night, a series of window glasses producing reflected im-

ages of the bright luminaires of the room gives the impression of a black hole outside the room. This may produce visual noise as well as, in special cases, act as the second source of veiling reflections. The effect is at its maximum if there are windows at opposite sides, reflecting images of each other.

To solve this problem select low brightness luminaires and/or hang draperies or curtains. Illuminated objects on the exterior for visual relief is another solution.

REFERENCES

Boyce, P. R. *Human Factors in Factors in Lighting.* New York: Macmillan, 1981.

Flynn, J. E., T. J. Spencer, O. Martyriuck, and C. Hendrick. "Interim Study of Procedures for Investigating the Effect of Light on Impression and Behavior." *Journal of the Illuminating Engineering Society 3,* 87 (1973).

Flynn, J. E. "A Study of Subject's Responses to Low Energy and Non-Uniform Lighting Systems." Lighting Design and Application (July 1977).

Hawkes, R. J., D. L. Loe, and E. Rowlands, "A Note Towards the Understanding of Lighting Quality." *Journal of the Illuminating Engineering Society, 8,* 111 (1979).

APPLICATION: OFFICE ENVIRONMENT

18

Task Lighting

The concept of task lighting is not new. For centuries candles, oil lamps, and kerosene lanterns were the means employed. In a crude sense task lighting may be defined as the amount of light that is needed to make a task visible. In this respect it can be an independent source of light located close to the task or a part of the general room lighting that illuminates the ambient as well. Ever since the invention of electric lamps incandescents have served both purposes (task and ambient); recently, however, fluorescent lamps took over that position. The use of fluorescent luminaires at the ceiling for task and ambient lighting has been common practice for years and is still popular because of their high light output, long lamp life, and high efficiency; yet the arrangement has revealed a number of flaws. Poorly designed luminaires and unplanned locations produce direct glare, inadequate amounts of useful (quality) light, veiling reflections, and reduced contrast. The introduction of table lamps was done out of necessity. For sedentary tasks, like working at a desk, reading, writing, or drafting a supplementary amount of light was needed not only for an increment in the quantity but also to improve visibility. Table lamps today not only provide supplementary light they are also decorative.

A number of factors should be considered in the improvement of visibility of the horizontal task (hereafter referred to as task).

TASK CONTRAST

The contrast between the visual task (e.g., the printed lines of a book) and the background (the paper) must be high. If the lines are printed light gray and the background is white, they will certainly be more difficult to read than if they were black on a white background. Research shows that for each 1% loss in contrast between visual task and background there is a need for 15% more light to maintain the same degree of visibility. Visibility is a maximum when the luminance contrast of the details in the background is maximum (see Figure 18-1).

SIZE OF THE VISIBLE TASK

The size of the visible task must be large and clear enough to be easily read. Figure 18-2 shows that reading the paragraph in the box becomes increas-

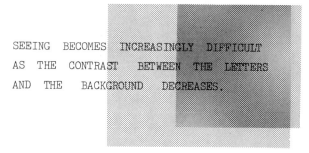

SEEING BECOMES INCREASINGLY DIFFICULT AS THE CONTRAST BETWEEN THE LETTERS AND THE BACKGROUND DECREASES.

Figure 18-1. Task contrast is important to comfortable vision. Visibility is maximum when the luminance contrast of the details in the background is maximum.

ingly easier as the size of the type gets larger. The type sizes shown range from 6 to 12 point; 8 point type may be regarded as the minimum if the quality of light is satisfied to the fullest extent. For most purposes, however, 10 point or larger is recommended for prolonged reading.

SPEED AND ACCURACY OF READING

The speed of reading of the visual task depends a lot on the eye's ability to focus on the word, adjust to it, and pass the message to the brain. Inadequate type size, low level of light, lack of contrast and luminance will hinder visibility, hence affect the speed and accuracy of reading.

AGE OF VIEWER

Aging of the eye has a serious impact on vision. All of the foregoing factors are of particular interest if the viewer is an older person.

Experiments conducted by lighting research centers show that vision decreases drastically as the eyes age. The older they get, the higher the amount of

quality light required for the same visibility. Figure 18-3 shows how younger workers outperform the older in terms of speed and accuracy at all illuminance levels.

LIGHTING FOR TASK

This, by far, is the most important factor of all. For the task to be visible it is necessary that the light concentrated on the task be sufficient in (a) quantity and adequate in (b) quality. This is explained in detail because these terms are the most frequently used in interior lighting.

(a) Quantity

The word quantity of light usually implies the amount of light falling on the task plane, measured by a footcandle meter. It is a measure of the raw or conventional lighting that may or may not make the task adequately visible. The unit of quantity of light is the footcandle.

To help the lighting designer decide on the quantity of light level the Illuminating Engineering Society has researched and adopted recommended levels of illumination for indoor activities. These data are listed in the Reference Volume of the 1981 IES Lighting Handbook. Because the exact illumination level for any activity will depend on a number of variables IES divides them into "lighting categories", which give a range of footcandle levels for a certain type of activity. The exact level can be determined by the age of the workers, speed and/or accuracy needed, and task background reflectance. The following example illustrates the procedure in its simplest form. (For detail the reader is advised to refer to the *IES Lighting Handbook,* 1981, Reference Volume, pp. A-1 to A-22.) Let us say that we are to determine the illuminance level on a desk that is used for studying books

Figure 18-2. Vision becomes difficult when the size of the task is small. (Reprinted from IES Lighting Handbook, 3rd ed.)

The use of 6-point type is not desirable for continuous reading even by persons with normal vision.

Eight-point type may be regarded as the minimum size tolerable if visibility and ease of seeing are of any consequence.

A more reasonable type size and, fortunately, one finding ever-increasing use for prolonged or continuous reading is this 10-point size.

Studies indicate the desirability of 12-point type size for continuous reading over long periods of time.

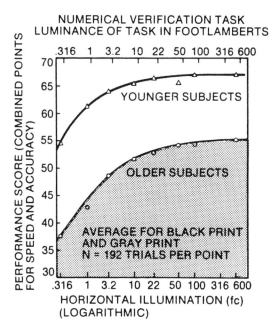

NUMERICAL VERIFICATION TASK
LUMINANCE OF TASK IN FOOTLAMBERTS

YOUNGER SUBJECTS

OLDER SUBJECTS

AVERAGE FOR BLACK PRINT
AND GRAY PRINT
N = 192 TRIALS PER POINT

PERFORMANCE SCORE (COMBINED POINTS
FOR SPEED AND ACCURACY)

HORIZONTAL ILLUMINATION (fc)
(LOGARITHMIC)

Figure 18-3. *The ability to see is drastically decreased as the eye ages. Younger workers outperform older workers in terms of speed and accuracy at all light levels. (Courtesy of Illuminating Engineering Research Institute.)*

(white paper, 80% reflectance). The observer or the worker is 45 years old and the demand for speed and accuracy is important. The first step is to identify the illuminance category, which varies from A to I, for different activities. From Table 18-1, part II, we find that it is E under "Reading" and "Desk: Primary task plane, Study". The letter E indicates that the recommended level of illuminance varies from 500 to 1000 lx (50 to 100 fc), from which a precise selection has to be made. For this and the final step we refer to Table 18-2b and find that for the age of the observer (45 years), demand for speed and/or accuracy (important), and the task background reflectance (80%), the level of illuminance is 750 lx (75 fc). The fc value is found by dividing the illuminance (lx) by 10. Ambient lighting levels are determined in the same way, except that, instead of the task background, room surface reflectances must be considered. Once the level of illuminance is known, point-by-point, lumen, or empirical methods can be used to determine the number of luminaires required to meet the footcandle level.

This new method of determining a level of illuminance undoubtedly provides a more precise answer than the old method in which only one number was given for an activity. But it still raises some questions;

for example, what happens if the room is for multipurposes and/or the ages of the workers vary widely? What about merchandizing areas in which artistic effects are desired? Advertising? Here are some words of relief: according to the IES, "This illuminance selection procedure is intended for use in interior environments where visual performance is an important consideration . . . the selection procedure is not used to determine the appropriate illuminances when:

1. Merchandising is the principal activity in the space and the advantageous display of goods is the purpose of lighting.

2. Advertising, sales promotion or attraction is the purpose of lighting.

3. Lighting is for sensors other than the eye, as in film and television applications.

4. The principle purpose of lighting is to achieve artistic effects.

5. Luminance ratios have a greater importance than adaptation luminance, as when it is desired to achieve a particular psychological or emotional setting rather than provide for visual performance.

6. Minimum illuminances are required for safety.

7. Maximum illuminances are established to prevent nonvisual effects, such as bleaching or deterioration due to ultraviolet and infrared radiation in a museum.

8. Illuminances are part of a test procedure for evaluating equipment, such as for surgical lighting systems."

It is important to note that the light level determined by this procedure represents the quantity only. It does not take into account the quality aspects of lighting, such as the glare produced by luminaires, which may have an adverse effect on the sight process. For most situations, in general ambient lighting, meeting the quantity is sufficient. For task lighting, however, it is essential that it meet quality as well.

(b) Quality

Quality in task lighting relates directly to the shadows and glare present in the lighting system. Sharply defined shadows reduce visual efficiency. Proper light diffusion and high-reflectance matte-finished surfaces

TABLE 18-1. A PARTIAL LIST OF CURRENTLY RECOMMENDED ILLUMINANCE CATEGORIES AND ILLUMINANCE VALUES FOR LIGHTING DESIGN—TARGET MAINTAINED LEVELS[a]

I. Illuminance Categories and Illuminance Values for Generic Types of Activities in Interiors

Type of Activity	Illuminance Category	Ranges of Illuminances		Reference Work-Plane
		Lux	Footcandles	
Public spaces with dark surroundings	A	20–30–50	2–3–5	
Simple orientation for short temporary visits	B	50–75–100	5–7.5–10	General lighting throughout spaces
Working spaces where visual tasks are only occasionally performed	C	100–150–200	10–15–20	
Performance of visual tasks of high contrast or large size	D	200–300–500	20–30–50	
Performance of visual tasks of medium contrast or small size	E	500–750–1000	50–75–100	Illuminance on task
Performance of visual tasks of low contrast or very small size	F	1000–1500–2000	100–150–200	
Performance of visual tasks of low contrast and very small size over a prolonged period	G	2000–3000–5000	200–300–500	
Performance of very prolonged and exacting visual tasks	H	5000–7500–10000	500–750–1000	Illuminance on task, obtained by a combination of general and local (supplementary lighting)
Performance of very special visual tasks of extremely low contrast and small size	I	10000–15000–20000	1000–1500–2000	

II. Commercial, Institutional, Residential and Public Assembly Interiors

Area/Activity	Illuminance Category	Area/Activity	Illuminance Category
Offices		Electronic data processing tasks	
Accounting (see **Reading**)		CRT screens	B[12, 13]
Conference areas (see **Conference rooms**)		Impact printer	
Drafting (see **Drafting**)		good ribbon	D
General and private offices (see **Reading**)		poor ribbon	E
Libraries (see **Libraries**)		2nd carbon and greater	E
Lobbies, lounges and reception areas	C	Ink jet printer	D
Mail sorting	E	Keyboard reading	D
Off-set printing and duplicating area	D	Machine rooms	
		Active operations	D
Post offices (see **Offices**)		Tape storage	D
		Machine area	C
Reading		Equipment service	E[10]
Copied tasks		Thermal print	E
Ditto copy	E[3]	Handwritten tasks	
Micro-fiche reader	B[12, 13]	#3 pencil and softer leads	E[3]
Mimeograph	D	#4 pencil and harder leads	F[3]
Photographs, moderate detail	E[13]	Ball-point pen	D[3]
Thermal copy, poor copy	F[3]	Felt-tip pen	D
Xerograph	D	Handwritten carbon copies	E
Xerography, 3rd generation and greater	E	Non photographically reproducible colors	F
		Chalkboards	E[3]

[a] Reprinted, with permission, from the *IES Lighting Handbook*, 1981, Reference Volume.

TABLE 18-2. ILLUMINANCE VALUES, MAINTAINED, IN LUX, FOR A COMBINATION OF ILLUMINANCE CATEGORIES AND USER, ROOM, AND TASK CHARACTERISTICS (FOR ILLUMINANCE IN FOOTCANDLES, DIVIDE BY 10)[a]

a. General Lighting Throughout Room

Weighting Factors		Illuminance Categories		
Average of Occupants Ages	Average Room Surface Reflectance (per cent)	A	B	C
Under 40	Over 70	20	50	100
	30–70	20	50	100
	Under 30	20	50	100
40–55	Over 70	20	50	100
	30–70	30	75	150
	Under 30	50	100	200
Over 55	Over 70	30	75	150
	30–70	50	100	200
	Under 30	50	100	200

b. Illuminance on Task

Weighting Factors			Illuminance Categories					
Average of Workers Ages	Demand for Speed and/or Accuracy[*]	Task Background Reflectance (per cent)	D	E	F	G[**]	H[**]	I[**]
Under 40	NI	Over 70	200	500	1000	2000	5000	10000
		30–70	200	500	1000	2000	5000	10000
		Under 30	300	750	1500	3000	7500	15000
	I	Over 70	200	500	1000	2000	5000	10000
		30–70	300	750	1500	3000	7500	15000
		Under 30	300	750	1500	3000	7500	15000
	C	Over 70	300	750	1500	3000	7500	15000
		30–70	300	750	1500	3000	7500	15000
		Under 30	300	750	1500	3000	7500	15000
40–55	NI	Over 70	200	500	1000	2000	5000	10000
		30–70	300	750	1500	3000	7500	15000
		Under 30	300	750	1500	3000	7500	15000
	I	Over 70	300	750	1500	3000	7500	15000
		30–70	300	750	1500	3000	7500	15000
		Under 30	300	750	1500	3000	7500	15000
	C	Over 70	300	750	1500	3000	7500	15000
		30–70	300	750	1500	3000	7500	15000
		Under 30	500	1000	2000	5000	10000	20000
Over 55	NI	Over 70	300	750	1500	3000	7500	15000
		30–70	300	750	1500	3000	7500	15000
		Under 30	300	750	1500	3000	7500	15000
	I	Over 70	300	750	1500	3000	7500	15000
		30–70	300	750	1500	3000	7500	15000
		Under 30	500	1000	2000	5000	10000	20000
	C	Over 70	300	750	1500	3000	7500	15000
		30–70	500	1000	2000	5000	10000	20000
		Under 30	500	1000	2000	5000	10000	20000

[*] NI = not important, I — important, and C = critical
[**] Obtained by a combination of general and supplementary lighting.

[a] Reprinted, with permission, from the *IES Lighting Handbook,* 1981, Reference Volume.

Figure 18-4. (a) *Direct glare is associated with heads-up-position.* (b) *Indirect or reflected glare is associated with the heads-down-position.*

minimize them. Although shadows are not desirable on task, their presence on the perimeter are sometimes preferable to add depth or to create an aesthetic effect.

Glare can be divided loosely into two types: the direct and indirect. Direct glare is associated with tasks in heads-up position, in indirect glare is associated with the heads-down position (see Figure 18-4). Direct glare is measured in terms of visual comfort probability (VCP), which is discussed in Chapter 19.

For the task to be clearly visible it is necessary to improve the quality of lighting by minimizing the effect of indirect glare that results mainly from light emitted in the 0 to 45° zone (see Figure 18-5), reflected by a shiny or specular surface on the task and pointed toward the eyes. The patches of light visible on the surface are the images of the light source(s) that cause a loss of visibility, commonly known as the veiling reflection (see Figure 18-6). Depending on the angle and direction of the light rays, the reflected glare can be distracting. Research shows that in an office atmosphere people work in a wide range of viewing angles, from 0 to 40° and peaking at 25° (all angles measured from perpendicular to task). Because the angle of incident ray is equal to that of the reflected ray, the light rays arriving at 25° from the luminaire are responsible for veiling reflections.

EQUIVALENT SPHERE ILLUMINATION (ESI)

Many years ago it was recognized that the key to quality task lighting is reflected glare control. After years of research equivalent sphere illumination was introduced in the fifth edition of the *IES Handbook* as a measure of visibility that would take illuminance and contrast into account.

By definition ESI is "the level of sphere illumination which would produce task visibility equivalent to that produced by a specific lighting environment." In this concept illumination inside a sphere is taken as the reference and the visibility of the task in regular lighting is compared with it; for example, let us say that to be able to see the task a light level of 100 fc is needed. Now the task is placed inside the uniformly illuminated reference sphere and observed at the same angle and direction. For the same level of visibility the light level inside the sphere may be different, say 50 fc. In this case for the same visibility the

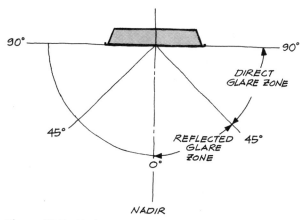

Figure 18-5. *Nadir is at the bottom of the luminaire at 0°. Measured from the nadir, 0 to 45° is the reflected glare zone; 45 to 90° is the direct glare zone.*

task is said to have 50 ESI. (Note that the sphere illumination does not necessarily represent the ideal lighting system; it is used for reference because it is easily reproducible and experiments show that placement of the task within an evenly illuminated spherical surface produces good task contrast).

The determination of an ESI value is a complex process based on many contributing factors; for example, the type of task (pencil, pen, and print on paper or mylar), task contrast, observer's orientation in the space (viewing angle and direction), and effects of veiling reflections must be considered. The procedure is so complex that analytical methods become impractical and the use of a computer is essential. A number of computer programs now available on the market will determine good ESI locations in a given layout. (These programs are provided by the luminaire manufacturing companies, usually free of charge, as an inducement to buy their equipment.) But unfortunately, even with a computer fed with the most accurate data, the results are applicable only to fixed conditions. A slight change in the observer's viewing angle or direction or in the type of task and its position would require a new set of calculations. In addition, a reverse process, for example, to determine the luminaire locations for ESI readings and work areas, is almost impossible at this time because of the complexity of optimization, and no attempt has been made here to provide mathematical models; only practical points are considered:

1. No matter what type of luminaire is used, installation away from the offending zones establishes good ESI. Consider a minimum of two luminaires placed at each side of the task area. Figure 18-7 gives the results of the orientations

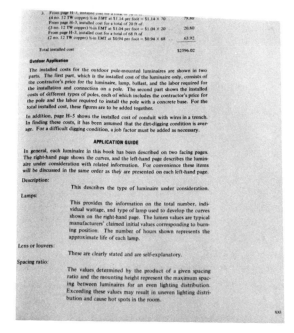

(a)

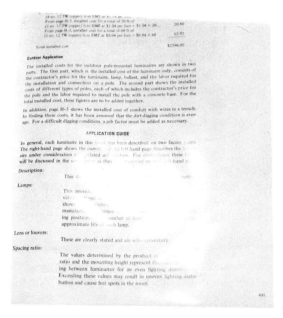

(b)

Figure 18-6. (a) *No veiling reflection,* (b) *Veiling reflection.*

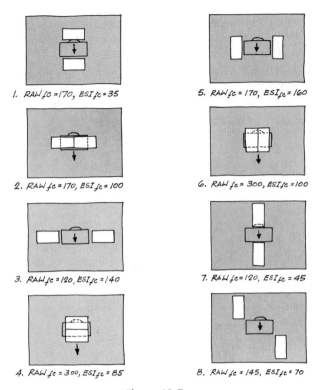

1. RAW fc = 170, ESI fc = 35

2. RAW fc = 170, ESI fc = 100

3. RAW fc = 120, ESI fc = 140

4. RAW fc = 300, ESI fc = 85

5. RAW fc = 170, ESI fc = 160

6. RAW fc = 300, ESI fc = 100

7. RAW fc = 120, ESI fc = 45

8. RAW fc = 145, ESI fc = 70

Figure 18-7.

in a small room of two 2 × 4 ft fluorescent troffers, each with four lamps and a standard acrylic prismatic lens. The highest ESI is obtained with No. 5, in which a luminaire is placed at each side of a desk. The least favorable is No. 1, which produces the lowest ESI with a luminaire in the offending zone. Also note that an increment in raw footcandle value does not necessarily mean that the ESI footcandles at that location will improve (e.g., Nos. 4 or 6). The same concept applies to larger rooms. Figure 18-8 is an ESI footcandle study of Problem 6-12 in which ESI footcandle levels are determined at four points (A, B, C, D) and four viewing directions (north, south, east, and west). Note also, as expected, that the highest ESI footcandles are obtained at point B even though the raw fc at this location is the lowest.

2. Experiments show that light emerging between 0 and 30° is a source of veiling reflection; ESI improves as light emerges from the upper angles. (Caution: light from upper angles may produce direct glare! A number of expensive, high ESI-producing lenses are victims of this condition.)

3. The degree of veiling reflections from the light control media of various light sources are as follows:

Diffusers

Diffusers tend to follow the lambertian law spreading equal amounts of brightness all around. From this standpoint there is a relatively small amount of glare in the close angles and only small veiling reflections.

Standard Prismatic Lens

Prismatic lenses, which have female grooves on the bottom surface, produce a concentration of light in the closer angles (0 to 30°) that causes high veiling reflections.

Louvers

Louvers can be loosely divided into three groups: translucent, opaque, and parabolic wedge. Louvers are physical barriers to light output; in this respect they are excellent for glare control at high angles (45° and higher), but they do reveal abundant lighting in the lower angles which causes veiling reflections that increase in the following order: parabolic, opaque, and translucent.

Polarizer

Polarizers are excellent for reducing glare produced by a single ray of light. Available materials of the flake or layer type used for area sources provide diffusion and reduce veiling reflections.

Daylight

Depending on its intensity and location, natural light (daylight) from windows can produce substantial veiling reflections. The glare can be controlled by the use of blinds or draperies.

4. Improvement of visibility or ESI is often no more difficult than repositioning a desk, seating arrangement, or luminaire by 90° to avoid veiling reflection. With the proper combination of angles reflected glare can be almost entirely eliminated by polarizing the light as it leaves the light source.

5. In existing buildings lighting can be judged with the help of a mirror about the size of a typical task (8½ × 11 in.) positioned on the work plane. If no luminaires are visible at the

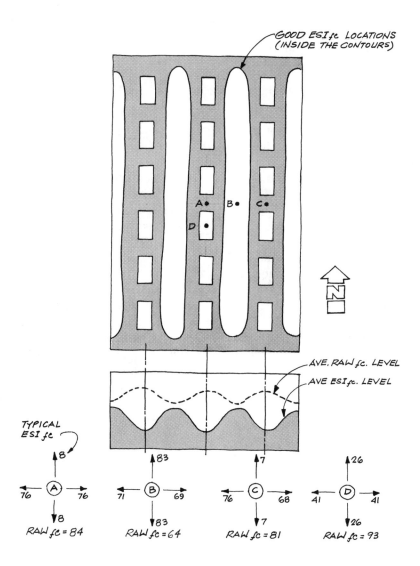

GOOD ESI fc LOCATIONS
(INSIDE THE CONTOURS)

AVE. RAW fc. LEVEL

AVE ESI fc. LEVEL

TYPICAL
ESI fc

	8		83		7		26
76	(A) 76	71	(B) 69	76	(C) 68	41	(D) 41
	8		83		7		26
	RAW fc = 84		RAW fc = 64		RAW fc = 81		RAW fc = 93

normal viewing angle, it is likely to have a high ESI.

6. Consider the use of supplementary light from a table lamp, light stand, or clamp-on source to wash off the veiling reflections caused by other luminaires.

In the latest *IES Lighting Handbook* (1981) the levels of illuminance for tasks subject to veiling reflections are no longer listed in ESI because "currently, insufficient experience in the use of ESI target values precludes the direct use of Equivalent Sphere Illumination in the present consensus approach to recommend illuminance values. Equivalent Sphere Illumination may be used as a tool in determining the effectiveness of controlling veiling reflections and as a part of evaluation of lighting system."

VERTICAL TASK—CRT LIGHTING

Contemporary offices and other commercial areas are becoming increasingly dependent on CRT, a short form for cathode ray tube, which is the generic term for the latest revolutionary application of high-tech: desk-top computers, word processors, and other video display terminals.

With CRT the task has been raised from desk level to the glossy surface of the screen. This presents unique problems that cannot be solved by traditional task lighting alone. A wide variety of models is available in a proliferation of styles with characters and backgrounds of various colors and contrasts and screens that can be convex to flat, vertically positioned to a 15° tilt. With no officially accepted standardization, the lighting designer is faced with the challenge of creating a new lighting system that will not only be satisfactory for conventional work on a horizontal plane but also for the vertical screen.

Recognizing Problems

It is important that the designer recognize the potential problems a CRT may present (see Figure 18-9), the biggest of which, perhaps, are the reflected images of the luminaires facing the screen. The brightness of the luminaires visible on the screen makes it almost impossible at times to read the characters. Images of other surfaces, such as windows, specular documents, lighted paintings or sculptures, work surfaces, and even the operator's clothes distort the field of view on the convex screen and reduce its contrast. The difference in lighting levels required for the two types of tasks is another problem. Characters on the screen can be read with ease in a dim environment of about 20 fc but reading, writing, typing, or viewing the keyboard may need 60 to 70 fc. Rays of light appearing from a luminaire behind the viewer has always been considered an excellent position for horizontal tasks. With CRT lighting, however, it is the worst. In addition, because the head remains in the up position, direct glare from the luminaires in front of the eyes is of great concern.

Finding a Solution

All CRT stations can be divided into three general categories. The first is "one-CRT-per station," which constitutes 90% of the installations. The second is "medium intensity situations" in which as many as 10 units in one general location constitute 5% of the installations. The remaining 5% is the third category, known as the "large data center," in which more than 10 CRTs face in various directions in groups or scattered all around.

Because of the complexities involved, it is obvious that one solution cannot hold true for all applications. On-site experience, however, led to the following conclusions, which may be used as guidelines for efficient CRT lighting:

CRTs in an Existing Room

1. If only one CRT station (first category) is to be installed in a room with a ceiling full of bright fluorescent luminaires, consider its placement in a subdued corner where the ambient lighting

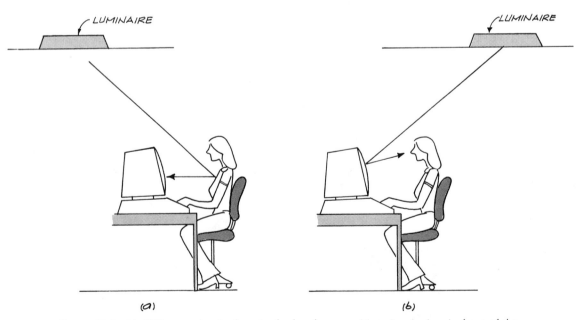

(a)   *(b)*

Figure 18-9. (a) CRT operation is done in the heads up position. Luminaires in front of the operator cause discomforting glare and those above contribute to a reflected image of the surroundings. The convex-shape screen projects an exaggerated image of the rear field of view and reduces screen contrast. (b) Light rays arriving from behind create an excellent contrast to the horizontal task; but on the vertical screen the effect is just the opposite. Reflected images of the rear luminaires appear on the screen, causing a veiling reflection and reducing screen contrast.

is fairly low. Position the CRT screen facing a nonglossy wall or a vertical surface that does not reflect light and no luminaires are in the operator's immediate field of view. If that is not possible, use a bookcase, file cabinet, or room divider to obstruct the glare (see Figure 18-10). This "sandwich" concept is probably the easiest means of getting good CRT lighting.

2. The sandwich concept can also be applied successfully in medium intensity situations in which only a few CRT units occupy one general location.

3. Perhaps the biggest problem is in dealing with "large data centers" in which a great number of CRTs are scattered all around the room, facing in multidirections. If the sandwich concept is impractical here, replacement of the existing lenses with "low-glare-producing" models should be considered. A variety of materials is available on the market, among which the most effective are $\frac{1}{2} \times \frac{1}{2} \times \frac{1}{2}$ in. small-cell, specular aluminized plastic louvers and (b) $1\frac{1}{2} \times 1\frac{1}{2} \times 1$ in. multicell, anodozided aluminum, specular silver, parabolic louvers (Chapter 12). The first kind cuts the glare to almost nothing, thus offering excellent CRT screen contrast but at the expense of reducing the general light level to about 50% or less, which may be too low for other activities. Its cost is the lower of

the two, but so is its efficiency (about 35 to 40%). Use of the parabolic louver offers a better solution by providing a compromise between glare and light output requirements.

4. If no changes can be made in the location of the CRTs or luminaires, screen filters can be added. These devices are available from Polaroid Corporation, Cambridge, MA, Optical Coating Laboratory Inc., Santa Rosa, CA, Sun-Flex Company Inc., Nanato, CA, and Inmac, Santa Clara, CA.

5. Reflections from a window can be eliminated by covering it with a blind or dense drapery.

6. The mirror-scanning technique can be used to identify the objects that reflect on the screen.

CRTs in New Applications

1. Uniform illumination of the entire ceiling can be done economically by indirect lighting. The luminaires may be pendant from the ceiling, self-standing on the floor, or furniture integrated, but care must be taken that no "hot spots" are visible. Luminaires that create a "radial batwing distribution" should be considered.

2. No objects or areas that exceed 500 fL or are less than 100 fL in brightness should be visible on the screen.

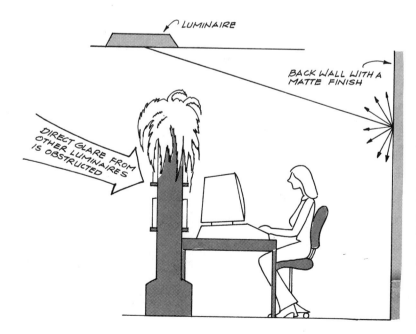

Figure 18-10. The sandwich concept works satisfactorily for CRT lighting. Place the CRT station between a wall and a low-height vertical surface, such as a room divider, file cabinets, or bookcase. The furniture allows ambient light to appear from the top and sides but obstructs direct glare from the luminares in front. The rear wall should have a matte finish and a medium reflectance surface to avoid any possible reflection on the screen. Wearing clothes to blend with the background minimizes the reflection on the screen.

3. All surfaces (including the operator's clothing) in and around the station should have a non-glossy or matte finish. Bright colors should be avoided.

4. Apply the basic concept of creating good ESI on vertical as well as horizontal surfaces. The mirror-scanning technique can be most effective for this purpose.

5. If direct luminaires must be used, the luminance ratio of the bright and dark surfaces of the ceiling should not exceed 5 : 1 from the field of view. Consider low-glare-producing but efficient luminaires when a large number of CRTs must be positioned in multidirections. Deep cell, specular finish, parabolic-louvered luminaires, or coffer ceilings may be a good solution.

6. Perhaps the best solution to CRT lighting is its installation inside low-partition modular booths, which in essence create the sandwich concept. The wall in front of the unit interrupts the direct glare from the luminaires at the back. The other tasks can be carried out by ceiling-mounted lighting, which must have the quality outlined earlier. A combination of task ambient lighting, indirect ambient, and furniture-integrated task lighting is another good solution (see Figure 20-1*b*). Care should be taken however, to make certain that the backwall reflectance is low enough not to interfere with the contrast of the screen.

7. The designer should follow the recommendations provided by National Institute of Occupational Safety and Health (NIOSH), which are the conclusions drawn from a series of experiments and research in the human engineering aspects of CRT operation. These recommendations include mandatory vision tests of the operator, work–rest regimens, flexibility in workstation design, optimum viewing angles,

Figure 18-11. *CRT dimensions and angles recommended by the National Institute of Occupational Safety and Health (NIOSH) are H = keyboard height = 29 to 31 in.; D = viewing distance = 18 to 20 in.; φ = viewing angle = 10 to 20°; bottom edge of the screen = 10°.*

viewing distances, keyboard height, and glare control. According to NIOSH, in CRT viewing the keyboard height from the floor should stay within 29 and 31 in,, the viewing distance, 18 and 20 in., the viewing angle between 10 and 20 in., and the bottom edge of the screen, 10° (see Figure 18-11).

REFERENCES

DiLaura, D. L. "On the Computation of Equivalent Sphere Illumi-nation." *Journal of the Illuminating Engineering Society, 4* (January 1985), 129.

DiLaura, D. L., and S. M. Stannard, "An Instrument for the Measurement of Equivalent Sphere Illumination." *Journal of the Illuminating Engineering Society, 7* (April 1978), 183–187.

Florence, N. "Comparison of the Energy Effectiveness of Office Lighting Systems." A paper presented at the 1976 IES Annual Technical Convention, Cleveland, Ohio.

Kaufman, John E., Editor. "Illuminance Selection," *IES LIGHTING HANDBOOK*, 1981 Reference Volume, pp. A-1–A-20.

Ngai, P. Y. "Veiling Reflections and Design of the Optimal Intensity Distribution of a Luminaire in Terms of Visual Performance Potential." *Journal of the Illuminating Engineering Society, 4* (October 1974), 53–59.

19

Ambient Lighting

Ambient lighting may be defined as the lighting in an area that produces general illumination. Its main function is to provide "clear vision" of the surroundings for "safe" circulation. In an office environment it may also contribute to task and perimeter lighting. When the head is in the up position, the luminaires are in view. Placement must be arranged to avoid veiling reflections on the task and to provide glare-free, comfortable lighting.

Ideally, however, ambient lighting does more than that. When the head is in the up position, the room's perimeter is in view. Every object, including walls, draperies, furniture, and luminaires, is a part of it; light and color of the surroundings are also major considerations in ambient lighting. The various factors that are of concern for ambient lighting are as follows:

ROOM STRUCTURE AND DIMENSIONS

Most rooms are rectangular and ceilings are flat, although other shapes are possible. The shape of a room and its dimensions, luminaire mounting height, and surface reflectances are important to illumina-

tion. Formulas used for lighting calculations in Chapter 6 (zonal cavity method) assume that a room's configurations are such that the luminous flux generated by the luminaires reaches every corner. If the room configuration meets that criterion, an average horizontal illumination can be determined by the lumen method of calculations.

If the structure of a room does not meet this standard or the room is multipurposed, more than one lighting system may be necessary such as track, accent, wall wash, or spot. The point-by-point method, based on the invers-square law, can then be used.

COLOR SURFACE REFLECTANCES

Whatever type of luminaire is selected, ambient lighting is largely dependent on surface reflectances. In the lumen method of calculation, the exact reflectances of the ceiling, walls, and floor are needed to determine an accurate coefficient of utilization (CU). If the lighting system is indirect, ceiling reflectances, followed by floor and wall reflectances, are essential to its distribution. Whatever the lighting system or method of calculations, it is obvious that the higher the surface reflectances, the greater the amount of light. Technically, then, colors must be selected to provide the maximum reflectance that will optimize lighting efficiency. (For office interiors, the I.E.S.-recommended surface reflectances are: ceiling, 80–90%; walls, 40–60%; and floor, 20–40%).

But color selection must go beyond meeting "high" reflectances. We must consider other related factors such as the visual, physiological, and psychological effects before making a final decision. Color selection should never be based on reflectance alone. Some of these points have already been discussed in Chapters 3 and 16; there is more information in Chapter 21.

DAYLIGHT

Use of daylight for interior lighting has been a principal feature of building design from the very beginning. Although it is beyond the scope of this chapter to describe the techniques of daylighting, for all practical purposes the following should be considered as the minimum requirements.

1. Designing for daylighting should be done with adequate illumination under overcast skies in mind.
2. Position and shape of the fenestration must be planned to complement the surroundings and increase the efficiency of the workers.
3. Controls for bright-sky, cloudy, and sunlit conditions should be provided to give the eye muscles the opportunity to relax by focusing on distant objects.
4. An artificial lighting system must compensate for or work with a daylight system when natural illumination falls below recommended levels.
5. Heat gain or loss due to fenestration must be considered.

Needless to say, because most office work is done during the daylight hours, it is particularly advantageous to design fenestration that will take advantage of the maximum use of daylight.

PHYSIOLOGICAL EFFECTS OF LIGHTING

Glare is undesirable not only for clear vision but also for physical and emotional comfort. According to Fa-

ber Birren regarding environmental brightness, "Prolonged exposure to high brightness can also cause damage to the visual organ . . . it can aggravate muscular imbalance, refracting difficulties, nearsightedness, and astigmatism. Avoid conflicting areas of severe brightness differences, which may force the eye to undergo tiring muscular adjustments." Although adequate, noncompromised light is a must for safety and clear vision, a minimum amount of glare is just as important.

Glare from Artificial Light

Direct glare derives from two sources. The first is an excessively bright luminous source that is aimed directly at the eyes and reduces the ability to see clearly. It is also known as a "disability glare." Looking straight at the headlights of an oncoming car is an example of disability glare (see Figure 19-1). The other type of direct glare is due to stray peripheral light that is not aimed at the eyes; for example, a cluster of fluorescent troffers in a large open office space (see Figure 19-2). This is known as the "discomfort glare." In an office environment discomfort glare is more of a problem than a disability glare.

Direct glare is measured in terms of visual comfort probability, or VCP, which takes into account the discomfort factor of direct glare. Research shows that discomfort glare due to excessive luminance in the normal field of view is directly associated with the stress produced in the eye muscle that regulates pupil size and induces fatigue. It therefore should be avoided. VCP is the method of measuring the discomfort glare of a lighting system currently accepted by

Figure 19-1. *Looking straight at the headlights of an oncoming car is an example of "disability glare."*

Figure 19-2. *Discomfort glare in the field of view caused by a cluster of luminaires on the ceiling in an open office.*

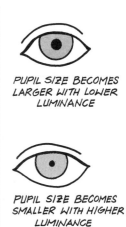

PUPIL SIZE BECOMES LARGER WITH LOWER LUMINANCE

PUPIL SIZE BECOMES SMALLER WITH HIGHER LUMINANCE

Figure 19-3. *Looking up, down, and around causes constant eye adaptation to varying luminances. As each occurs the size of the pupil changes within a finite time and settles on a size that is perfect for that vision.*

the IES. It is not a measure of the physiological effect, but it does represent a statistical prediction of the percentage of people who will be expected to find a lighting system acceptable in terms of discomfort glare. Based on the format and procedure of the IES, VCP data are available for most area type luminaires (e.g., 2 × 4 ft fluorescent troffers), usually free of charge, from the manufacturers. Its values, as expected, vary for different room sizes, light distribution of the luminaires, and height of luminaire mounting planes.

Higher VCP values mean a higher probability of comfort (lower discomfort glare). After conducting a number of experiments the IES recommends that for visual comfort the lighting system of an office environment meet the following three requirements:

1. A VCP of 70 or more.
2. A ratio of maximum-to-average luminance of no more than 5 : 1 (preferably 3 : 1) crosswise and lengthwise.
3. Maximum luminaire luminances, crosswise and lengthwise, of no more than the following values:

Angle Above Nadir (°)	Maximum Luminance (cd/m²)	(ft-L)
45	7710	2250
55	5500	1604
65	3860	1125
75	2570	750
85	1700	495

For this the designer must examine the photometric report of the luminaire he intends to use.

Glare from Objects and Transient Adaptation

Another type of glare that may induce fatigue is caused by the reflections of the objects and surfaces in the field of view by transient adaptation. Transient adaptation is a process by which the eyes adapt themselves to a vision of a certain luminance and then proceed to the next vision of another luminance. As each occurs the size of the pupil changes within a finite time and settles on a size that is perfect for that vision. If the luminance ratios of the visions are substantially different, the transient adaptation is proportionally longer and uncomfortable (see Figure 19-3). Starting from the background of the task, the desk top, the materials on the desk, the furniture, floor, walls, ceiling, and images, the accentuated lighting on objects and paintings, the fenestration, all are contributing factors of the transient adaptation.

To keep the disability glare and transient adaptation within a comfortable limit the luminance ratios should not exceed the following: task to immediate surround, 1 : ⅓, task to remote dark surfaces, 1 : ⅕, task to remote light surfaces, 1 : 5. In addition, the luminance ratio between an accentuated object and its background should not exceed 5 : 1.

DISAGREEMENT BETWEEN THE ESI AND VCP PRINCIPLES

Finding a lighting system that produces high ESI and VCP presents a unique problem because their principles of operation are in opposition. The direct glare zone is between 45 and 90°, concentrating mainly between 60 and 90°. For a high value of VCP it is necessary that the luminance associated with this zone be as low as possible and that the light emerge between 0 and 45°. The indirect glare zone, however, lies between 0 and 45°, concentrating mainly between 0 and 30°. For a high value of ESI it is necessary that the luminance associated with this zone be as low as possible and that light emerge between 45 and 90°. In the circumstances the lighting designer will have two choices: (1) to evaluate the importance of each application and to create a design after setting the priorities; (2) when ESI and VCP are of equal importance, to provide a luminous system that will produce light between 30 and 60° in a "batwing" candlepower curve (Figure 19-4).

AMBIENT LIGHTING SYSTEMS

A variety of standard and creative ceiling patterns is possible in architectural ambient lighting. Here are a few.

Uniform Lighting: Standard Ceiling

For many years uniform lighting was the only practical approach to office illumination (and still is). Although uniform lighting is possible with any form of luminaire, the most commonly used for commercial interiors is the recessed troffer, placed to follow a predetermined grid pattern. The system is ideal for (a) perceptual clarity; (b) densely occupied work areas (100 ft^2 or less per worker); (c) tenant spaces in which the occupants change frequently; and (d) buildings in which workstations can be located anywhere in the space over the building's life cycle. Some noted disadvantages, however, are (a) it wastes energy by providing more light than needed for many tasks; (b) the uniform illumination is generally regarded as visually boring.

If a uniform lighting pattern is a must, the designer should consider (a) louvers or lenses designed to improve visual comfort and task contrast; (b) a low-glare-producing medium on the ceiling and supplementary lighting (table lamp) on the desk to wash off veiling reflections; (c) use of a flexible power-distribution system (Chapter 12) to provide mobility in luminaire relocation.

Uniform Lighting: Luminous Coffers

A coffered ceiling usually means a domed ceiling with a concealed luminaire. The luminaire is typically a fluorescent troffer or a surface-mounted wraparound. Done with care, a luminous coffer can provide glare-free task lighting with high visual comfort; use luminaires with batwing distribution and SC between 1.5 and 1.6 (Chapter 12). Some disadvantages are (a) a coffered-ceiling can be expensive; (b) luminaire locations cannot be changed; and (c) special luminaires are sometimes needed to fit into the coffer at added expense.

Uniform Lighting: Luminous Ceiling

A luminous ceiling is a large area with louvers or translucent panels in various shapes, sizes, and col-

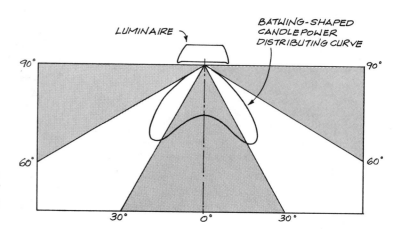

Figure 19-4. Luminaires or lighting systems that produce maximum light in the 30 to 60° zone are good solutions to the conditions when ESI and VCP are equally important.

ors. The panels act as a low brightness source of diffused illumination. Lamps are typically fluorescent and are installed in the cavity above the panels or louvers. The diffusing material should have high transmittance and an absorptance as low as possible. The cavity should be deep enough to provide the proper relation between the spacing of the fluorescent lamps and the vertical distance from the panels or louvers to produce the required uniform brightness. (More on design tips in Chapter 14). The several advantages of a luminous ceiling are (a) produces uniformly diffused illumination which yields high visual comfort and good task contrast; (b) work stations can be located arbitrarily without losing the quality of ambient (or task) lighting; (c) with proper selection of the louvers or panels the ceiling can be dramatically attractive; and (d) it serves the dual purpose of providing light and hiding structural beams, pipes, or ducts.

Nonuniform Lighting

Nonuniform lighting is the present state-of-the-art, the main purpose of which is to provide light only where needed. It can accommodate any type of luminaire, including direct, indirect, and direct-indirect. Its main advantages are (a) light and shadow add depth and an aesthetic effect; (b) energy saving is possible because light is provided only where needed; (c) it is economical because fewer luminaires are needed, (d) luminaires do not necessarily need expensive louvers or lenses to improve visual comfort or task contrast because they can be placed for the best effect. One disadvantage is that a nonuniform ceiling pattern may not be pleasing for some applications.

Longitudinal Lines: Luminous Beams

Symmetrically spaced, longitudinal lines can be created with recessed troffers or surface-mounted wraparounds, placed end to end. The continuous wraparounds give the impression of a luminous beam. The advantages are (a) the parallel lines emphasize length and can be utilized in rooms that require the appearance of depth; (b) workstations can be placed in between the lines to avoid veiling reflections; and (c) wiring costs of surface-mounted luminaires can be minimized (a feeder is brought into one end). Note that the use of a nonglare medium will improve VCP but the emphasis on length may be sacrificed.

Horizontal Lines

Like the longitudinal lines, recessed troffers or wraparounds can be used for horizontal lines and luminous beams. The advantages are (a) the lines of light across the room emphasize width; (b) wiring costs may be minimal for surface luminaires. One disadvantage is a serious glare problem, visually and on the task, when the workstations face the horizontal lines.

Pendant Fluorescents

This lighting still enjoys wide acceptance for the modernization of offices and institutions with high ceilings; it is seldom used in new construction because the trend today is decidedly toward low, uncluttered ceilings. The luminaire can be direct, indirect, or a combination. The luminaires are suspended from the ceiling by stems (or chains) to a minimum distance of 8 to 10 ft above the floor. Some advantages are the following: (a) they are highly practical for dark ceilings or when structural elements such as beams or exposed joints are present and other elements such as mechanical ducts and pipes fill the space; (b) pendant luminaires visually lower the ceiling. Disadvantages are (a) too many pendants may clutter the ceiling; and (b) pendants collect environmental dirt and maintenance is a constant problem. The quality of lighting depends on the location and type of distributing medium selected.

Luminous Cornices

In this system luminous panels are located at the intersections of the walls and ceiling. Diffusers typically are opalescent acrylic over fluorescent strips. Luminous cornices are usually sufficient for quality ambient-cum-task lighting in small rooms; for larger rooms their use is mostly for aesthetics; supplementary lighting must be considered for adequate task and ambient lighting.

Coves

Coves can be designed for lighting as well as for architectural emphasis. A fluorescent (cold cathode or neon) lamp is concealed behind a structural element (wall recess or projection), from which light is emitted toward the ceiling to be redirected downward (see Chapter 14). In small rooms cove lighting produces glare-free visual comfort. In larger rooms, however, coves, like luminous cornices, are more adaptable to aesthetics than utility. When combined with supplementary light, such as the downlights, track lights, or spotlights, they can be quite attractive and a source for quality task and ambient lighting. For straight runs fluorescent strips should be used and staggered to avoid shadows; for nonlinear (curved) lines cold cathode or neon lights are acceptable but they should not be used in combination.

REFERENCES

DiLaura, D. L. "On the Computation of Visual Comfort Probability." *Journal of the Illuminating Engineering Society*, 5, 207 (July 1976).

Guth, S. K. "Computing Visual Comfort Ratings for a Specific Interior Lighting Installation." *Illuminating Engineering* (October 1966).

Helm, Ronald N. "Energy and Lighting Design—Part One." *Electrical Construction and Maintenance*, 62–70 (November 1979).

Helm, Ronald N. "Energy and Lighting Design—Part Two." *Electrical Construction and Maintenance*, 61–67 (December 1979).

Kaufman, John E., Editor. *IES Lighting Handbook*, 5th ed., 1972.

McNamara, A. C., and Andy Willingham. "The Concept of Visual Comfort Probability." *Plant Engineering*, 141–144 (June 12, 1975)

20

Task-Ambient Lighting

In large offices in which task locations are unknown but quality light in terms of good task contrast and visual comfort are important "task/ambient" lighting is probably the best answer. In this system a large space is divided into many small movable booths (modular) with low partitions. Each booth is provided with a task light for normal office work and the partitions are low enough to take advantage of the general lighting system. Because of the small area configuration that obstructs glare, this arrangement is also ideal for CRT operation. See Figure 20-1 for an overview of a modern modular work station equipped with task/ambient lighting.

The modular concept offers several advantages; for example, it provides privacy, a pleasing environment, flexibility, quietness, and above all, energy-effective lighting.

A number of manufacturers offer this system today in various quality levels. The introduction of furniture-integrated, task-ambient lighting systems was so sudden that most of them offered nothing but aesthetic value. Only a few of these manufacturers took the time to engineer their products before releasing them on the market. Let us discuss this system in detail.

The ambient unit of this system can be direct or indirect. For direct ambient lighting the calculations are done by the conventional lumen method. Widely spaced, ceiling-mounted luminaires provide a low level of light of about 20 to 30 fc. The indirect system, on the other hand, makes use of indirect or semidirect luminaires, either that hang from the ceiling, stand on the floor, and rest on the furniture or are built into it (Figure 20-2). Lamps are fluorescent or HID (mercury vapor or metal halide). Between the two HID is the most popular because of its compact size and ease in light control. Regardless of the type used, the following should be considered for indirect ambient lighting:

1. Placement of the luminaires should be above eye level to avoid direct glare. If the cabinet height is low and/or the source is visible, it is necessary to use low-brightness shielding to avoid direct glare. This, however, may reduce luminaire efficiency to as much as 50%, depending upon the shielding used.

2. A sufficient distance between the ceiling and luminaires must be allowed to avoid a concentration of light above the luminaires. A reflect-

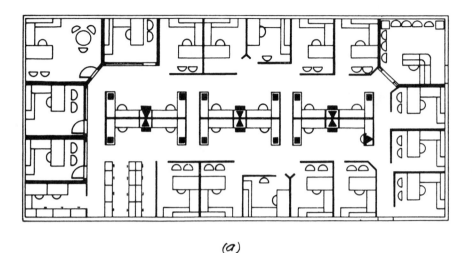

(a)

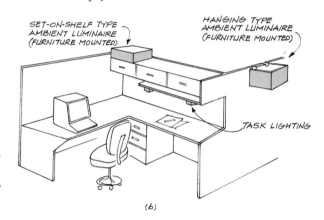

(b)

Figure 20-1. (a) *An overhead view of a typical modern office modular work station with low partition walls and task/ambient lighting. (Courtesy of the Halo Lighting Division, McGraw-Edison Co.) (b) A modern office module with task/ambient lighting.*

ing surface that is too close will make the ceiling the dominating feature and may be unpleasing. Distribution of light should be well spread in a radial batwing fashion by the use of a properly designed refractor, reflector, or both.

3. The ceiling surface should be made of a highly reflective diffusing matte material. If the ceiling is a tee-suspended exposed grid, the tees should be matte finished, preferably in the same color as the ceiling panels. Textured rather than smooth panels diffuse the light more efficiently.

4. Select luminaires with tempered glass tops. A flat horizontal surface provides easier maintenance. Properly enclosed luminaires will prevent exposure to ultraviolet rays if the lamp should shatter; the glass, however, will reduce efficiency by approximately 10%. Use of clear Teflon may be considered; 5-mil Teflon will reduce efficiency by only 5%. Sealed and gas-

keted Teflon luminaires will eliminate dirt accumulation inside, yet allow the lamps to ''breathe.''

5. CRT location must be considered. Neither the bright surface of the source nor the reflected light on the ceiling should be visible on the CRT screen.

6. The location of the luminaires should be such that their hot bodies cannot be touched accidentally and plenty of clearance is provided for heat dissipation.

7. Ballast noise is another consideration. Select ballasts that are low in noise and avoid placing them in a location in which the sound may be amplified by the furniture.

The main purpose of using an indirect system is to produce uniform luminance across the ceiling area and uniform, diffused, shadow-free light throughout the room. This will increase visual comfort, but the effect may be boring. Furniture in attractive colors

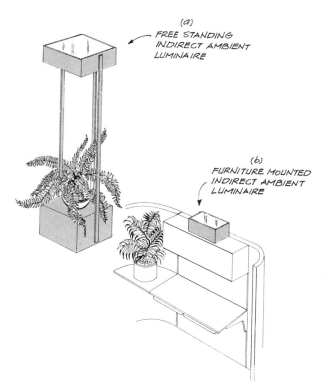

Figure 20-2. Typical examples of free-standing and furniture-mounted indirect, ambient luminaires.

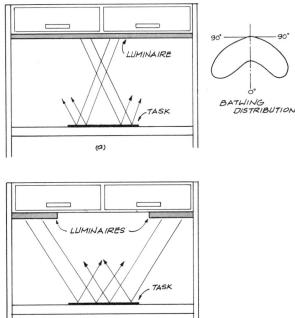

Figure 20-3. (a) A batwing distribution redirects reflected rays away from the offending zones. (b) Light rays arriving from two lamps, one at each side, provide abundant light on the sides and less in the middle. This condition can be cured with special lenses that emit light toward the center of the task.

and accent lights to highlight decorative items will provide visual relief from the uniform diffused illumination produced by an indirect lighting system.

Furniture-integrated fluorescent lamps are used for task-lighting. The enclosure is usually equipped with a conventional prismatic, plastic refractor or an open bottom. Others have specially designed refractors that produce batwing distribution. Although the location of most lamps is directly above the user and parallel to the task, others are side-mounted or in combination. Figure 20-3 shows some typical examples.

Furniture-mounted task lighting should be properly designed and equal importance should be given to aesthetic and technical aspects. The following are some considerations for a good technical performance:

1. If two lamps are used, place one at each side to reduce veiling reflectance on the task. Because the lamps are located so close to the task level, this may produce high levels of light concentrated on two sides. This may be minimized by using a special refractor to push light toward the center of the desk. The task area should have even, uniform light.

2. Some manufacturers locate a single bare lamp at the back of the desk. This is undesirable for two reasons: (a) it produces veiling reflectance on the task and (b) the back surface becomes the dominant feature of the system. Use of a conventional, prismatic refractor will diffuse the light but may still result in high veiling reflectance.

3. For most single-person task systems one lamp is sufficient, but it must be located above the task area with a batwing refractor underneath. The batwing refractor virtually cuts the lamp output in half and reflects the light away from the center (see Figure 20-3a).

4. High luminance contrast between the task and the immediate furniture-surface area should be avoided and limited to a 3 : 1 ratio. Most tasks are done on white paper of approximately 85% reflectance. The reflectance of the furniture surface should not be any lower than 30%. If

the luminaire is located at the rear and light spills on the vertical surface at the back of the workstation, it is important that this surface be uniformly lighted and produce luminance within the 3 : 1 ratio.

5. From the standpoint of ease of maintenance there should be access for lens, louvers, or lamp removal. The plastic selected should be acrylic, as opposed to polystyrene, to avoid yellowing. The luminaire finish is important; if it is glossy, it will be highly reflective; if it is too porous, it will hold fingerprints. A semigloss finish is usually the best selection.

6. The luminaire should be carefully concealed to eliminate direct glare.

7. Ballasts that produce the least noise should be selected. Furniture-integrated luminaires have ballasts that are too close to the user. Any ballast noise in these circumstances will be louder than in the ceiling-mounted system. All wiring must be concealed and must comply with applicable electrical standards. The total assembly should not have exposed sharp edges, which are hazardous, or corners that can damage the electrical cord.

Some aesthetic considerations in task/ambient lighting are the following:

1. To avoid a feeling of claustrophobia, which module walls, may invoke, consider low-height partitions. Arrange the sitting area to give an unobstructed view of the open areas of the room from any angle. It should be glare-free, open, and pleasing.

2. The material and finish (color) of the furniture, floor, and walls should complement one another and the visible peripherals of the room should be decorated with color to provide visual relief and break the monotony of uniform ambient lighting. (see Chapter 21).

3. All luminaires that are a part of or are placed on the furniture should have a surface finish that blends with the furniture and the surrounding decor. Avoid introducing new color; too many may be confusing.

4. For ambient lighting the lamp color should be carefully selected to enhance the beauty of the room in general. If mercury vapor or metal halide is used, phosphor-coated lamps, as opposed to clear, will diffuse light. Clear lamps may produce light streaks, especially on low-height ceilings.

The greatest advantage that a task/ambient lighting system can provide is the right amount of light wherever required. A nonsacrificed amount of quality light is available for the task in any location, whereas a low level of glare-free ambient light creates a perfect atmosphere for CRT and circulation lighting. Nonwasting ambient light saves energy and supplementary lighting enhances the beauty of the perimeter.

REFERENCES

Nuckolls, James L. "Furniture-integrated Lighting—Equipment Reviewed." *Lighting Design and Application,* 22 (January 1979).

Shmitz, Sylvan R. "Evaluating the Quality of Task/Ambient Lighting." *Lighting Design and Application,* 25 (January 1979).

Sorcar, Prafulla C. *Energy Saving Lighting Systems.* New York: Van Nostrand-Reinhold, 1982.

21

Perimeter Lighting

Perimeter lighting serves walls, windows, paintings, sculptures, draperies, mirrors, bookshelves, displays, and other elements frequently found in commercial interiors. Because much of this lighting is a part of the ambient and the determination of the ambient light level is largely dependent on the perimeter-surface reflectances, it is virtually impossible to draw a line between the two. The term perimeter lighting is used here to include all perimeter surfaces (ceiling, walls, and floor) and objects in the normal field of view.

The eyes demand constant variety in the field of view. It is therefore necessary to select objects and areas in the perimeter to be illuminated with varying but balanced brightness. When the eyes are lifted from the task, they naturally search for a sight that is opposite in nature; for instance, if the task is performed under abundant light, the eyes will seek out objects or areas of lower brightness; if the task is colorful, the eyes look for areas or objects that are ''flat''; if the task is extremely sedentary, the eyes will focus on distant objects to give the eye muscles a rest. The mind will also seek similar relief. In the middle of a sedentary task, when the eyes encounter a beautiful well lighted object, (e.g., flowers or a painting) the viewer achieves a sense of emotional satisfaction as well as visual relief. The beauty of the object momen-

tarily takes the mind away from the task, reduces fatigue, and renews energy. It is a constant cycle. In an office environment, when quality light is provided for the task, safe and glare-free light for the ambient, and an adequate amount of light on the perimeter, a visual balance in the lighting system is accomplished.

COLOR OF LIGHT

For offices, drafting rooms, libraries, and laboratories, where work is sedentary and a high level of light is required, color should be neutral with a slight leaning toward the warm. The cool white or deluxe cool white fluorescent, deluxe white mercury, or phosphor-coated metal halide should be considered. For rooms with low-level illumination requirements (e.g., restrooms, lounges, powder rooms, cafeterias) the color of light should be provided by incandescents or deluxe warm-white fluorescents.

COLOR OF THE SURFACES

For private offices or other areas in which a single accupant is served the color selection may be made to suit individual taste; but when masses of people gather colors must be carefully selected to satisfy the psychological and physiological needs of the majority, for which Chapter 16 should be consulted. The ceiling should be white or off-white. It should have a high reflectance between 70 and 90%. The floor may be a light or medium-light color to suit the atmosphere, and its reflectance should be between 15 and 30%. The walls should be a color, with 50 to 55% reflectance, and they should never be white. According to Faber Birren, "Except for ceilings, white or off-white should not be used on walls where groups of persons are assembled. High environmental brightness not only handicaps seeing (by introducing a form of interior "snow" blindness) but also severely constricts the pupil opening of the human eye, an action that is muscular and very fatiguing." The accent colors can be medium-deep, with patterns as described in Chapter 16.

Additional considerations are the following:

1. Perimeter lighting (peripheral) must counterbalance all sterile effects created by task and ambient lighting. If the task lighting is uniform and color consistent, the perimeter lighting must be nonuniform and color-varied. Conversely, if the task lighting is nonuniform and multicolored, the perimeter lighting should be uniform and color coordinated.

2. A contrast in color and light is probably the most important feature of perimeter lighting. By choosing the correct level of color and brightness for the perimeter an object near it can be made obvious or inconspicuous. This phenomenon can highlight certain selected objects or expand a room visually with a lot of furniture.

3. Use of light to accentuate an object can be pleasing, but indiscriminate use of high or low lighting can defeat the purpose. It must be remembered that visual conditions improve with increased brightness up to a point at which diminishing returns are quickly reached. This applies not only to the visual task and its background but also to all objects in the peripherals. For comfortable vision the following luminance ratios should be observed:

   2 : 1   Perceptible brightness difference (contrast) for focus

   3 : 1   Between task and adjacent darker objects (e.g., the book and the surface of the table, typewriter, computer, and word processors)

   5 : 1   Between the task and remote darker surfaces (e.g., the book and the dark areas between bookshelves and under furniture)

   1 : 5   Between task and remote brighter surfaces

   20 : 1   Between windows, luminaires on ceiling, and luminous columns and large adjacent surfaces

   7 : 1   For highlighting a three-dimensional object; between objects and adjacent darker surroundings

   5 : 1   Between a flat object (paintings, murals, and carpet) on walls and adjacent darker surfaces.

4. Accent-lighting techniques (diffusing, backlighting, highlighting; see Chapter 14) are a major contributor to good perimeter lighting. For proper accent lighting the following must be observed: (a) The object or surface illuminated should be visible—not the source; (b) The reflected light from the object must not aim at the eyes (unless glittering is desired); (c) if the illuminated surface has a specular finish, the luminaire must be located to obscure its image at a normal angle and to prevent its reflected light from reaching the eyes.

5. Visual comfort is better if the objects in the peripherals are arranged in an unobstrusive and unconfusing setting. Overbrightness, too much color variation, clashing design, and darkness are confusing. Avoid creating situations in which the eyes must adapt too quickly to a wide range of brightness or color variations.

6. To keep the eyes alert they need constant variety. A perimeter lighting system that provides a perfect visual balance at present may become monotonous after a few months of use. Occasional rearrangement of the objects in the peripherals and a change in color and lighting arrangement on the perimeter will continue to stimulate interest. Use of luminaires like tracklights and eyeball and directional luminaires with dimming switches is an excellent, economical solution to these problems.

22

Office Environment: Room-by-Room Analysis

PRIVATE OFFICES

Private offices are those that accommodate one-person activity and are most often small-to-moderate in size. The key to the success of office lighting is (a) quality task lighting, (b) glare-free ambient lighting, and (c) interesting perimeter lighting for visual relief. More than one lighting system, some incorporated with regular or dimmer switches to create a complete visual balance may be required. For smaller offices the designer is challenged to accomplish the objective with a minimum number of luminaires.

No matter how small the room, the designer should consider a minimum of two luminaires. Each may contain half the number of total calculated lamps and each should be located at one side of the desk (see Figure 22-1a). In a fluorescent luminaire most of the light is produced in a plane perpendicular to the length of the lamp; therefore the luminaires must be placed to permit most of the light to focus on the desk. Because light appears on the task from the sides, no veiling reflections appear in the angle of view; the result is high contrast. Based on this principle and with a satisfactory finish on the walls, virtually any type of lighting system, including indirect,

cornices, and cove, can be used successfully for quality task light. In small rooms VCP is not a major consideration because the luminaires are located above the head and no direct glare exists in the normal field of view.

If pendant indirect luminaires are used, care should be taken that the reflected light on the ceiling is not the room's dominant feature or does not spread into the offending zones (Figure 22-1b). This system is best adapted to rooms with medium-to-high ceilings and to ceilings with a smooth finish. If it is used on grid-suspended ceilings, the grids should be finished in the same color as the ceiling panels, which should have a matte, preferably textured finish.

Cove lighting can be a built-in architectural feature or mounted separately on the walls (Figure 22-1c). Light from the opening at the top reflects from the ceiling and appears on the task area. With a proper selection of the luminaire in terms of its design, intensity, and color rendition, this arrangement can be aesthetically pleasing and energy-effective. As in pendant luminaires, here, too, the grids of the suspended ceiling should be the same color as the ceiling panels.

Perimeter decor, color, and light fixtures must be

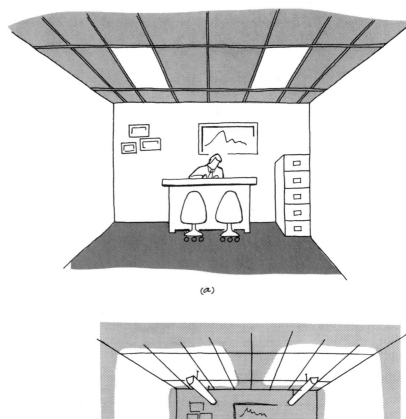

(a)

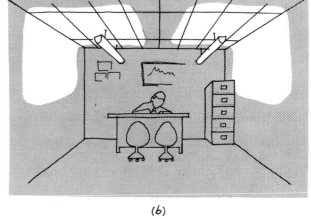

(b)

Figure 22-1. *(a) Ceiling-mounted luminaires: A minimum of two luminaires should be installed in small offices, one at each side of the desk. In this arrangement the shadows are minimized and high contrast is achieved. (b) Pendant luminaires: Care should be taken that the reflected light in the ceiling does not become the room's dominant feature or appear in the offending zone. This system is best suited to rooms with a medium-to-high ceiling. (c) Coves can be built-in or separately mounted on the walls. Light from the opening at the top reflects from the ceiling and appears on the task area as a diffused source. With proper selection of luminaire in terms of decor and color, this arrangement can be aesthetically pleasing and energy effective.*

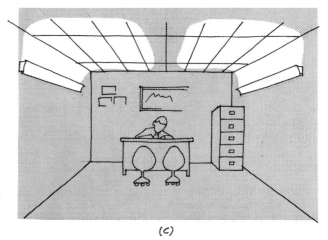

(c)

Figure 22-2. A carefully calculated lighting system for visual balance: (a) Ceiling luminaires have low brightness and their location provides quality light on the task; (b) glare-free ambient lighting from low-bright luminaires; (c) interesting perimeter light for visual relief.

selected to provide visual relief and create a balanced interior. Ceiling-recessed or track-mounted directional incandescent lights can highlight walls, draperies, wood paneling, or pictures. Emphasis should be given to low brightness on ceiling elements and to highlighting interesting features. (See Figures 22-2 and 22-3 for related interest.)

Because many offices are designed for key personnel, the environmental impression must often be one to reflect their personal tastes. The designer must provide a lighted environment to meet their working needs. Chapters 16 and 21 should be reviewed for color selection and other factors that will help to create the desired result.

GENERAL OFFICES

General offices are designed to accommodate a number of people and are moderate to large in size. They are, in general, either areas in which task locations are known or unknown. When they are known, the techniques mentioned earlier can be successfully applied to provide good task and ambient lighting. If the desks are arranged in rows, the luminaires should be located in between them (Figure 22-4). The luminaires can be placed intermittently or end to end as required. Direct glare, which may be a problem in the normal field of view, can be minimized by using

Figure 22-3. The same room is lighted with a continuous fluorescent troffer at the peripheral. Note that (a) the arrangement minimizes veiling reflection on the task, providing more flexibility in desk location; (b) there is sufficient ambient light with little glare at the normal direction of view that can be further minimized by using low brightness (louvered) luminaires; (c) the perimeter is highly illuminated. Although dramatic, the uniform, diffused shadowless white fluorescent light all around the perimeter may appear monotonous because it lacks focal points.

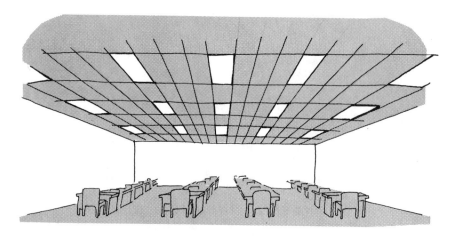

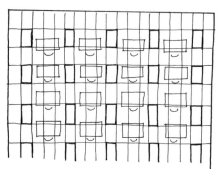

Figure 22-4. *In large rooms in which task locations are arranged in a row the luminaires should be placed intermittently, or end to end, between the rows.*

parabolic-louvered troffers or units equipped with low-glare-producing media.

When task locations are unknown and must be selected arbitrarily (this is normal in most office buildings), the choices are (1) uniform lighting to serve for task and ambient simultaneously, and (2) uniform lighting for ambient and supplementary portable lighting for the task.

In choice No. 1, the following are options and design considerations (many are covered in Chapter 12 and 19; here we review the related items):

1. Parabolic louvered luminaires, recessed or surface-mounted on the ceiling.
   - Excellent for visual comfort (VCP ranges from 65 to 95) but not so great for veiling reflection control.
   - Deeper cells and non-specular reflectors produce higher VCP.
   - The efficiency decreases inversely with the number of cells and their depth.
   - Luminaries with batwing-shaped candle-

power distribution are the best for satisfactory task and ambient light.

2. Acrylic lensed luminaires; recessed or surface-mounted on the ceiling. Some specially designed lenses (extruded/refracted, Chapter 12) are capable of producing excellent task contrast radially but unfortunately they are poor in direct glare control. Conversely, there are other lenses that are excellent for direct glare control but poor for task contrast. The few lenses on the market that are good for both unfortunately have very low efficiency (between 30 and 45%). A loss in efficiency and light control usually occurs simultaneously with the use of thicker material that has been chosen for lens strength. Here, too, luminaires with batwing candlepower distribution are best for quality task and ambient lighting.

3. A coffer lighting system.
   - The luminaire must be concealed deep enough inside the pocket to render it invisible from normal viewing angles.
   - The light distribution from the luminaire must

be a radial batwing type so that good task contrast is available at all sides of the luminaire.

- The majority of the light must emerge through the 30 to 60° zone and the angle of the dome must intercept and reflect all light above 60°.
- The reflecting surfaces of the dome must be matte; color and texture must match the rest of the ceiling. (reflection: 70–90%)
- To create a ceiling of uniform low brightness the number of lamps per luminaire may be reduced and spread into an increased number of domes.

Because of the ceiling modification needed, a coffer lighting system may be quite expensive.

4. Luminous ceilings, in general, are merely aesthetic; but with proper selection of the lens and/or louvers, they can be made effective for quality interior lighting. This system contains fluorescent strip lights in the cavity above the luminous ceiling (Chapters 14 and 19). A luminous system is expensive and usually has low efficiency.

The concept of uniform lighting for ambient and supplementary lighting for task parallels the task-ambient lighting discussed in Chapter 20. Ambient lighting may be done with low-glare-producing direct luminaires (or indirect luminaires), which will be the only permanent feature of the system. Task lighting can be obtained from portable units like table lamps, clamp-on type sources, lampstands placed by the worker as needed or from track lights. The main advantages of this system are (1) substantially lower energy use compared with the first choice, (2) quality task and ambient light, and (3) abundant flexibility in task locations. The latest style in this system is the pendant type slim, cylindrical channel with attractive finish (paint or chrome) housing indirect fluorescent lamps for ambient and track lights for task lighting. The ambient light can be uniform or non-uniform and virtually glare-free because of their hidden location; track lights provide mobility in task lighting avoiding veiling reflections. High initial cost is their main disadvantage.

No matter what type of light system is used, it should be remembered that large offices may be subdivided at some future time; therefore the designer should determine in advance whether special precautions should be taken to meet future needs; for example, the utilization of light (utilization factor) reduces proportionally with room size and the circuits at the area of interest must have some reserve power to meet the requirements. Beam, column, and air-handling diffuser locations on the ceiling should be well defined and ascertained before the design is begun. Close coordination and cooperation between the architect, mechanical engineer, and lighting designer is the only solution.

To break the monotony of uniform lighting the peripherals should be carefully organized with selected colors, lighting equipment, furniture style and finishes, upholstery, and decorative accents. Wall reflectance should be between 40 and 60% with colors that are satisfactory aesthetically, psychologically, and physiologically (see Chapter 21). When color is selected for style, a light, neutral shade with bright accents, used intermittently, can be very effective. Texture in the wallpaper (if any), furniture trim, and wall accents can be in the same bright colors. With somewhat deeper hues on the floors and with planters, paintings, wall plaques, and upholstery, all together will complement the neutral wall surface and offset the sterile effect of diffused lighting.

DRAFTING ROOM

All of the criteria mentioned for large offices (general offices) are applicable here, and more so, because drafting is sedentary work that needs concentration of mind and eyes and requires an abundance of quality light. The additional areas in which the designer must exercise special care are the following:

- The whole drawing board is the task area: the possibility of reflective glare is much larger. The drafting table can be properly positioned to avoid the glare. For those with an inclining mechanism, the board can be tilted to a more comfortable angle. Note that for a tilted board the offending zone is closer to the task area (see Figure 22-5).
- All drafting tools—a tee-square, parallel bar, triangle, and template—should have a matte finish in a bright color for easy accessibility.
- If additional light is required, table lamps (the clamp type that takes a minimum of space on the board) may be considered. Proper positioning

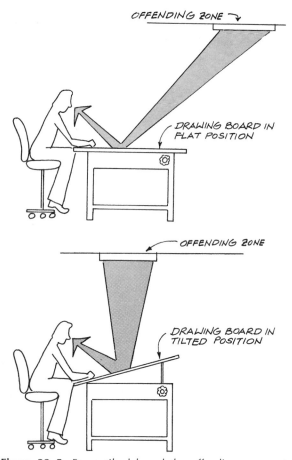

Figure 22-5. *For a tilted board the offending zone gets closer.*

will increase light and "wash off" any existing glare from ceiling lights.

- Positioning the board opposite a window will increase the glare. Whenever possible, however, window(s) should be at one side, counterbalanced by luminaires on the other. Avoid windows at the back; they will cast a shadow of the body on the task.

- One unavoidable problem in drafting is the fine shadow that a straight edge, tee-square, or plastic triangle casts on the drawing—often misleading the background information. This problem can be minimized effectively by adjustable supplementary lighting attached to the board.

- A drafting room with a CAD (computer-aided design) system needs some special precautions. Placing the screen in a subdued area or in a sandwich concept helps to reduce glare (refer to

CRT-lighting in Chapter 18 for details). The plotter should be placed in a well lighted area.

- A transilluminating drafting table, which incorporates a light source behind a translucent surface panel, should have a dimming system. The degree of luminance required varies with the type of task and the light level of the room. To avoid direct glare the areas that are not being used for drafting should be covered with an opaque material.

CONFERENCE ROOM

Although a conference room is used mainly for meetings, the duration and variety of the associated activity suggest the need for a flexible, as opposed to a fixed, lighting system (Figure 22-6). The main points are the following:

- The ceiling light must shed quality task light directly on the conference table and should have a separate switch for its control.

- To create a pleasant environment the perimeter should have wallpapered, or richly paneled walls or murals "washed" by ceiling recessed, surface, or track-mounted incandescent lights equipped with a separate dimmer switch.

- Supplementary lighting, on a separate dimmer switch, should be provided for maps, boards, and displays on or near a predetermined wall. The location of the luminaires should be such that they cannot reflect the light toward the viewer's eyes.

- The luminaires should be coordinated with the switching arrangement. In the event that a film or slides are shown the overall light can be dimmed to a level low enough in the screen area for good projection but high enough for taking notes in other areas.

RECEPTION ROOM

- From an aesthetic standpoint this probably is the most important room in the entire office environment because it builds the image of the company. Like the conference room and the executive offices here, too, close coordination between the architect, interior decorator, and

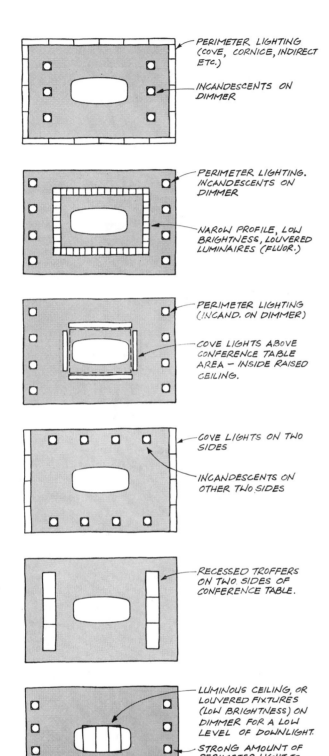

Figure 22-6. *Conference-room lighting with various systems.*

lighting designer is required to create an "atmosphere" or "impression" of this image. A non-uniform light level is desirable.

- The receptionist (secretary) is often the operator of the CRT. Coordination should be such that the screen is free of glare; this includes the reflection of the operator.

- If a logo is used on the wall, the perimeter color should be selected to complement it. If raised letters are used, a shadow effect from a single source (or multisources) may be highly desirable. In any event, a dramatic appearance achieved by focused sources, directional light, wall wash, sparkle, or glitter can be put to best use in a reception room.

- The sitting room for guests should have sufficient light, critically located to make reading material easily visible, yet not overpowering.

- If a glass wall separates the reception room from an adjacent area, such as a conference or a board room, care should be taken that the visibility in one does not interfere with that in the other. A glass wall will give an impression of space which is often desirable in reception or conference rooms (Figure 17-2). Plants, other self-standing or ceiling-hung displays will provide sufficient privacy. When the conference room is not occupied, the lights on its far walls may be left on to maximize the dramatic effect. If all lights in the conference room are turned off, the effect may be cavelike. Lights highlighting objects such as paintings, sculpture, or plants can be highlighted and should remain on to define boundaries.

FILING ROOM

- Filing areas need a high amount of lighting because they deal with reading materials that vary in contrast from excellent to poor. In addition, there is no specific task location; files may be read sitting or standing, depending on the location of the cabinets. Illumination at any angle, including vertical and horizontal, is of equal importance.

- Indirect lighting, intensely diffused direct light from large sources, or in combination may be considered. The main ideas is to create lighting in which reading from any angle will be glare-free and comfortable.

- The activity in a filing room is normally temporary. Perceptual clarity is important. Therefore the walls and ceiling should have high reflectance and the floor should be a light color for maximum effect. Abundant uniform, as opposed to nonuniform, lighting is preferable. The furniture, too, should be a light color.

- In rooms in which the file cabinets are placed in rows, an economical yet effective way of lighting provides linear sources (or long and narrow area sources) between the rows. Low, direct-glare-producing louvered luminaires with high SC (1.5 or higher) yield excellent vertical and horizontal illumination. Care should be taken that the luminaires have enough candlepower at the lower angles to give adequate light at the level of the bottom drawers.

COMPUTER ROOM

A computer room has three main areas that have three types of operation; programming, key punching, and machine operation.

- In the programming area work is done mainly with printed material and writing with pen or pencil. The quality and level of the light should be similar to those of an office.

- The key punching area may have a number of units, in all of which reading of fine print is required. Quality light is important here because it minimizes mistakes in program reading and key punching.

- The machine area normally does not need excessive amount of light because most of its work is automatic and other activities involve short time visual tasks like feeding and removing tapes and reading labels. For repairing purposes, however, a high amount of light may be necessary. For this reason, machine areas should be designed for higher level of light with multiple switching or dimming mechanism to vary its level as needed. For repairing purposes it is often necessary that the light level be low enough for the CRT screen to be distinctly visible.

- Because a high level of light and a low ambient temperature are simultaneously required in a computer room, fluorescent light with low-power consuming ballasts and lamps may be considered. Room surfaces, including the floor, should have a high reflectance.

- The indicator lights and lighted pushbuttons must be bright enough to be clearly visible in the general room lighting.

UPS BATTERY OR GENERATOR ROOM

To provide uninterrupted power supply (UPS) some computer systems are backed by storage batteries or generators located in a separate room, usually adjacent. If batteries are used, the lighting fixture should be gasketed and vaportight to prevent damage from the fumes.

In generator rooms vibration and heating are biggest problem. Although use of an exhaust fan can remove the generator heat, the luminaires should be selected and fastened to withstand the continuous vibration. If incandescents are used, filaments with multiple supporting rods, suitable for these applications, should be considered. If fluorescents are used, it should be made sure that the continuous vibration cannot move the lamps from their sockets.

Luminaires should be provided wherever light is required in a uniform or nonuniform layout. In any case, the perimeter of the room should be painted white (or off-white of high reflectance) for good visibility and utilization.

WASHROOMS OR RESTROOMS

A well lighted, color coordinated, cheerful washroom or restroom is important not only because it allows users to make adjustments to their appearance, but also to their minds; it restores energy by reducing fatigue obtained from sedentary office work.

Several important points must be considered (Figure 22-7). The first is that the light should fall on the person, not on the mirror, for proper visibility. Second, it should be aimed from angles that do not cast shadows on the face. Third, the color of the light should complement the color of the skin, and fourth, the whole environment must be cheering.

Ambient light should be approximately 20 fc. If the room is small (8 × 8 ft or smaller), task light (50 fc) is enough to provide ambient lighting as well. For larger rooms additional ceiling or wall-mounted lighting may be necessary.

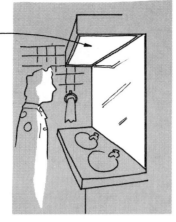

IF LIGHTED SOFFIT IS USED, THE LENS OR LOUVER SHOULD BE SUCH THAT IT REFLECTS LIGHT ON THE FACE; NOT ON MIRROR. THE SOFFIT SHOULD RUN ENTIRE LENGTH OF THE MIRROR OR VICE-VERSA.

THEATRICAL MAKE-UP ROOM LIGHTS (INCANDESCENT BULBS) ABOVE MIRROR ALONE, OR ALSO ON THE SIDES. LAMPS SHOULD NOT EXCEED 25 WATT TO CUT GLARE.

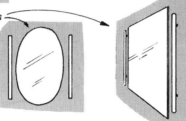

TUBULAR INCANDESCENTS ONE AT EACH SIDE OF SMALL MIRRORS WILL PROVIDE A PLEASING APPEARANCE.

Figure 22-7. Some considerations in restroom lighting.

The walls may be wallpapered, painted, or paneled, in warm colors. On painted walls avoid the use of a consistent color by introducing a complementary accent color to treat the eyes and moods to moderate variety.

A number of different lighting arrangements can accomplish these objectives:

1. Wall-mounted fluorescent luminaires or incandescents above the mirror.

2. Wall-mounted fluorescent or incandescent (theatrical dressing room effect) above and on the two sides of the mirror.

3. A combination of wall and ceiling-mounted luminaires above the mirror.

4. Soffit lights equipped with fluorescent lamps and louvers extending above the length of the mirror.

5. Ceiling-pendant luminaires with luminous sides flanking the mirror.

Incandescents are the best sources for mirror lights because of their excellent color rendition. For theatrical lights, a cluster of lower wattage lamps is preferred not only to cut glare but also to provide the warmth of low-wattage incandescence. If fluorescents must be used, its color should be warm white, or deluxe warm white.

CORRIDORS

The principal concern in corridor or hallways is safety. Typically one-third to one-fifth of the adjacent office lighting level (not less than 20 fc) is sufficient. Perimeters of high reflectance are desirable.

In the design of a lighting system the width and the length of the corridor should be taken into consideration (Figure 22-8). If the corridor is long and narrow, horizontal light patterns or linear luminaires on the two sides washing the walls will give a visual impression of greater width. On the other hand, a wide corridor can be made to look narrower by installing a row or rows of linear sources down the middle of the ceiling. Long corridors, which resemble tunnels can be broken to seem shorter by using different tones and lighting intermittently. High ceilings can be lowered visually by creating scallops on the walls from ceiling recessed downlights or by creating dark areas above cornices.

Because of their long life and efficiency, fluorescents are most suited to corridors than any other source. Selected luminaires or lamps of some luminaires should be connected to the emergency power supply of the building to provide ingress or egress lighting in case of a power failure.

Corridors usually terminate at an elevator and/or staircase. To move traffic automatically, these areas should be slightly brighter than the corridors.

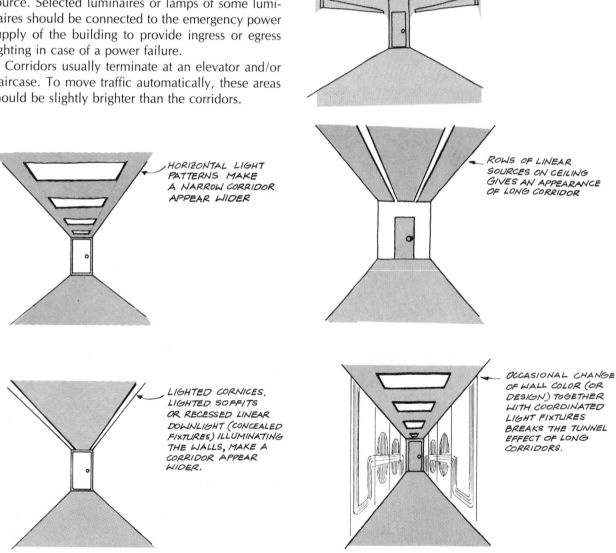

Figure 22-8. Some considerations in corridor lighting.

STAIRWAYS

In addition to being a means of getting from one floor to another, stairways are an essential escape route in case of fire. From this standpoint there should be sufficient light (20 fc) for all normal and emergency uses.

The luminaires should be mounted high enough not to "blind" the eyes as one moves up or downstairs. In addition, lighting should be ample enough to prevent harsh shadows that might cause misjudgment of the height of the steps.

LOBBY

This is actually the termination point of the corridors and hallways that lead to stairways and elevators. Here, too, the light level should be one-third to one-fifth of the adjacent areas and in no circumstances less than 20 fc. The perimeters should define the boundaries and give an impression of spaciousness. Floors near the elevators should have plenty of lighting to be clearly visible. The floor of the elevator lobby should never be glossy because it would reflect the luminaires and encourage a false step (Figure 22-9). The floor should be covered in matte finished

Figure 22-9. *Avoid a glossy floor in an elevator lobby. This reflects the images of bright surfaces and causes confusion in floor elevation.*

tiles or with carpeting in a complementing color. The perimeter of the lobby should be well lighted in a soft color to heighten a sense of security. Selected luminaires including those near the elevators, should be on standby power to provide lighting during emergency situations.

EQUIPMENT ROOM

No matter how much planning is done beforehand, the lighting layout for some rooms cannot be completed until the equipment layout is known, or in place (e.g., the generator, mechanical, electrical, and telephone rooms).

- The ceiling is usually cluttered with ducts, pipes, gaslines, water pipes, and structural beams, which prevent the use of ceiling-mounted luminaires in the right locations. Pendant luminaires are the best solution.

- If vibration is a major factor, incandescents (filaments with multiple supports) suitable for these locations should be used. Fluorescent strip lights also meet this problem if the lamps are securely joined in their sockets.

- Overall lighting should be direct, uniform, or nonuniform but sufficient to reach every corner.

- The perimeters should be painted white for better light reflection and for the reduction of shadows.

- The equipment room may need an exhaust fan to reduce the ambient temperature which has an impact on fluorescent lamp performance. Typically, an optimum light output is obtained when the bulb wall temperature of the fluorescent lamps is operating at 100°F.

In electrical equipment rooms, the floor-standing main distributing panels (switchgear) or wall-mounted panel boards have labels in fine print (e.g., circuit index) for which a good vertical illumination is a must. Proper ventilation with a louvered door or exhaust fan may be required to remove heat from the room (usually generated by transformers or motors). The lighting systems of these rooms should be connected to emergency power circuits.

APPLICATION: MERCHANDISING ENVIRONMENT

23

Sign and Show-Window Lighting

A merchandising environment can be widely varied from a tiny shop to a large shopping center, selling hairpins to automobiles and covering the entire color spectrum. Lighting is one of many factors but is perhaps the most important in creating that special environment, the ultimate goal of which is increased sales. The trend today is to present the merchandise in a self-service or limited service format, both of which are designed to reduce sales personnel. The designer's challenge is to present the merchandise so that it will sell itself and the customer will return for future shopping.

There are three basic requirements in the lighting design of merchandising areas:

1. The initial impression must be strong enough to persuade the customer to enter the store.
2. Inside the environment must be comfortable and the material of interest, easily available.
3. The overall impression must be such that the store will be remembered.

In this chapter we discuss the first point; the other two are covered in Chapter 24.

INITIAL IMPRESSION

The sign and the show windows create the first impression. Their main objectives are (1) to draw attention; (2) to hold attention despite competition from other displays; (3) to develop interest and persuade the shopper to enter the store; (4) to leave a long-lasting and favorable impression.

SIGNS

The many types of sign can be divided into four groups (see Figure 23-1). The first is self-lighted like neon, cold cathode, or exposed incandescent lamps whose designs or logos are made with light sources. The second has a raised or flat design of translucent material illuminated by light sources (fluorescents, neon, etc.), concealed inside a box. The third type has an elevated design with a luminous background which produces a silhouette effect. The fourth is lighted with flood lights.

Whatever the technique, the size of the design or the logo should be large and brightly colored for easy visibility. The selection of colors, material, script, or

223

Figure 23-1. *Signs can be divided into four groups: (1) Self lighted (a) incandescent lamps, with or without motion or blinking, (b) neon light. (2) Translucent characters illuminated from the back. (3) Opaque characters (flat or raised) illuminated from the back producing a silhouette effect. (4) Flood lighted sign. The characters may be flat or raised. Raised letters produce shadows which add extra depth. The last sign shows that no matter what kind of technique used, distinctiveness and individuality make it easy to remember.*

artwork should identify with the merchandise and should have a general appeal. Choice of color is important. Although all bright colors, such as red, orange, yellow, and blue, are excellent for the purpose; other colors of less intensity are suitable also as long as they contrast or blend with the other colors. Blue is excellent for signs that are close by, but not for those at a distance. This is especially true of blue neon signs on which the eyes have difficulty focusing because of their "halo" effect.

Signs self-lighted by clusters of incandescent lamps should be considered only for applications that must be seen from a distance (e.g., along the roadside). Their use inside shopping malls or shopping centers may produce an uncomfortable glare unless powered by very low wattages. Blinking such as on and off or motion can also be effective, depending on the application. Bulbs for this purpose are available in 6-, 10-, 11-, 15-, 20-, and 40-W ratings, both clear and in color. For motion effect gas-filled, 20-W lamps are the usual choice.

Fluorescents as backlighting for "plastic" letters or "boxed" signs with translucent materials is common. The main thing to remember is that the translucent material and lamp locations should diffuse the light evenly and the fluorescent ballast must adapt to extreme temperatures. The variance in light output of the lamps caused by temperature change should be considered (Chapter 4).

Luminous background signs are excellent for indoor application as long as the silhouette effect is created in front of a uniformly distributed, diffused, soft light. Neon or fluorescents are ideally suited to this purpose.

Flood-lighted signs are designed for exteriors. They can be effective indoors if the sources are not visible and an even light distribution is directed at the entire sign.

The desired legibility range, store-front dimensions, and brightness determine the size of the sign and that of its characters or design. The brightness between the luminous and nonluminous areas must be high but not discomforting to the eye. Brightness and contrast created by light and color are the factors that attract attention. Distinctiveness and individuality contribute to its memory value. The selection of color and style should be such that they blend with the subject of the sign to create a pleasing, favorable impression with a lot of public appeal. Blinking and motion increase the power of attraction and memory value even further; but indiscriminate use often defeats the purpose. Success of the sign depends largely on its uniqueness and creativity, which is limited only by the designer's imagination.

Some shopping centers and merchandising areas have set rules that govern size, style, and color. In such situations the show window bears most of the responsibility of creating the first impression—so vitally important to merchandising success.

SHOW WINDOWS

A show window is extremely desirable if not essential, because it provides a bridge between the shoppers' expectations outside the store and the goods available inside.

Show windows, in general, come in two different forms, the first with a closed background, the second open at the back. In both cases, large areas of glass are used up front to protect the displayed material from external abuse and, of course, to provide optimum visibility. In the modern trend its purpose goes beyond mere display. It is used to show present and upcoming styles of merchandise; that is, what is new today and what is coming in the future. What is "in" and what is "out." To dramatize the effect some stores hire live models to walk about inside the show windows to promote the sale of their merchandise.

The main difference between the two types of show window is their backgrounds; the closed background features a wall at the back, which creates an isolated space, whereas the open background has no barrier and merges with the total selling space. Each has advantages and disadvantages. The closed type draws the onlookers' attention and forces them to concentrate on the display but it does not necessarily "invite" them to enter. The open type cannot get the onlookers' full attention but it can lure them in by revealing part of the interior. The closed type can be highly effective if the adjacent part of the store is also walled in glass through which the customer can get a view of the interior.

GLASS FRONTS

Although large glass fronts are a great asset and of paramount importance in making displays visible, they produce some annoying problems, one of which is the reflections they create during daylight hours. Images of the street background, including that of the

onlooker, are reflected on the glass and reduce visibility. Three general techniques are there to control this condition (Figure 23-2). The first is by increasing the light inside the show window to a level at which the brightness of the merchandise is greater than that of the reflected external images. A false concept is held by many that to do so the light level inside the show window must be equal to or greater than that outside. The designer must note that the competition is between the brightness of the displayed merchandise and the external reflected images on the glass (not with the brightness of the external articles). Experiments show that the photometric brightness of the reflected image is approximately 10% of that outside. On a sunny day, when the average brightness outside

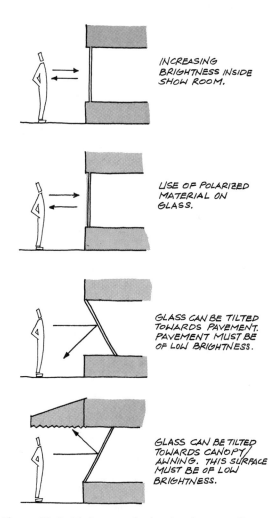

Figure 23-2. Various methods of reducing reflection on showwindows.

is 1000 fL, the reflected image brightness is approximately 100 fL. On a cloudy day this may decrease to 40 fL or less, depending on the light outside. To make the displays inside properly visible the illuminance level inside should be such that their photometric brightness is equal to or larger than 100 fL (based on a sunny day). Therefore if the average reflectance of the articles is, say, 40% the illuminance level inside should be at least $100 \div 0.4 = 250$ fc.

The second method uses polarized glass. A sheet of polarized material is attached to the glass which holds the horizontal vibration of the unpolarized rays to reduce glare.

The third, and possibly the least expensive, method uses some external means such as an awning or canopy with a dark undersurface to cast a shadow on the window. The orientation of the glass should be such that it reflects only the dark surface.

SHOWROOM INTERIOR LIGHTING TECHNIQUES

The showroom interior may use one or more of the following systems (see Figure 23-3):

General Lighting

This is mainly to provide general illumination and to reduce reflections on the glass. The lamps can be incandescent, fluorescent, or HID. Sources must be concealed to avoid any direct glare.

If the interior is bright, other lights may provide sufficient spill to be considered as general light, in which case no separate general light is necessary. Use of fluorescent lamps, with proper color rendition, concealed above a louvered ceiling are often the most economical.

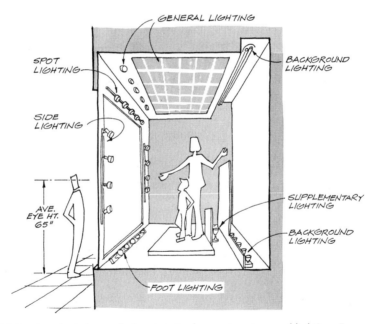

Figure 23-3. *A typical show window interior has various types of lighting. For general lighting, the luminaires in the ceiling should be glare-free since this surface is largely visible from the viewer's angle. The ceiling should be as uncluttered as possible. Spot lights highlight the merchandise and also produce sparkles. For sparkles, the sources must be positioned so that the reflected light from the shiny surfaces are directed at the viewing angle. (The eye height of the average viewer is approximately 65 in. above the floor.) Foot lighting is essential to erase shadows left by ceiling lights; this is a major consideration because of the viewing angles. Background lighting can be smooth wallwash or nonuniform. The intensity of wallwash regulates contrast between the merchandise and its background. A nonuniform pattern is sometimes necessary to break the monotony of even lighting. Supplementary (portable) lighting accents or highlights difficult areas (areas that cannot be reached by other lights).*

Side Lighting

This method provides light from the sides for special effects. Fluorescent strips are mounted vertically or incandescent spot or flood lights are mounted on vertical tracks. Luminaire aiming flexibility and the use of colored lamps provide the infinite possibility of dramatic effects; for instance, on three-dimensional objects effects of light and shade can be created by aiming light from one side and a reduced amount from the other. For a more dramatic effect red or pink light can be aimed from one side and blue or green from the other. A number of fixtures with a variety of colored lamps and dimming switches, individually controlled, should be considered for each side. For versatile flexibility red, blue, and green should be considered as the minimum. Their combination at various intensities will produce many other tints.

Spot Lighting

These are incandescent lights with aiming flexibility, normally located at the ceiling near a window. They can be installed individually on the ceiling or track-mounted. Spot lights can produce highly concentrated light to be aimed at an article or element of a display that must catch the attention of shoppers.

Background Lighting

Background lighting is necessary only when pattern or color is needed to create a contrast with the merchandise under the spot light or to create a silhouetted effect. Fluorescents or incandescent flood lights are suitable for this purpose.

Footlighting

Footlights are needed to erase undesirable shadows under three-dimensional objects, often produced by ceiling-mounted spots or general lights. They can be unidirectional fluorescents or a row of incandescents mounted on the floor near a window.

Supplementary Lighting

Self-standing incandescents or fluorescents sometimes provide supplementary lighting of the main display or other areas from obscure angles. Hidden behind objects, they produce vertical lights in areas to which footlights normally cannot reach. In addition, they are sometimes used to illuminate standing panels or screens to produce a silhouette effect or to reduce window reflections.

MODERN TRENDS IN SHOW WINDOWS

Uncluttered appearance, sharp contrast, and colored lights are the latest trends in show windows. White light is essential to reveal the true colors of the merchandise, but colored light can heighten the dramatic effects. Tinted backgrounds, colored shadows, day-time-nighttime variation, psychic lighting, and a gradual change of atmosphere by tint variation are only a few effects in use.

To add further interest to colored light special properties such as leaves, snow, rain, sunrise, sunset, or a rainbow are sometimes projected at the background to represent a season or a special time that relates to the displayed merchandise. The slide is actually located at the center of a 4 × 4 in. steel mat, which is then mechanically held in front of the light fixture for projection.

Multicolored phosphor tubes are used effectively for special background designs or to define the perimeter of an object in space. The tubes do not produce the light but glow in brilliant colors under long-wave UV light sources in an effect similar to neon. They are coated with phosphor, and wires are inserted to form any desired shape.

Use of laser beams to create a volume of light is another technique that dramatizes a show window. The source is moved mechanically in a predetermined manner to produce a three-dimensional volume of light which is used to enclose to isolate the main display (Figure 4-41).

OPEN-BACKGROUND SHOW WINDOWS

A lighting design for an open-background show window is somewhat challenging because closed-background techniques cannot be used unless modifications are made. The main problem is to hide the light sources from both sides of the window; for this the total effect is dependent primarily on light emerging from the ceiling, sides (deeply concealed), and supplementary (self-standing) sources. Footlighting can be used (on both sides) only if it is concealed in recessed chambers and located below normal viewing angles. Colored lighting effects, as described earlier, with laser beams and phosphor tubes can be produced here with equal success because the sources can be located in the ceiling. Fiber optics and electroluminescent lamps are some of the other sources that can be used for dramatic effects in difficult applications (Chapter 4).

REFERENCES

Feltman, Sidney. "A Designer's Checklist For Merchandise Lighting." *Lighting Design and Application,* 18–21 (May 1986).

Kaufman, John E. *IES Lighting Handbook, 1981 Application Volume.* New York: Illuminating Engineering Society, 1981, Chapter 8.

24

Store Lighting

Needless to say, the architect, interior designer, and lighting designer must coordinate their efforts to provide a harmonized environment that will present the merchandise in its most attractive form. Apart from the aesthetic values, good lighting can produce many other related benefits; for example, it can (1) help the merchandise to sell itself (self-service stores); (2) attract customers to selected items; (3) provide safety and security; (4) move traffic in a specific pattern; (5) create a mood; and (6) leave a lasting impression. All points are dependent on quantity and quality of lighting; the last two are particularly related to the aesthetic and emotional responses of customers. If the environment is pleasant and comfortable, they will be inclined to spend more time inside, thus increasing the possibility of sales; if it is inviting and memorable, they may be repeat customers.

The amount of light required varies with the merchandise and each application; it must be flexible. The designer should refer to the *IES Lighting Handbook,* 1981 Reference Volume, for the levels of illuminance currently recommended but should use them only as a guide. Current practice indicates a strong trend toward variations in illumination for different stores and for the various departments within

them. These considerations, plus those of competition, need for distinctive effects, and store design, may make it desirable to vary the levels at specific locations over the values recommended.

For the actual levels of light the designer must exercise skilled judgment based on the circumstances. The following are some practical points and design guidelines:

1. The circulating areas (areas that are not used for display or appraisal of merchandise or for sales transactions) should have an illuminance between 10 and 30 fc. In high traffic stores (such as self-service department stores) a higher level (100 to 150 fc) is desirable to allow rapid customer appraisal of the displayed merchandise. The general lighting can be achieved by direct or indirect or their combination. The indirect system provides a uniform diffuse light on vertical and horizontal surfaces alike, with almost no shadows. This effect may be beneficial for merchandise appraisal, but may lend monotony in the environment that can be overcome only by using it as a foundation for other types of lighting system such as sparkles, glit-

ter, cases, niches, and brightly lighted displays. The direct lighting system, on the other hand, can produce dramatic effects by providing strong light and shadow; it may also produce direct glare.

2. The merchandise should be located strategically throughout the selling area under display light. This invites the customers to move around and to examine it while making a choice. Nonuniform, as opposed to uniform, lighting is the state of the art. Whether horizontal or vertical, all display areas should be illuminated three to four times higher than the levels of the circulating areas. A variety of basic displays is possible:

   (a) Concentrated light from the ceiling that utilizes spot or floodlights aimed at specific areas. A variety of incandescent and high-intensity discharge luminaires (Chapters 11 and 13) is applicable and should be considered when merchandise is displayed on an open table. The illuminance should be four times that of the adjacent area.

   (b) Departmentalized lighting is done by displaying the merchandise in a self-standing booth under its own low-height roof. Fluorescent lamps, concealed under the roof should be used to illuminate the merchandise. The luminance ratio between the displayed surface and its immediate surrounding should not exceed 4 : 1.

   (c) Valances and cornices are used mainly at the perimeters where merchandise is stacked on shelves and vertical illuminance is important. Valances and cornices can be opaque, luminous, or perforated. Fluorescent lamps are most suitable and should be located far enough from the wall to provide sufficient light on the bottom shelf. The average illuminance level should be three to four times that of the circulation area and the illuminance ratio between the top and bottom shelves should not exceed 3 : 1.

   (d) Showcase lighting utilizes fluorescent lamps alone or in conjunction with incandescents. Fluorescents are used to provide a continuous line of light and to minimize the heat inside the enclosed space. Small-diameter lamps are preferred because they occupy a smaller space. For irregular-

shaped cases (such as circular or curved) cold-cathode tubes or neon can be used. Incandescent lamps add dramatic effects such as glitter, shine, shadows, highlights, and warm colors and are often selected for displays of ornaments or pottery.

Some words of caution apply to these displays. All products do not possess the same color stability. Some merchandise may fade under direct exposure to high illuminance (heat) or, for extended periods, under UV rays of fluorescent lamps. Frequent interchange of merchandise is often the most economical solution.

3. The feature display must have maximum power of attraction and must utilize intense brightness for dramatic effects. Its illuminance level may be as high as five to six times that of basic displays. When an article is taken from one display location to another for appraisal, the illuminance between the two locations should not exceed a 3 : 1 ratio and their color rendition should be the same.

4. For modeling lighting more than one accent light should be used at various angles to emphasize color and detail from all sides. Strong shadow will darken one side if it is lighted by only one source. If the facial expression of the model is important, the sources should be placed at an angle approximately 45° above the head. Sources directly above may produce telltale shadows. The illuminance ratio between the model and surrounding areas should not exceed 5 : 1.

5. Counter lighting should be between two to five times that of the circulation area. Although a counter is used as the point of sale and for the completion of paper work, it should not be lighted like an office. Techniques of accent lighting in conjunction with direct luminaires may be used to provide glare-free light and for good contrast on task. Quality of color rendition from the sources is important because customers often wish to check on their merchandise at the last moment.

6. Lighting at a mirror is probably the most important, yet the most neglected area in merchandizing. It must be remembered that for merchandise like dresses and coats the final appraisals are done in the fitting room where the decision to purchase is made. Two factors

are important here: the appearance of the merchandise and coordination with the person's complexion.

Materials look different under varying light sources (a phenomenon known as metamerism). A pink dress that looks gorgeously attractive under the color-balanced light of fluorescent and incandescent spots on the selling floor may be totally disappointing in the fitting room under cool-white fluorescent strips. In addition, the rendition of lamp color must flatter the skin tone. The psychological implication is that if the appearance of customers is enhanced they will be more inclined to purchase. To meet this objective the following points should be considered:

(a) Use large mirrors that show the complete figure from the front and sides. The customer should be able to admire the merchandise from the back as well.

(b) Select sources like incandescents and deluxe cool-white fluorescent lamps which have balanced wavelengths.

(c) Locate the sources to eliminate harsh lines and shadows on the face. Soft lights should be aimed from the sides and top of the mirror.

(d) The sales item, as worn, should be adequately lighted in its entirety. Light should be aimed at the face and body, not at the mirror.

(e) Do not overflatter a tone; this may result in the return of the article after examining it at home under different lighting.

(f) Consider the reflectance, color, and illuminance of the background; these elements should not be overpowering or distracting.

7. Ceiling patterns of light can serve many related purposes; for example, (a) a change in the direction of traffic can be indicated by lines of light on the ceiling; (b) a cluster of downlights can flood the escalator; (c) show tables and counters can be downlighted; (d) merchandise areas can be separated; and (e) floor layouts can be indicated.

It must be remembered that the overall lighting of the merchandise area should project an interesting and comfortable environment. Eyes demand constant variety and cycling stimuli to remain alert to the surroundings. Nonuniform patterns varied in brightness of light and color are helpful in this regard. Excessive rates of brightness between areas must be eliminated to avoid eyestrain. Comfort and an agreeable atmosphere are normally related to moderate, not radical, variation. Overstimulation can often be as ineffective as severe monotony.

PERIMETER COLORS

Perimeter colors should be chosen to help to create a mood or atmosphere that is comfortable and inviting to the customers. A color that will promote a favorable aesthetic and emotional response is the key to success. (Chapters 15 and 16).

Floor color, perhaps, is the most important because it makes the first impression. It is also important in that the wall and ceiling colors are largely dependent on it. Soil (and stains) from foot traffic is another factor. All points considered, its selection is mainly a compromise of aesthetic, emotional, and utilitarian aspects. Some factors to consider are the following:

1. Warmer tones are cheering and cooler tones are soothing. This concept may be applied in the selection of a color that is also good for hiding normal stains. Floor-covering reflectance should be between 15 and 25%.

2. A plain or lightly textured pattern is preferable to large designs in gaudy colors because it can serve more effectively as a background for the merchandise. The key word here is contrast. If the merchandise is colorful (e.g., clothes, or carpets), it should be displayed against a plain color.

3. Consider using more than one color for large areas to reflect the layout of the floor. Merchandise may be separated by different background colors and coordinated lighting. The traffic areas can be done in another color to isolate stains and soil.

4. Avoid a specularly finished flooring near the escalator, stairwell, or elevator landing. A shiny or glossy surface may encourage false steps.

From a utilitarian standpoint white or off-white ceilings are most suitable for stores in which diffused light is used for task and ambient lighting. For others, however, they can be a continuation of the floor or wall colors, but reflectance must not exceed 70 to 75%. Multicolors can be used to emphasize the special architectural features of a ceiling; for instance, if there is a sudden change in ceiling height (e.g., soffit or drop ceiling), texture, or shape, these features can be treated with separate colors. Coordination between architecture, color, and lighting can improve the appearance of displayed merchandise and create a dramatic effect; for example, a light blue dome ceiling with a cove light surround and pinhole incandescent downlights can achieve an outdoor effect, especially for such items as camping equipment. A cathedral ceiling in a furniture store may be painted white, but its exposed beams will benefit by the application of a color that matches the general decor.

Some designers prefer a dark ceiling (black) in order to focus attention on the display. This arrangement should be used in rooms in which ducts, pipes, or beams are exposed or in which ceilings are high enough to eliminate direct or discomfort glare from the luminaires. If a dark color must be used on a low-height ceiling, accent lights directed away from the field of view should be considered. Area sources should never be used with black, low-height ceilings.

Wall colors should follow or complement the floor treatment and reflectances should never exceed 60%. Most merchandising areas have insufficient open wall space because of the need for display materials such as murals, pictures, rugs, showcases, shelves, and posters. Regardless of room size, however, wall colors should conform to the mood that is intended and should complement the merchandise. Large open wall spaces should never be white.

When displays are primarily confined to floor space and the walls are largely visible, a single color may be used. If a consistent color is chosen, accenting with the same color in varying lightness and saturation will help to break the monotony. Contrasting hues are most successful in small areas. The philosophy of using dark colors in a light surrounding and light colors in a dark surrounding should be considered. Use of one or more hues, in contrast to the dominant color, usually provides more interest.

COLORED LIGHT FOR DECORATION

Use of colored light, the latest decorative development in merchandising environments, originated in theatrical applications in which colored light was used to create a mood and other dramatic effects.

Nightclubs, restaurants, and discos are familiar users of colored light. Merchandising areas have now been enthusiastically adapted to this sophisticated approach.

Faber Birren defined color in three types: surface, film, and volume. Surface colors are those that distinguish forms; film and volume are related to light. Film color is atmospheric (sunrise, sunset) and volume color appears in space like a fog. Colored light, used in merchandising areas, constitute a third category. Apart from its decorative aspects, some experts claim that people actually see more clearly through volume color than under white light.

Reaction to colored light is not the same as to pigments; for example, green pigments are accepted as tranquilizing influence, most restful to the eyes; but green light produces a ghastly effect on the skin and is to be avoided. Many years ago M. Luckiesh, in his book *Light, Vision and Seeing,* showed that yellow light is the most psychologically pleasing and the easiest to focus. In terms of choices, C. E. Feree and Gertrude Rand placed yellow at the top and followed it with yellow-orange, yellow-green, and green. Deep red, blue, and violet were the least desirable. Stanley McCandless showed that the eyes are more sensitive to yellow and green light, which always appear brighter than blue or red. According to Faber Birren, in an extreme dark adaptation the eyes seem to have the best acuity under red light. Blue is the most difficult for the eye to focus on because of the halos that seem to surround it.

Whatever the physiological or psychological effects, colored lights, for now, are used in merchandise areas only for decorative purposes. From this standpoint the use of colored light is manyfold. The following are some examples:

1. Show cases, or low-partitioned booths, each lighted with a different color, can be used for merchandise display. To provide a balance in the psychological and physiological reactions, colors that have opposite effects should be selected; for instance, to counterbalance the exciting effects of red or yellow soothing colors such as blue or green should be adjacent. With a little imagination, these combinations can result in dramatic effects; for example, in a furniture store a red or yellow light will give the effect of daylight on a bedroom set, whereas a blue light will simulate the night hours.

2. By using the above concept red and blue lights

can be used to emphasize the effects of light and shadow on merchandise.

3. Colored lights in specific designs can be projected on a wall to substitute for wallpaper or murals. The design can be abstract or realistic to coordinate with the merchandise.

4. The color of a wall can be changed instantly or gradually to suit the mood of the environment or the color of the merchandise.

5. Representations of three-dimensional objects can be created in space by moving laser beams in a predetermined manner. This treatment can be used in show windows to highlight merchandise by surrounding it by a circular wall or cone of light (see Figure 4-41).

The decorative effects of colored light in public areas appear to have generated a new wave of excitement in modern lighting design. Merchandising provides the public with the latest fads and developments in every aspect of life—whether for food, clothes, or style; so why not decoration with colored light? It is more than welcome as long as it is done tastefully and serves the main objectives—customer appeal and higher sales!

REFERENCES

Birren, Faber. *The Story of Color.* Crimson Press, CT 1941.

Birren, Faber. "Color and Man-Made Environment: The Significance of Light," *Journal of the American Institute of Architects* (August, 1972).

Birren, Faber. *Color and Human Response.* New York: Van Nostrand-Reinhold, 1978.

Ferree, C. E. and Gertrude Rand, "Lighting and the Hygiene of the Eye." *Archives of Opthalmology* (July 1929).

Luckiesh, M. *Light, Vision, and Seeing.* New York: Van Nostrand, 1944.

McCandless, Stanley. *A Method of Lighting the Stage.* New York: Theatre Arts Books.

INDEX